PARNELL

THE POLITICS OF POWER

Edited by Donal McCartney

WOLFHOUND PRESS

First published 1991 by
WOLFHOUND PRESS
68 Mountjoy Square
Dublin 1

British Library Cataloguing in Publication Data
Parnell : the politics of power
  I. McCartney, Donal
941.5081092

  ISBN 0-86327-317-3
  ISBN 0-86327-321-1 pbk

This book is based on papers read to the Parnell Society at Avondale.

Front cover portrait of Parnell by Robert Ballagh, courtesy of the artist and of the Kitty O'Shea pubs, Dublin, Brussels and Paris.
Cover design: Jan de Fouw
Typesetting: Wolfhound Press
Printed in Ireland by Colour Books

Contents

Acknowledgements

The Parnell Society was founded in 1986 with three aims:

— to stimulate interest in the life, work and times of Charles Stewart Parnell;

— to promote Avondale as a centre which will reflect Wicklow's historic association with Parnell and his family;

— to explore the relevance of Parnell and the politics of his era to modern Ireland.

The Society has organised a Spring Day and an Autumn Weekend each year since its inception, and its first Summer School was held in 1991. The essays included in this book are a selection of the papers read to the Parnell Society. The Committee wishes to express its appreciation to the editor, to the individual contributors and to Louise Richardson for her help in preparing the material for publication. It also wishes to express its gratitude to Allied Irish Banks, an Bord Bainne and Cement Roadstone for making possible the publication of this centenary volume.

Preface

Donal McCartney

Charles Stewart Parnell wielded more power than did any other Irishman during the long and often bitter struggle between Ireland and Britain. In the pursuit and exercise of that power he exhibited not only a rare political skill but a fascinating and complex personality. Peasants, poets, politicians and priests were mesmerised and captivated by him, or by the myth that surrounded him. Where others had failed, he united all of nationalist Ireland in an agitation which came to bear his name. 'Parnellism' may have meant different things to different people but all were agreed that it represented a powerful force at a particular stage in the development of nationalist Ireland. What role did Parnell's own personality play in this historical process? How much can be explained by his family background or by the milieu of his own Co. Wicklow landlord class, or by the political circumstances of the time? These are questions that are worth asking again and again, and are worth approaching from a variety of angles.

His success in uniting all shades of nationalist opinion behind his leadership has to be balanced by his failure to win over Unionist Ulster to Home Rule. The Ulster question, which had yet to emerge into its most sinister aspects, he had hoped to solve in the wider context of Anglo-Irish relations. When and how did Parnell come to realise that Ulster was a problem? What was the reaction in Unionist Ulster to the emergence of Parnell and the *ism* that he represented. It may well be asked to what extent the failure to achieve Home Rule in Parnell's time made the issue of Northern Ireland intractable to ours. We can never know whether Home Rule backed by a Liberal government led by the great Gladstone and fully supported by a powerful Irish Party led by the equally great Parnell would have been — however reluctantly — acceptable in Unionist Ulster. But it is arguable that under Parnell, the protestant landlord, and in all the circumstances of the time, Home Rule for a united Ireland had then a better chance of success than in any subsequent period or under any other leadership.

From his earliest years in parliament Parnell grasped the supreme significance of the Irish land question. He realised that it could carry him who dared to political leadership, and help him fashion country-wide a national agitation. If not properly controlled and directed it could just as easily destroy both man and movement. Parnell's relationship with the land agitation was ambivalent and merits re-examining. He distanced himself from the more extreme agitators and from those who would see the solution to the land question as an end in itself. His achievement, and that of the Land League over which he presided, was in smashing the old landlord system and transferring the ownership of the land of Ireland to the tenant farmers. 'The magic of property which turns sand into gold', was one of Parnell's rare poetic phrases. It was also his most prophetic. For the class which, through his labours, inherited the gold grains of landed property was the same class that came to have a vested interest in political and social stability.

Parnell is the politician's politician. He found an outlet for his ambitions, urges and needs in practical politics. Through a combination of circumstances and talent he found himself at the head of a powerful political machine. The stage he had to play on — the parliament of the United Kingdom when the British Empire was at its zenith — was a much larger stamping-ground than that played upon by Irish politicians who succeeded him. This gave immense scope for the political artist and his work. It involved him in the closest possible exchanges with the Liberal and Tory leaders of his day in Britain. It also led to contacts with other imperial leaders like Rhodes of South Africa. The question that has to be asked of all politicians has to be asked of him: what was it that motivated him? Clearly it was not the patent nationalistic idealism of a Pearse. Just how much did patriotism, the love of Ireland and the Irish people propel his actions? To what extent was he inspired by a social conscience, or how much can be attributed to self-aggrandisement? How much was sacrificed for something called Ireland or were these apparent sacrifices made more for Charles Stewart Parnell? One is reminded of that word-portrait of Napoleon which saw him grooming his horse, *France*, with loving care; but whether it was in the interests of the horse or of the rider remains in question. Like Napoleon was Parnell too, after the divorce controversy and the crisis of confidence in his leadership, demanding of his mount that one jump more, which finally destroyed both rider and mount? Parnell's career is also an object lesson in the fickleness of party and personal loyalty.

The decline and nature of the fall of so powerful a figure as Parnell left a deep impression on the political and literary imagination of the nation. Perhaps it is a sense of guilt because of our rejection of him in the last year of his life that has haunted the Irish conscience ever since. It is certainly remarkable that he, the least literary of all Irish political figures, has been the most celebrated in the immortal writings of our two most famous literary sons — Joyce and Yeats. His political opponents in Britain and Ireland, his liaison with Katharine O'Shea and his own personality all contributed in their various ways to that fall. The role played by Gladstone and the non-conformist conscience has often been examined. It is worthwhile too, however, looking into the role which a Conservative ideology may have played in the overthrow of Parnellism. Then one has always to ask was it sheer pride and pig-headedness and the power which corrupts absolutely that account for his behaviour at the most critical point of his career. Parnell has been portrayed by F.S.L. Lyons, C.C. O'Brien and others as the tragic hero who was brought down by the weaknesses in his own personality. Could it be, however, that he was brought down rather by a grand alliance — the combination of petty narrow-mindedness, strait-laced Victorian attitudes, and the bourgeois values of Gladstonian Liberals, Irish bishops, ambitious Home Rule colleagues and tenant farmers who had suddenly become as conservative as they had so recently been radical once they were on the way to acquiring ownership of the land? Could it be that the 'Uncrowned King' was swallowed up in the quick-sands created by these giants of bourgeois circumstance? Or probing more deeply into the heart of the man, did he sacrifice his most cherished political cause of an independent Ireland, his own political career, and his country into the bargain, for the love of a woman and the family life she gave him? His affair with Mrs O'Shea, the most tragic love-story in Irish history, also raises the great issue of the standard of private morality expected from our public figures.

When one remembers that Parnell was dead at the age of 45, his achievements, by comparison with recent Irish politicians appear all the more impressive. He remains one of the most intriguing leaders in modern Irish history. Though he is dead a century, it is far easier for many today to identify with him than with other, more recent heroes. Part of the explanation for this lies in the fact that Parnell and our generation have close political affinities, placed as we are on each side of the intense Irish nationalism of the first half of the 20th century. If one smoulders so intensely nationalistic as Pearse did, then 1916 and the blood sacrifice are the only predictable end to his career. If one is influenced by Pearse's idealism to the extent that de Valera was, then however shrewd a practising politician he might also be, his idealism separates him from the more pragmatic concerns of today's politics. This is one of the reasons why idealistic nationalists, like Pearse and de Valera have been subjected to the so-called revisionism of recent years, while the more pragmatic Parnell on the other hand has remained relatively safe.

The following essays, in which some of these questions are explored, were originally delivered as lectures in Avondale to the Parnell Society. So long as these and similar questions can be posed about his achievements, personality and motivation, so long will we continue to be fascinated by Charles Stewart Parnell.

Charles Stewart Parnell

TOP LEFT: Parnell's mother, Delia Stewart
Parnell, and RIGHT: his great-grandfather
Sir John Parnell, former Chancellor of the
Exchequer in Ireland. ABOVE: Parnell.
RIGHT: Parnell as a boy.

Parnell and Parnellism

Donal McCartney

Charles Stewart Parnell belonged to a typical landlord family which had come to Ireland at the time of the Restoration. His father had lived the very ordinary life of the country gentleman on his estate at Avondale, Co. Wicklow. Of the 11 children, five boys and six girls, of the family of John Henry Parnell and his wife Delia Stewart who survived birth, Charles was the seventh.

In June 1846, when Charles was born, it would have been impossible to foretell, if one were to judge by the non-political career of his father, that this child was destined to become a tremendous force not only in Irish politics but indeed in the politics of Britain and the British Empire. Historians and other commentators have wondered how this Protestant landlord came to be idolised by a Catholic peasantry at a most critical stage in the development of Irish democracy, and how his leadership was totally accepted, at least for a time, by men of many talents like Davitt and Devoy emerging out of that peasantry, or Justin McCarthy, Tim Healy, William O'Brien, T.P. O'Connor and John Dillon, who belonged to a more middle-class background. He has been regarded as a charismatic figure, something strange and mysterious that had hit the Irish scene out of the blue, as it were.

When one probes a little deeper into his family background, however, his interest in politics becomes less surprising. His great-grandfather, Sir John Parnell, was Chancellor of the Exchequer in Grattan's parliament; although very much committed to the idea of the Protestant ascendancy, he was prepared pragmatically to support the admission of Catholics into parliament although he was more doubtful about giving Catholics the right to vote. He was described as a lazy man but with plenty of talent. He opposed the Union strongly and bitterly. Sir John's son, Henry, Parnell's grand-uncle, was if anything more intelligent and more successful than his own father. Henry also strongly opposed the Act of Union and on the Catholic question was a more liberal emancipationist than Sir John. He served in what was called the Ministry of all the Talents in the United Kingdom parliament (1806-7). As Lord Treasurer, or Commissioner of the Treasury of the Irish province, he was considered a financial wizard. The library at Avondale included several works which he had authored. His *History of The Penal Laws against the Catholics* (1808) is an important document showing the opposition that this liberal Protestant had to the penal laws and to the Protestant ascendancy as it then existed in Ireland. Catholics like O'Connell borrowed illustrations from this book for their speeches. A book which he wrote later on financial questions anticipated the reforms of Sir Robert Peel and Gladstone. He served in a number of Whig ministries in the first half of the 19th century, acting as Paymaster General in the last of these governments in which he served. In 1842 when in his mid-sixties, he committed suicide.

Henry's younger brother, William, was Parnell's grandfather. For a brief spell, 1817-21, he represented Wicklow in the United Kingdom parliament. His writings on Irish problems profoundly influenced the development of Irish nationalism and the cause of Catholic emancipation. His *An Enquiry into the Causes of Popular Discontents in Ireland* (1804) very carefully analysed the reasons for political and social agitation in Ireland. He examined issues like sectarianism, the long memory of the Irish, the broken treaties between Ireland and England in the past and the ill-treatment of the peasantry. Like, perhaps, all of the Parnells, he had the reputation of being a good landlord. Even before O'Connell had made his mark, William Parnell was advising the Catholics to 'be angry and sin not'. He harangued them by telling them that they had as much spirit as would support a sixteen-year-old virgin on her entry into life. His *Historical Apology for the Irish Catholics* (1807) was another strong polemic in favour of Catholic emancipation. Employing the sort of argument that O'Connell would use later, he placed the Treaty of Limerick firmly in a nationalist tradition, describing it as a treaty, made between two sovereign nations, which had been broken by the British. He was also anti-British in his interpretation of the 1641 rebellion. These books by Henry and William Parnell and the spirit that lay behind them were very much behind the tradition of Avondale when Parnell was still a child.

On his maternal side, too, the family had been deeply involved in politics. His mother, Delia Tudor Stewart, belonged to an important family in the Boston area of America, which claimed kinship with the Tudor monarchy. Delia's grandfather was Secretary of State for a brief time in the US Senate. Delia's father, Admiral Stewart, 'Old Ironsides', as he was called, had been a famous naval commander in the 1812 war against the British. Parnell may well have inherited some of his anti-English feelings from his grandfather Stewart. Given his family background, both American and Irish, it is after all not so surprising that he should emerge into political leadership in 19th century Ireland.

Some oft-repeated stories from his childhood and his early manhood may be apocryphal but they do give an indication of the man he was to become. It was noted that one of his favourite pastimes as a child was to engage in mock-battles with toy soldiers. On one occasion his sister Fanny noticed that her soldiers were always being knocked down while Parnell's remained standing despite the number of direct hits which she scored. Eventually she discovered that Charlie had glued his soldiers to the floor of the house. He was always more interested in winning than in adhering to the rules of the game. The same characteristic exhibited itself during his cricket days. By county standards he was regarded as a good cricketer and he was captain of the Wicklow XI. On one occasion when playing against the Phoenix Club in Dublin a row broke out between Charlie and the captain of the Dublin team. Despite his own team's protestations Parnell was not prepared to give in so he marched his men off the pitch. His team had gone to Dublin just to play a game of cricket but he had gone there to win, and was prepared to stick rigidly to the letter of the rules when that was seen to give him the advantage.

Because his mother moved around a great deal with her family, Parnell's formal education left a good deal to be desired. Yet he managed to be accepted to Magdalene College in Cambridge. He never got his degree because of a bout of fisticuffs in which he was engaged. Charles and some of his fellow students had been out celebrating and while they were waiting for a cab to take them home they got involved in an argument with a manure merchant and one of his workmen. Insulting language led to punches. The manure merchant, who had sustained a bleeding nose and mouth, torn trousers and a dislocated arm, took legal action against Parnell and sued for 30 guineas. Parnell's counsel admitted to some wrong on his client's part and the jury found for damages for 20 guineas. Because the affair had come before the courts Parnell was sent down for the remainder of the term, but he never returned to Cambridge. 'These English,' he used to say to his brother John, 'despise us because we are Irish, but we must stand up to them, that's the way to treat the Englishman — stand up to him.'

After travelling for a year in America, where his brother had gone to live, the two Parnells returned to Ireland and Charles decided to enter politics. It was in Dublin that Parnell began his political career, as the unsuccessful candidate in the parliamentary by-election of 1874. Although he never sat for Dublin the relations between him and the city, to which he intended to restore an Irish parliament, were of the closest kind all through his stormy seventeen years in politics. And when death ended his career in 1891, it was Parnellite Dublin that clasped him to her bosom, as 100,000 people followed his funeral from City Hall to Glasnevin Cemetery.

It was no disgrace to have been beaten for the Co. Dublin seat. In every election since 1841, two Conservatives had always been returned for the two seats for Dublin County, beating off every challenge from the Liberals. Indeed in the general election of 1874 two Conservatives were returned unopposed, so strongly embedded was the Conservative-Unionist interest. When one of these MPs had to seek re-election, following his appointment to a government office, Parnell, then 28, offered and was chosen to run against him in a contest that the Home Rulers did not expect to win. But Parnell was a Protestant landlord with a reputable name who would be able to pay his own election expenses. He received £300 from the Home Rule

League, which he handed back when the election was over. The contest cost him £2,000.

In the Rotunda where he made his political debut he embarrassed his political colleagues. A.M. Sullivan said: 'To our dismay, he broke down utterly. He faltered, he paused, went on, got confused, and, pale with intense but subdued nervous anxiety caused everyone to feel deep sympathy for him . . . many on the platform shook their heads, sagely prophesying that if ever he got to Westminster, no matter how long he stayed there, he would either be a "silent member", or be known as "single-speech Parnell".' T.W. Russell said that he was struck with Parnell's 'extraordinary political ignorance and incapacity. He knew nothing, and I thought he would never do anything'.

O'Connor Power said: 'He seemed to me a nice gentlemanly fellow, but he was hopelessly ignorant, and seemed to me to have no political capacity whatever. He could not speak at all. He was hardly able to get up and say, "Gentlemen, I am a candidate for the representation of the county of Dublin". We all listened to him with pain while he was on his legs, and felt immensely relieved when he sat down. No one ever thought he would cut a figure in politics. We thought he would be a respectable mediocrity'.

But the daring Parnell had been the first to carry the Home Rule flag into the Conservative stronghold of Co. Dublin. Although he was defeated his 1,200 votes against his Tory opponent's 2,100 was no disgrace; and when a vacancy occurred in the more nationalistic Co. Meath constituency one year later, Parnell had earned the right to the nomination, and was duly elected at the head of the poll.

Isaac Butt had predicted, 'Unless I am mistaken, the Saxon will find him an ugly customer, though he is a good-looking fellow'. In parliament that was precisely what Parnell turned out to be — an ugly customer. From the start he associated himself with that little group of ex-Fenians who were determined to obstruct the business of parliament. There was nothing very noteworthy about his short maiden speech, except the determined pronouncement: 'Ireland is not a geographical fragment of England. She is a Nation.' (From Parnell, at least, there was never any talk about 'mainland Britain'.) What really attracted attention was the altercation he had with the Chief Secretary for Ireland, who had referred to the 'Manchester murderers'. 'No! No!' said Parnell, with a vehemence that startled the House. The Chief Secretary paused, and then solemnly said, amid cheers: 'I regret to hear that there is an honourable member in this House who will apologise for murder'. Parnell, with all of that dignity of which he possessed a great deal, replied in his most icy manner: 'I wish to say, as publicly as I can, that I do not believe, and I never shall believe, that any murder was committed at Manchester'.

Parnell was not a revisionist: he was an unashamed nationalist, combining in his political attitude the constitutional and physical force traditions. He did not approve of assassination, of the Phoenix Park murders kind; but by the same token he was not prepared to kick the Manchester martyrs when they were down. This was to be one of his great strengths as spokesman for the whole nationalist tradition.

His remark had drawn on himself the fire of British ministers. He was a marked man — the most dangerous among the Irish parliamentary party, one that had to be watched carefully. The remark re-echoed, too, around the Irish world. The Fenians in Ireland and Britain sat up and took note of this mysterious landlord who dared defend their cause in parliament. John Devoy, the god-father of the Fenian organisation in America, wanted to learn more about this impressive new star that had arisen. Within two years of his entry into parliament Parnell had asserted his leadership over the obstructionist wing of the party; he was elected President of the Home Rule Confederation of Great Britain in place of Butt; and he was already being talked about as a man likely to succeed Butt as leader of the party.

When Michael Davitt and other Fenians were released from Dartmoor Prison (at the end of 1877) it was Parnell who invited them to a public breakfast, once again snatching the headlines as the friend of Fenianism. The meeting took place in Morrison's Hotel, No. 1 Dawson Street. Parnell always stayed in this hotel when he was in Dublin, and some of his most historic meetings took place there.

It was in Morrison's Hotel, too, that Parnell held those meetings with Michael Davitt and John Devoy in 1879 which led to the policy known as 'The New Departure' — one of the most critical developments in the history of Irish nationalism. It was in Morrison's that he was arrested in 1881, for opposition to the Land Act, and taken to Kilmainham. It was in Morrison's, after his release in 1882, that he and Healy drafted the constitution of the Irish National League which replaced the suppressed Land League.

Essentially what the New Departure meant was the bringing together for the first time in Irish history of three powerful forces: constitutionalism, physical force nationalism, and agrarianism.

Constitutional nationalism stretched back from Parnell through Butt, and through Daniel O'Connell to Grattan. What it aimed at was an Irish domestic parliament with a sisterhood relationship with England under the same crown. Under Butt and O'Connell it had always denounced physical force as a means, and renounced a separatist Ireland as its objective.

The Republican physical force tradition, which in these talks John Devoy represented, went back through the Fenian Rising of 1867 and the Young Ireland rebels of 1848 and Robert Emmet in 1803, to Wolfe Tone and the United Irishmen in 1798. It aimed at the establishment of a separatist Irish Republic. The republicans had despised the constitutionalists for thinking that Irish independence could ever be won by simply reasoning with the English in their own parliament in London.

The third force was that of agrarianism for which Michael Davitt, with the establishment of the Land League, was then the spokesman. It stretched back through the Famine, and Fintan Lalor, to the inarticulate secret agrarian societies of the eighteenth and early nineteenth centuries. The social radicalism of the land agitation was something that constitutionalists like Daniel O'Connell or republicans like the Fenians, O'Leary and Kickham, had always fought shy of.

But now in the New Departure these three forces, often in the past opposed to each other, were fused together under the superb political skill of one man. It was in the manipulation of the extremes of constitutionalism and revolution that Parnell excelled. And by not setting bounds to the march of the nation he held together his grand alliance. 'He goeth furthest,' Oliver Cromwell had said, 'who knows not whither he is going.' By any standard, his was a remarkable achievement; and it gave to Irish politics a power such as had never before been experienced. The amalgamation of these three separate forces under his leadership is best described as Parnellism.

And Parnell maintained the balance of power between these three forces for the benefit of nationalist Ireland as a whole, as surely and skilfully and autocratically as Bismarck was maintaining the diplomatic balance of power in Europe for the benefit of his Germany.

Parnell firmly believed, and had often said, that the only thing which the English would respond to was power. 'You must never expect the English to be enthusiastic about Home Rule . . . They will find Ireland impossible to govern, and then they will give us what we want . . . We must show them our power. They will bow to nothing but power,' he assured R. Barry O'Brien. That three-pronged weapon he now possessed in Parnellism.

To make it effective, Parnellism demanded a very high degree of talent, hard work, total devotion and great courage. It was not a weapon for the faint-hearted. And it landed him in Kilmainham jail for seven months. The cause absorbed his time and energies, it involved long and frequent absences from Avondale, much travel in Ireland, Britain and America, frequent stop-overs in Morrison's Hotel and in hotels in London. It meant, of course, the neglect of his own business interests, serious financial difficulties, and the threatened sale of all his Wicklow property to pay off his mortgages.

That is why a subscription for Parnell was organised, which led to that extraordinary scene in Morrison's Hotel when the Lord Mayor called on Parnell to present him with a cheque for £37,000. The Lord Mayor, as is the nature of Lord Mayors, had also come with a speech for the occasion. Parnell cut him short, saying: 'I believe you have got a cheque for me'. The Lord Mayor said he had, and tried to resume his oration. 'Is it made payable to order and crossed?' interrupted Parnell a second time. Parnell took the cheque, put it in his waistcoat pocket, and that was one Lord Mayor's speech that was not delivered.

Later that night at a crowded banquet in the Rotunda, Parnell concentrated his remarks on the political situation, and made only the briefest reference to the subscription. He said: 'I don't know how adequately to express my feelings with regard not only to your lordship's address, not only to the address to the Parnell National Tribute, but also with regard to the magnificent demonstration. I prefer to leave to the historian the description of tonight and the expression of opinion as regards the result which tonight must produce'. Sexton's whisper to Healy: 'a labourer would acknowledge the loan of a pen-knife more gratefully', depicted Parnell as a most ungrateful cad. Nearly all contemporary accounts agree that Parnell was a man of almost ostentatious courtesy, and was very sensitive to any kindness done to him.

F.S.L. Lyons, who could be quite critical of Parnell in some respects, has explained his behaviour. He argues that Parnell on this occasion was exhibiting two of his chief characteristics — his pride and his dedication to politics. Reticent about his private affairs in the extreme, the gift of money could only have been deeply humiliating to him; and his remarks to the Lord Mayor, and at the banquet, were almost certainly the reaction of a highly embarrassed man. His instinct, at the same time, was to make the maximum political capital out of the event. So he underlined the political significance, not only of the tribute, but of the fact that it had been collected in the face of Roman opposition. It represented less a form of outdoor relief for the landlord, than a massive vote of confidence in the political leader. The little incident always made an impression on Lord Spencer, the Lord Lieutenant. He said the fact that nobody was offended by the acceptance of the handsome cheque without the least expression of thanks only showed the immense power of the man. Less than two months later Dublin's Lord Mayor had consented to stand at the special request of Parnell, and with the approval of the Bishop, as parliamentary candidate for the safe seat of Meath.

Parnellism unleashed saw Parnell perform the greatest acrobatic act ever in Irish history. He balanced coolly on his tight-rope between its two supports, constitutionalism and revolutionary agrarianism. The boycott, the no-rent manifesto, the plan of campaign, Captain Moonlight, parliamentary obstruction, the disciplined party machine of about 80 MPs holding the balance between Liberals and Tories — these were the moral equivalents of Fenian dynamite, and in the long run much more effective than their attempts to blow up public buildings in London, including the House of Commons, with utter indifference to the presence there of Parnell and his party. Does nothing change in Irish history? The dynamiters were organised by an extreme wing of the American Fenians. They included, incidentally, the 25-year-old Tom Clarke, the future 1916 man, who was jailed for his part in these dynamite outrages, the purpose of which was to lay London in ruins.

Parnell regarded the campaign as sheer lunacy, and its organisers as damn fools. But he only smiled at the hypocrisy of the English politicians who condemned the violence. When the London *Times* fulminated against Patrick Ford's New York *Irish World* which had approved of the dynamite policy, he laughed it off as a case of the pot calling the kettle black. His concern was to keep Irishmen united in the grand alliance of Parnellism, which he succeeded in doing. Its achievements included the smashing of landlordism in Ireland; the beginning of the Land Acts, creating a peasant proprietorship; the conversion and commitment of Gladstone and the Liberals to Home Rule; and the introduction by the Tories of good government measures in their attempt to provide a substitute for Home Rule.

'Parnell', said Mr Gladstone, who had been in parliament for 60 years and Prime Minister on four occasions, 'Parnell was the most remarkable man I ever met . . . He did things and he said things unlike other men. His ascendancy over his party was extraordinary. There has never been anything like it in my experience in the House of Commons. He succeeded in surrounding himself with very clever men, with men exactly suited for his purpose . . . In his time he had a most efficient party, an extraordinary party. I do not say extraordinary as an Opposition, but extraordinary as a Government. The absolute obedience, the strict discipline, the military discipline, in which he held them was unlike anything I have ever seen . . . and Parnell was supreme all the time.' He might have added that like Bismarck he had no colleagues, only subordinates.

The magic spell of his fascination, which he cast on his lieutenants and foot-soldiers alike, would nowadays be vulgarly called 'charisma'. But the mystique he possessed for them is widely attested to, even by those who later became his most bitter enemies. It had, of course, something to do with his charm, and his honoured name, and with the fact that he was a Protestant landlord leading a Catholic peasantry. It had something to do with the fact that unlike your stereotyped Irish politician, he used words sparingly, but effectively. It had something to do with the fact that when he discovered he was regarded as a mystery man he consciously cultivated the mysterious image. And it had a lot to do with his indomitable will and courage, his sheer political instinct, and his skills as a political leader. He had some of those qualities of his great contemporaries: Gladstone's grasp of the essential point, and command of detail; Bismarck's iron will and command of men.

A middle-aged Englishwoman caught the eye of the Chief as he performed the most daring acts on his tight-rope. The acrobat lost his balance and fell. He fell first in love, and then from his political high-wire. The fall was majestic, tragic, devastating. Samson Agonistes brought down with him the whole structure that he had designed. The grand alliance of constitutionalists, agrarians, Fenians, Irish Americans, bishops and Gladstonians shattered into their elemental parts never again to be re-united in that same combination which Parnellism had fashioned. And without its leader Ireland lost its way.

I do not intend to say much about the most tragic love-story in Irish history, beyond reminding ourselves of how very natural it all was. Parnell had never had much of a home-life in his youth. And as a politician he had spent much of his time in lonely hotel rooms. Katharine O'Shea provided him with all the comforts of a home life that he had not known, and a companionship that allowed him to open up his heart and his mind in a way that he never did with his political colleagues.

People asked then, and have asked ever since: How could Parnell have allowed his pride to ruin Ireland's chances of getting Home Rule? Why didn't he resign from the leadership when Gladstone, and later the bishops and the party, demanded it? It needs to be stressed that although Parnell did not resign, he was effectively removed from the leadership by the defection of the great majority. And yet, Home Rule did *not* come. Nor indeed was it possible that Home Rule could be achieved as long as the Tory-dominated House of Lords possessed a veto which would not be removed until twenty years after the death of Parnell.

Besides, it is worth asking whether some possible Home Rule measure was *so* important that an individual like Parnell had to be sacrificed for this particular political possibility. Was not the Ireland that he wanted, which would respect the individual's liberty of a private life-style, more important than some formula about a Home Rule government?

'If you are going to throw me to the wolves make sure you get my price first.' Parnell, himself, was quite realistic about the chances of getting Home Rule. He granted that Gladstone meant to establish Home Rule of some kind. But Gladstone was an old man, and *any* kind would satisfy him because he could not wait. But Parnell said he wanted an Irish parliament that we would be able to keep and work, and that if we didn't get it this year or next we could wait half a dozen years. He said it would not come in Gladstone's time. And when he looked at Gladstone's likely successors — Morley, Asquith, Campbell-Bannerman, Rosebery, Harcourt — he said that none of them cared enough about Home Rule to risk anything for it. They would bow to nothing but power — the power of Parnellism. And who can say that his prediction was wrong? Ireland did *not* get Home Rule. And Parnell having been sacrificed for it, who can blame the 1916 generation for its determination not to accept so miserly a concession?

Between the divorce case in November 1890 and Parnell's death almost a year later, in October 1891, Parnellites and anti-Parnellites fought three bitter by-elections: the first of these was Kilkenny North (22 December 1890); the second was Sligo North (2 April 1891) and the third and last by-election which Parnell ever fought was Carlow County (7 July 1891). In Kilkenny North the Parnellite candidate got 35% of the vote against the anti-Parnellite's 65%. In Sligo North the Parnellite candidate did somewhat better and got 43% against 57% for the anti-Parnellites.

Parnell had married Katharine O'Shea on Thursday 24 June in a registry

office in Sussex. By Sunday he had arrived in Carlow. The election was a
rowdy affair. When the result of the Carlow by-election was announced
Kettle had only got 29% of the vote cast, against 71% for the anti-Parnellite
(local merchant John Hammond). It was Parnell's last election — four
months later he was dead at the age of 45. In the general election the
anti-Parnellites won 71 seats and the Parnellites, decimated, won only nine.
Nearly half, or four out of that total of nine, were elected for Dublin city or
county. Less than a year before his death Parnell had said: 'I rely on Dublin.
Dublin is true. What Dublin says today, Ireland will say tomorrow'.

The Parnellite split discredited constitutional politics — and politicians,
whether Parnellite or anti-Parnellite, came to be a despised class. Parnell had
led a great national front which had released powerful energies and hopes.
After Parnell's fall these now spilled over, or were diverted from parliamentary politics into other areas like the Gaelic League, the Anglo-Irish literary
revival, Sinn Féin and the IRB. In a certain sense, the fall of Parnell made
the Easter Rising possible — perhaps, from the standpoint of some
contemporaries, even necessary.

Parnell, Wicklow and Nationalism

R.F. Foster

What made Parnell the kind of politician and public figure he was? One way to an answer lies through a consideration of his background before he became a public figure: establishing the dimensions of the world he came from, rather than seeing him retrospectively through the operatic tragedy of his last year, or even through the very high profile of the 1880s. I should like here to make the case that he can be located in a strain, a minority strain but still an influential one, which might be called the hard-headed landlord tradition. There was, I think, such a tradition of conservative, propertied, politically Protestant landlords, who formed a potential constituency for moderate nationalism in the 1870s, precisely the time Parnell enters politics.

Their ideological background is probably to be found, indirectly, in the ideas and writings of the people around the *Dublin University Magazine* in the 1830s whose guru, of course, was the brilliant young Isaac Butt.[1] This group was, politically speaking, dispersed by the Famine, but a certain continuity might be discerned; and Butt became the leader of the party to which Parnell attached himself in the 1870s. When we see Parnell simply as the man who displaced Butt, we forget that he was, before that, the man who followed Butt.

Throughout the development of articulate Irish nationalism in the later 19th century, there is a minor strain of unlikely figures: conservatives, Protestants, often landlords; interested in the potentialities of devolution, antagonistic towards English party politics, disposed towards education and land reform. Allegiances could be curiously confused, 'interests' hard to define, the circle often squared. Some of the unexpected identifications of Irish Protestants after 1868 may have been electoral red herrings.[2] But from early on, the Catholic clergy tended to prefer to work with Conservatives; and after Disestablishment the Tories, with no Irish church to defend, were freer to become a more 'Irish' party — as several of them saw in the late 1870s.

It is too often forgotten that Parnell entered politics at the same time as the element of Conservative Home Rulers whose sincerity has been trenchantly questioned by Dr Thornley. (And even after Irish politics had been clericalised and radicalised, under Parnell's direction, the recurring guests at his shooting-lodge, Aughavannagh — Esmonde, Redmond, Corbet — represented something closer to this strain than to the new men. It is tempting to wonder whether he felt politically as well as socially closer to this tradition.)

Nor were Irish Toryism and Irish proto-nationalism incompatible. The Home Government Association was, of course, strongly Tory and Protestant in its origins;[3] being, in many ways, a reaction to Disestablishment. Moreover, one should continue to beware of thinking 'Conservative', 'Protestant' and 'Unionist' synonymous, at least before the mid-eighties; Tories held out far more hope to the Catholics on the education issue, for one thing. By the early 1870s, however, the Tory Home Rulers are generally seen as headed for the dust-heap of history. They were, according to their severe historian, 'divorced from the main sources of Irish political energy',[4] and paid the penalty. Conservative 'taints' had to be purged; identification with popular liberal elements had to be made. Certainly, the body of Conservative Home Rulers withdrew soon enough: Sir John Barrington, a founder of the HGA, declaring that the initial 'efficiency' motivation, and the desire for federalism, had been swamped by repealers and agitation. Thornley castigated such attitudes as representative of the 'shallowness of Conservative Nationalism'.[5] He has shown how the issues of land and education, cautiously embraced after Disestablishment, came to worry other landlords and Conservatives, and put them off the HGA. But they were to accept both, if only tacitly, in ten years' time. Meanwhile, however, events had pressed the movement in a Catholic and anti-Conservative direction: while Gladstone's treatment of the hierarchy over education drove them into the arms of the Home Rulers.

A case can still be made for the fluidity of constitutional nationalist ideology in the mid-1870s, when Parnell entered politics. It was an era of the middle ground in politics supposedly being opened up.[6] Need the taking up of the Home Rule League's programme by the policy declarations of politicians like Chichester Fortescue (a supposed model of Trollope's Phineas Finn) have been necessarily insincere? Were the sprigs of the gentry who were returned in 1874 — like Lord Francis Conyngham, C.M. Vandeleur, Wilfred O'Callaghan — representative of a more thoroughgoing, if still idiosyncratic, nationalism than they were accused of? Thornley analysed the landed element and found a lack of 'genuine nationalist zeal' in their statements about 'not injuring the integrity of empire'.[7] But the point surely is that Home Rule at this time did not imply anything to injure 'the integrity of empire'. For many nationalists in the mid-80s, the same still held true. Devolution was the order of the day. Nor did it imply hard-line political discipline: the landed element objected to the whip, but this did not necessarily coincide with lukewarmness about the Home Rule principle.[8] A refusal to follow a pledged party line was part of the political culture of these members. And this argument against an imposed party discipline was repeated by another aristocratic young recruit three years later, when Butt tried to bring him to heel: if it strikes us as ironic that this member was

Charles Stewart Parnell, the irony is largely retrospective.

To evaluate the upper-class Home Rulers by their lack of 'genuine nationalism' seems a little off-beam. They would not have disagreed with Butt that their object was 'to make honest and intelligent Englishmen realise to themselves the deficiencies of their Irish government and Irish legislation'. Parnell himself, as history would show, took things further. He joined them for reasons of personality and ambition, as well as political principle; he was more maladjusted to the easy traffic between England and Ireland than were his peers in Anglo-Irish society. And he used the opportunity of public debates over what Home Rule meant, to emphasise that it entailed Repeal (and, in time, to imply Fenian sympathies). But he still used the archetypal Anglo-Irish weapon of arrogance in his wrangles with Butt, and we hear the authentic tone of the Big House in his cold dismissal of those who aimed at rapprochement with England as representing 'Irish snobbery, compelling some Irishmen to worship at the shrine of English prejudice'. And in his line against Butt he was supported by an improving landlord like Mitchell Henry, and an aristocrat like Lord Francis Conyngham.

There was widespread fear that Parnell's victory over Butt would mean the end of an important preoccupation of the early Home Government Association: the desire to represent as wide a spectrum of Irish society as possible.[9] And certainly, when Butt went, so did 'all-Irelandism' as well as federalism. With Butt went, too, much of the landed and Protestant support for the movement. It had always represented a minority element in the party. But such men remained as a suppressed strain in the Irish political culture. And in some ways Parnell, who is usually seen as having rooted out this growth, can be seen (with typical Anglo-Irish ambivalence) as continuing to represent the kind of 'efficiency Home Rule' that had brought landlords like Blennerhasset, Esmonde, Bowyer, King Harman and the O'Conor Don into the party before him. He was also an 'improving landlord' (by his own lights), whose politics suited his position: the sawmill buildings, viewed on your left as you come up the drive at Avondale, remain as vivid evidence of his real preoccupations.

In the wider context, his attitude becomes in many ways a logical one. For the attitudes that brought some landlords to Home Rule in the latter part of the 19th century were widely diffused. The more one reads in the rich literature of memoirs and letters, the more this appears to be the case. Examples abound, like John Hamilton, the good landlord of Donegal: born an ultra-Tory but progressing during his long life to favouring local Provincial Councils, a peasant proprietary, joint-stock farming, and sweeping land reform.[10] It was the same attitude, strongly laced with self-preservation, that fuelled the later devolution initiative on the part of Conservative landlords in the early 1900s and the notion of federalism so warmly propounded by Erskine Childers round the same time: Home Rule as 'an indispensable preliminary to the closer union of the various parts of the Empire'. Butt and *his* contemporaries were articulating a 'responsible government' claim which was in tune with contemporary developments elsewhere.

And in these counsels, we can hear the voices of those (few) landlords who saw the way things were going: the doom of the Irish land system, as spelt out by land values, agricultural price movements, and uneconomic rents. For all the recent argument on the issue, many contemporary landlords anticipated Professor Donnelly's judgements that by 1879 it was 'as clear as the shine on their best-polished silver' that without reorganisation their time had come.[11] Pamphlets from the 1850s on had been reiterating that the landlord system was doomed. 'Their day is nearly gone; the incumbered estates act has sealed their doom', wrote 'An English Clergyman' in 1851. Five years later a different kind of visitor, Friedrich Engels, described the Anglo-Irish in a much-quoted letter to his friend Marx:

> These fellows are droll enough to make your sides burst with laughing; of mixed blood, mostly tall, strong, handsome chaps, they all wear enormous moustaches under colossal Roman noses, give themselves the false military air of retired colonels, travel round the country after all sorts of pleasures, and if one makes an enquiry, they haven't a penny, are laden with debts, and live in dread of the incumbered estates court.[12]

Such impressions describe only an element of the landowner class; on other levels, the Famine 'acted as a Darwinian selector of the fittest' landlords.[13] But some of the politically minded among them began to see that land reform, and land purchase, might be their only hope. This realisation could have led them into the Home Rule movement in droves. One reason why it did not was the altering and broadening of Irish political organisation, at this very time. Another was rapid identification of the movement with a *revanchiste* Roman Catholic church, and with the drive for denominational education. Another was the rhetorical form that land reform took when it came, in the wake of the land war: the language of social revolution and expropriation (though not their realisation).

To view the land war as a revolution of rising expectations, concealed by the rhetoric of destitution, is no longer novel, and indeed is already up for reassessment: though Drs Bew and Ó Gráda have recently dealt the *simpliste* version a swingeing blow, and drawn out the various conflicts of interest which 'the tenantry' embodied. Nor was the 'rising expectations' theory completely new. It was articulated by some observers as early as 1880. One journalist saw the land war as an adroit takeover by the middling tenantry, manipulating a credit squeeze; Clifford Lloyd repeated (from the opposite political angle) Anna Parnell's analysis, that the tenant farmers never acted up to the letter of the Land League because they never needed to; Samuel Hussey noted how the church was worried by the land war because they held mortgages on so many landlords' properties.[14]

Probing back into the intervening years, between the 1850s and the land war, the pamphlet literature of the late 1860s includes many broadsides from enlightened landlords, calling on Gladstone to do the right thing and help the landlords out with a sweeping plan of land purchase. Implicit in many of these productions is a curious sense of angry apartness which suggests an anticipation of nationalism. One writer appeals to the Italian example of Cavour; another remarks:

> I write and will speak as one of those Irish classes which England has scarcely seen or heard of for seventy years — namely, the descendants of the Irish patriots of 1800, and the great body of the middle classes of all creeds. England for the last seventy years has only known and seen those who sold their country (and were glad to have a country to sell), and the labouring population, who want to earn a scanty livelihood; but she will now find, having bided our time, quite a different class of Irish to deal with.[15]

This author was a landlord, ex-High Sheriff, millowner; a defender of resident landlords; the subject of threats from Ribbonmen. And we find him calling for 'an Irish independent vote and voice', at least in local affairs, and — like so many of his kind, and like Parnell himself — constantly invoking the hallowed date of 1782. Another pamphleteer of the time, producing a 'Dialogue' on fixity of tenure and signing himself 'An Irish Landlord', moved easily from tenurial questions to a plea for financial Home Rule.[16]

Such men, whether or not they ever reached Parliament, were representative of the original element so marked in the Home Government Association. They were, of course, largely replaced by the 'new' Home Rulers, typical of the much-analysed party of the 1880s: professional men of lower-middle-class origin. This new element, partly through brilliant oratory, did much to obscure the tradition of the old landlord Home Government men; the rhetoric of the land war created a great divide. Even more potent propagandists entered the picture too, including Karl Marx. On a different level, popular Irish novelists anatomised a society which was certainly bizarre, but which subsisted on exaggeration; and one sometimes feels that each side of the landlord-peasant equation did its best to live up to the formidable literary tradition created for it by Maria Edgeworth, Lady Morgan, Lover, Lever, Banim, Griffin, Carleton, et al. Mr and Mrs S.C. Hall, indefatigably touring Ireland and as indefatigably finding themselves sent up by people enthusiastically responding to their own stereotypes, recorded this painstakingly in three volumes. Samuel Hussey's memoirs deliberately represented himself, according to literary convention, as the absolute type of feckless half-mounted gentry: 'I thought farming was the idlest occupation and suggested it should be my profession — an idea hailed with rapture, principally because it saved everybody the trouble of racking their brains about me'. Yet the facts show him a hardworking and flinty steward of his talent, obsessed with farming on the Scottish model.

In every contemporary account from the landlords' side, a lost Golden Age of good relations between landlord and tenant, Protestant and Catholic, is attributed to some stage of the recent past. W.R. Le Fanu, as befitted a clergyman's son, identified it as pre-1831 — 'before the Tithe War'.[17] Others looked back to the days before O'Connell; others, before the new landlords set up by the Encumbered Estates Act. Arthur MacMurrough Kavanagh spoke of it as being before the 1870 Land Act — a critical betrayal of the old sanctity of landlord-tenant relations. Finally and irrevocably, it was to be 'before the Land War'.

But there had always been 'improving landlords' — a feature of every nineteenth-century Irish novel, if only as an exception to point up the general rule. And the point that it was in the landlord's own interest to help his tenants improve their holdings was not missed by observers. The stereotypical landlord-tenant relationship often has to be modified.[18] Even in a county like Donegal, a parish priest declared at the height of the land war that several of the local landlords were the reverse of oppressive — and their lands covered a good deal of the county.[19] And Wicklow embarrassed its local Land Leaguers by the readiness of its landlords to swim with the tide.

Wicklow, indeed, confounds the stereotype — with its notable tradition of model estates and improving landlords. The Tighes and Fitzwilliams paid for improvements on their tenants' holdings; at mid-century, before the Famine, every visitor eulogised the 'improvements', the 'cultivation', the well-built houses at all levels of society. In the 'numberless fine residences and handsome family mansions' were to be found some figures who appear at an odd angle to the accepted landscape of 19th-century Ireland. One thinks of Mrs Smith of Baltiboys, an uncompromising Scots gentlewoman transplanted to Wicklow, whose marvellous diary[20] abounds in acid descriptions of her neighbours; Lord Downshire, 'weak, vain, pompous, self-important', but 'not a bad landlord if he would be quiet about it'; Lord Milltown, a representatively dissolute Irish peer, led astray by bad education, personal deformity, and an affected wife; Hugh Henry, whose estate could easily be reorganised to provide employment, if he could stay away from bad company like Charles Lever (whom he surely provided with a model).[21] And Mrs Smith felt overall that 'the Irish gentleman is at last waking from his dream of idle pleasure, which never satisfied, which deteriorated his character, impoverished his resources, spread distress round him, and left him to drown reflexion in the bottle'.

The same thing, the same year, was noted by the Halls. 'Of late a decided improvement has taken place among all classes throughout Ireland . . . the country is on the eve of a new era — from the one side jealousy and suspicion are rapidly removing, and from the other, prejudice is rapidly departing'.[22]

This, of course, did not happen; all these blithe prognostications were interrupted by the Famine. And there was in both judgements a certain lack of realism. But, though a novel like Carleton's *Valentine M'Clutchy* shows things necessarily black and white, and Maria Edgeworth's Lady Dashfort remarks that 'you must live with the people of the country or be torn to pieces, and for my part I should prefer being torn to pieces', the diaries and records of the gentry culture imply a more varied and subtle pattern of relationships: at least in Wicklow. Mrs Smith's diary discusses questions like the elastic social position of the land agent.[23] She also records what historians have inferred from statistics, the fact that an eviction notice did not necessarily impose any necessity to leave. And even Carleton, in 1872, remarked that 'the lower Irish *until a comparatively recent period* were treated with apathy and gross neglect by the only class to whom they could or ought to look up to for sympathy or probation',[24] but things were better now. After the trauma of the Famine, some of these themes re-emerged in strengthened form.

Change was on the way by the 1870s, only dimly perceived and analysed in a number of ways. One thing most observers noted was that the landlord system could not be sustained *ad infinitum*; another was that the change in the nature of the Irish parish priest since the growth of Maynooth's influence was the most obvious reason for the change in social relations in post-Famine Ireland.[25] The overall impression was different. The bitter criticisms of a Wicklow landlord and politician, James Grattan of Tinnehinch, had been poured into his diary throughout the 1830s. Irish society was 'ignorant, prejudiced, vulgar, brutal' — 'bad education and bad company' — 'a gentry embodying the character of a military without the discipline'. 'The people in many places are insufficiently civilised', he had written,

> pursued by tithes, habituated to see a great military force and to think that the law depended upon them; for the most part unacquainted with an active magistracy or an efficient police, kind or indulgent landlords, or a respectable clergy, they are what they have been and will continue to be until a milder government and system changes their character and education changes their habits.[26]

This was a rationalist belief shared by his neighbours like William Parnell (grandfather of Charles Stewart) and Lord Fitzwilliam: the sons of those who had prominently opposed the Union, believers in 'education open to all', critics of the effects of the Union on Ireland; all owning estates abutting on each other in Wicklow. The reasonable reaction of such people was to attempt to change the system, gearing it for more efficiency and greater reform. William Parnell and James Grattan had entered liberal politics (and had been opposed by their more predictable neighbours for doing so). The lessons of the Famine only amplified the reaction; Mrs Smith, significantly, supported Butt's first Home Rule initiative, because of the government's dereliction of duty over the Famine. However, especially after the 1860s, those landlords who opted for progressivism often tended to be marked down for local criticism; because too often, such attitudes went with consolidation of holdings, modernisation of farming methods, and other changes that disturbed the traditional integument of Irish country life. Threats of eviction were not necessarily part of such strategy: re-cropping, migration, realloca-tion and drainage were. These were generally summed up as 'English ideas', and resentment against them was articulated in the Land War. Staying with Wicklow, we find one of Lord Fitzwilliam's tenants telling the Land Commission in 1881:

> He has without a doubt introduced English ideas, contrary to the feelings and views of the Irish people. I do not know any landlord who has with greater determination attempted to carry out English ideas than he has.[27]

This was evidently something to be resented. And yet Parnell admitted in Parliament, as a neighbour of Fitzwilliam's, that 'as to the Fitzwilliam estate in Wicklow, I know a great deal about it; it is so well managed that the tenants up to the present refused to join the Land League'.[28] It is one of the instances where the improving Wicklow landlord speaks more clearly than the nation-alist politician. (As to the Fitzwilliams, their estate records indeed show a complex structure of administrative organisation, embracing teachers' salaries in free schools, widows' pensions, a Poor Shop run on a money basis, and the encouragement of tourism: as well as an element of social control. An agent's dictat runs: 'Edward Kelly is not to beat his wife Johanna any more and his wife is not again either to keep company with the Kirwans of Ballyconnell or to go into their house'. 'English ideas' could invade many areas. But when rent was increased with improvements, it was only by 5%; and the estate paid a half of all improvement expenses. Requests for rent reductions were often sympathetically met, especially if they involved reductions to subtenants in turn.[29] Thus one of Parnell's neighbours. Inter-estingly, another estate instanced in 1881 as being managed 'on the English model' was the Carysfort estate, practically next door to Avondale, where before 1870 free sale prevailed, and the tenants were encouraged to reclaim, fence and drain. Even after 1881, rents were paid without reduction. During the Land War, Wicklow's record was relatively peaceful.[30]

All this leads to the question of whether Wicklow had a special nature. Did the 'English' character of estate administrations, and names like Hume-wood, Belmont, Woodstock and Avondale indicate an ethos differing from the norm? Certainly, there was prosperity outside the model estates — to go by the records of the savings banks, the type of crime recurring at assizes, the speed of agricultural recovery after the Famine, the low illiteracy figures.

Individual estate records show wages well above the average. Grandees like the Powerscourts, in between acclimatising Japanese deer and afforesting the landscape, took good care to keep well in with local clergy and tenantry.[31] At least in the east of the county, there was a dominant 'estate culture'; one recent authority, discussing the way that estates 'landscaped' both physical and social geography in Ireland, refers to Wicklow for many of his examples.[32] And while in control, the Wicklow gentry bent themselves to making their mark on the populace: often through education. School accounts are prominent in estate records; Robert Truell of Clonmannin and Mrs Smith of Baltiboys were preoccupied by educational initiatives; the Halls were impressed by the Putlands' school at Bray, and the Latouches' at Delgany. In Wicklow, at any rate, we can isolate a gentry subculture: past the preoccupation of letters and diaries with religion, illness, visiting and the weather, we find a vein of analytical criticism of the stereotypical Irish landlords, generally coming from landlords who have *not* adopted the status quo. They may view their tenantry as mean, foolish, demanding and unreasonable with a condescension that makes our blood run cold. But they tend to argue that the *system* has produced this effect. These critics are as anti-English as any colonials. James Grattan criticised his and William Parnell's friend Tom Moore 'for eulogising the English character and institutions overmuch — a fault very usually found with those who have lived long abroad'.[33] The same strain found an interest in Irish history and tradition, and an annoyance with the way these were underplayed in comparison to fashionable Scots preoccupations. Antiquities and restoration became an obsession from the 1830s on. But 'Irishness' for these critical gentry was carefully defined. Grattan and Mrs Smith felt equal repugnance for violent Orangemen and violent Catholics, and were suspicious of the Repeal movement's associations.

How, then, to defuse dangerous passions and ensure social stability? A 'resident gentry' was the safer, recurring, panacea. Men like Parnell's own father tried to live up to this. His constant attendance at Poor Law Guardian meetings, his dutiful attitude to county affairs, can be followed in the Rathdrum Poor Law Union records.[34] Such attempts were often uphill work, struggling against not only a system that was already outmoded, but also against the expansive cynicism of local opinion. And this predisposition to good works often went with an aggressive Protestantism which negated their effect — in Wicklow no less than elsewhere (J.A. Froude, of all people, was won back to the church by a sojourn in a Delgany rectory). But the Fitzwilliam schools dispute shows an attempt to impose non-sectarianism (though his school committee was described as 'a set of whoremasters' because it included a Quaker and a publican).[35] Fitzwilliam's agent took issue with the Protestant Bishop of Ossory about anti-Catholic sermons. And Wicklow grandees like Powerscourt, Meath, Monck and Proby clubbed together to buy a house for the celebrated Father Healy of Little Bray, who appeared regularly at their dinner-parties; and they at his.[36]

Where then does Charles Stewart Parnell fit into this tapestry? The researcher feels an attractive glow in reading Lady Alice Howard's diary for 1873 and finding Charlie and Fanny Parnell, the future President of the Land League and the future muse of Irish-American nationalism, playing tennis at Shelton Abbey. Once again, the retrospective irony is worth savouring. But it is also an indication of the variety and ambivalence of the gentry culture. Schizophrenia, as a concept if not a word, recurs in contemporary descriptions of Parnell's position. But he certainly makes sense as the pragmatic, Tory-inclined landlord, just as much as a figure in the tradition of Lord Edward Fitzgerald, Erskine Childers, Maud Gonne, or Bridget Rose Dugdale; the zeal of the convert is not appropriate. Carson is nearer the type, or Bismarck (whom he admired). Sometimes he has the air of an arrogant colonial, fighting to preserve something. This ties in too with the anti-Union tradition. As Professor Lyons has shown, Parnell's identifiable preoccupation, up to 1886 at any rate, was with 1782: to the irritation of those who had thought Home Rule through to its logical conclusion.[37] And 1782 had been the apotheosis of the gentry culture. When he was appearing in parliament for nothing else, he turned up to contribute to questions that affected his stone-quarries in Wicklow; his only consistent correspondence with English politicians concerned similarly mundane 'improving policies'; recent work has demonstrated the essential conservatism of his stance throughout the Land War. In all this, he is the archetypal improving landlord in politics. He also carried on the tradition of Wicklow gentlemen who became demented about the chance of finding gold in the county. In his campaign on behalf of the Arklow harbour, he was closely connected with another Wicklow improving landlord, his kinsman Lord Carysfort. The 'improving landlord' persona often struck those meeting Parnell who expected it least.[38]

This brings us back to the connection between nationalism and Toryism — far warmer than Liberals could understand. The Land War identified Home Rule with Radicalism, but this was an erroneous connection. Even while it was dominant, the nationalists were engaged in elaborate parliamentary games with the Conservative 4th Party, who, despite historiography, more often took up ultra-Tory than neo-Liberal positions. (We find him, with obvious pleasure, supporting an obstructive move made by them on behalf of the owners of foxhound packs; Parnell speaking 'in the interests of the dogs themselves'.[39]) In November 1881, Frank Hugh O'Donnell, with characteristic ineptitude, attempted to form an Irish-Conservative alliance while Parnell was in jail; it might have stood more chance with him out of it. W.S. Blunt and others found to their sorrow that the Irish were more potentially conservative and imperialist than a people supposedly breaking the bonds of colonialism had any right to be; Labouchere used this very phenomenon as an argument to persuade wavering right-wing Liberals in 1885-86. In Terence McGrath's *Pictures from Ireland* (1880) one is struck by the fact that nearly all his selected stereotypes — agent, attorney, gentleman farmer, parish priest, distressed landlord — are basically Conservatives in politics. In the same year J.G. Swift MacNeill, a Home Ruler with a Conservative background, emphasised how the policy of Home Rule could be taken up by either party. And a certain element of English Conservatives were quite ready to speculate privately about the possibilities inherent in the Home Rule card during the early 1880s.[40] One thinks of the phenomenon of the Conservative Roman Catholic in Irish politics; of the success the Marlborough viceroyalty had in winning over influential Catholic opinion to the Conservative Party in the late 1870s. In the early 1880s Conservatives like Gorst, Wolff and Blandford all favoured versions of Home Rule from their various angles: in 1885 there were powerful arguments for Lord Carnravon's belief that he was widely supported. It was fear of Conservative rapprochement with Home Rulers in 1886 that produced the organised Ulster bloc in parliament.

This remained a minority trend. By the mid-1880s, a Conservative Catholic priest like Father Healy seemed an anomaly; a landlord like King Harman (old HGA man, instrumental in famine relief, proud of his 'good landlord' reputation) was pitilessly attacked in the *Freeman's Journal* as the whitest of sepulchres. Samuel Ferguson, a key figure in the Irish rediscovery of the past, had originally moved from powerful Tory associations and an Ulster gentry background to founding the Protestant Repeal Association in 1848; but first the 'plebeianising' nature of the Home Rule movement, and then the Phoenix Park murders (which moved him to lengthy poems in the Browning mode) stopped him going further. He had once called for 'a restoration of Grattan's Parliament' — as did Lecky, who then became the Unionists' intellectual champion — and as did Parnell.

And Parnell remained archetypally Anglo-Irish — a fact greatly appreciated by his party. The archetypal arrogance remained, to be found in his sister Anna too. He could address the electorate in the tones of a landowner demanding his due.[41] There was also the archetypal hard-upness; Dublin opinion decided that Parnell's trip to America in 1879 was undertaken in order to pay his bill to his tailor, and his perilous financial position comes more clearly into focus with every scrap of Parnell family material that comes to light. It is amusing to find the family solicitor writing in 1882 that he well understands Captain Boycott, since he has to collect Parnell's brother's rents protected by two armed constables. The Parnells, however, needed their rents; they were as reduced in circumstances as many other Wicklow gentry. Up to 1882, it is true, Parnell pursued a line in politics marked by Fenian flirtations and a well-publicised (and probably genuine) rejection of English mores and English politics. But at the same time, he remained firmly

identified with his background. It is apposite to find — though not in Barry
O'Brien — that on a visit to Waterford in December 1880, the joy-bells of
the Protestant cathedral were rung for him; and that he subsequently hunted
with the Marquess of Waterford's hounds. Or that, at a dinner with Victor
Hugo in Paris in February 1881, Parnell was the only Irishman in evening
dress. It is possible to see him as believing that land reform would bring the
landlords into the nationalist ranks. Ambivalence dogs his image throughout.
Certainly, Parnell may profitably be connected back to the Home Ruler
landlords, Tory and Protestant, who had 'joined up' in the 1870s, and whom
he had supported in classic Tory Home Rule issues like Grand Jury reform.[42]
Times, and politics, changed; and he helped to change them. As early as 1876
Richard Bagwell, the historian, could write a choleric article violently
indicting any landlords who were associated with the Home Rulers; and as
for Protestant Home Rulers, Bagwell wrote, 'let all imagine that can, what
sort of Protestants would support Mr Parnell'.[43]

But why did more landlords *not* follow Parnell's example, and accept the
radicalisation of the Home Rule demand as something that might work in
their long-term interests? Certainly, the rhetoric of the land war, and the
general polarisation of attitudes (religious as well as social) by 1886, worked
against this: subsequently cultural revivalism, and the revolutionising effect
of the First World War, transformed everything. By 1919 that attractive
novelist and incomparable observer, George A. Birmingham, could write
that 'the most striking feature of Irish politics is the stability of parties': the
lack of dialogue and fluidity between nationalists and unionists. Yet, Birmingham correctly surmised, before the 1880s there had not been this rigidity.
There had once been the strain of nationalism that believed in independence
for the increased efficiency of Ireland and of the Empire, and had closely
associated with the English Conservatives. But the new nationalism had to
exclude it.[44]

Elsewhere, Birmingham mused about the failure of the Anglo-Irish to take
up nationalism; he could not see them as a 'garrison', as Sinn Féin claimed;
and if Griffith had thought through his Hungarian parallel, he would have
seen that *they* were the Magyars. From 1800, the English had consistently
sold the Anglo-Irish down the river; why then adhere to the Union?

Largely, Birmingham answered himself, because they were distrustful of
'ideas' and 'enthusiasms', in the tradition of the eighteenth century which
they still represented. It is an inadequate answer, but the question is still valid.
A misplaced fear for property had more to do with it; Birmingham himself
was told by a local nationalist, 'Damn Home Rule! What we're out for is the
land. The land matters. All the rest is tall talk'.[45] By 1919, in any case,
snobbery, social superiority, deference and unionism had fused; since long
before, the connection of a unionist ideology with the gentry had been taken
for granted. But, as Birmingham pointed out with characteristic percipience,

it had not always been so.

The hardening and fixing of gentry attitudes is more immediately reflected in George Moore's haunting novel of the 1880s, *A Drama in Muslin*. Written from contemporary notes taken by Moore's brother, it reflects Moore's own ambivalence as a landlord and a hater of Gladstone, who still realised the exploitative basis of the Irish rural economy. And in this book, Parnell looms in the background: all the more threatening to the insecure gentry since he was once the kind of eligible young landlord who obsesses the scheming county ladies.[46] He is a baleful figure to the whispering girls, who belong to a class already doomed; he spells the end of what they have known. The news of the Phoenix Park murders interrupts a county picnic. 'I think they ought to hang Mr. Parnell', says one of the girls; 'I believe it was he who drove the car'. Lord Kilcarney, the encumbered landlord, explaining his dislike of Dublin society, says of the Castle: 'I used to hate it; I was as bad as Parnell, but not for the same reasons, of course. Now I am only afraid he will have his way, and they will shut the whole place up'.[47]

In fact, Parnell had once much enjoyed Castle society. But by the mid-1880s, no-one would believe that. And by then too, the vast majority of Irish landlords had retreated into fear. A failure of imagination had led to a fear of displacement: of *no place being left to them*. It is no accident that a favourite story in Unionist memoirs dealt with the jarvey who answered John Morley's remark that Home Rule would bring him 'great times': 'Yes, for a week: driving the quality to the steamers'.[48]

The 1880s, like the 1840s, occasioned a great spate of 'Irish observations' literature, in which the threatened landlord is a recurring figure. The hysterical note of the ILPU tracts from the mid-1880s is an eloquent reflection: it also solidified, and made (more or less) coherent, a party line. And this attitude had spread to Wicklow. Symbolically, an ILPU pamplet in 1886 forecast that under Home Rule, 'there would be nothing in the world, except the cowardice of the Parnellites, to prevent the loyalists of a secluded spot like Delgany from being massacred on any Sunday afternoon'.[49] And the loyalists of Delgany agreed.

Twenty years later John Synge's mother used to rent Casino, the dower house on the Avondale estate (now demolished: it stood where the car park is). Wandering around Wicklow, Synge found 'a curious affection for the landed classes' lasting on among those who remembered them in their heyday; the older country people saw them as the losers, though the younger felt differently. This may have reflected the difference between the nationalism of the Irish parliamentary party and of Sinn Féin. Exploring a ruined garden in the vicinity, which may well have been Avondale's, he mused:

Everyone is used in Ireland to the tragedy that is bound up with the lives of farmers and fishing people; but in this garden one seemed to feel the tragedy of the landlord class also, and of the innumerable old families that are quickly dwindling away. These owners of the land are not much pitied at the present day, or much deserving of pity; and yet one cannot quite forget that they are the descendants of what was, at one time, in the eighteenth century, a high-spirited and highly cultivated aristocracy. The broken greenhouses and mouse-eaten libraries, that were designed and collected by men who voted with Grattan, are perhaps as mournful in the end as the four walls that are so often left in Wicklow as the only remnants of a farmhouse.[50]

The note is, apparently, one of elegy rather than whining: which often obtrudes on the memoirs of those gentry who simply could not understand how rapidly they had come to be seen as dispensable. Parnell, to return to him for the last time, had been a product of this very background; the rupture of his career makes us forget that in many ways it was originally set on a course entirely consonant with this.

Of course, I leave out his sense of practical politics — his use of the Fenians — his American background. All this set him far apart from the Wicklow gentry culture. And I leave out the imponderable effect on him of the vivid Wicklow traditions of 1798, and the influence of his sisters and — possibly — his mother. All this is vitally important in the formation of the phenomenon. But so is that tradition of the continuity of anti-Union gentry families — Ponsonbys, Tighes, Grattans, Parnells; closely integrated into the circuit of interconnected Wicklow county society, with the Fitzwilliams, Carysforts, Smiths, Howards, and others; deeply interested in running their estates in a modern way, attempting to encourage responsibility and productivity, interested in plans for canals and railways, employing hard-headed Scots or Ulstermen as estate managers. Religious tolerance also distinguished them (Parnell was much less affected than most Irish Protestants by the stereotype of Catholics as at once childish and devious). Parnell, seen in this tradition, helps to illustrate a continuity in Irish history, from the (self-interested) opponents of the Union, through the improving county gentry, to the Tory and landlord supporters of early Home Rule.

And there the continuity ends. The pieces of the jigsaw were jolted and reshuffled, first by Catholic *revanche*, then the sudden and violent — if temporary — agricultural crisis of the late 1870s, and then by the identification of Liberalism, radicalism, Catholicism and Home Rule from the 1880s. Perhaps most of all, the social map of Irish politics was redrawn by the introduction of the secret ballot, and the franchise and redistribution reforms of 1884-85, which put paid to deference politics in the old style. Irish society did not provide a political party staffed by Parnells instead of Healys and O'Briens; though Parnell stayed on to lead it.

He broke and shaped moulds; he remains uniquely glamorous, and glamorously unique. But in some ways, he was originally a representative figure too. From the time he emerges into the spotlight in the 1870s he appears, as Yeats wrote, to be schooled in solitude. But some at least of what lay behind him involved the experience of a rationally minded gentry, putting — as they had always done — their instinct for survival first, realising the land system would no longer support them, cautiously attempting an initiative towards devolutionary independence, strongly conscious that things had to change in order to remain the same. This strain should equally be borne in mind — and not only because it had such a formative part to play in the making of Parnell.

Notes

1. The mental world of this group has been brilliantly explored in J.A. Spence's PhD thesis, 'The Philosophy of Anglo-Irish Toryism' (London, 1991).
2. As in the broad promises about land legislation and denominational education in the 1868 election. D. Thornley, *Isaac Butt and Home Rule* (London, 1964), pp. 30-2.
3. The tradition that the HGA was 'Tory nationalism' incarnate is enshrined in A.M. Sullivan's *New Ireland* (see 14th ed., 1881, p. 328). Sullivan himself was something of an admirer of Irish Protestant probity; he told Galbraith he would accept the Church of Ireland Synod as a parliament for Ireland, knowing that it would lead to full and equal Home Rule (J.G. Swift MacNeill, *What I Have Seen and Heard* (London, 1925), p. 126).
4. Thornley, pp. 96, 113.
5. Ibid., pp. 125-6. This was not restricted to 'Protestants with horses'; Bishop Delaney, who had cautiously supported the HGA, was one Catholic Conservative who had hoped it would lead to something like a 'national Grand Jury for Irish affairs' (ibid., p. 129).
6. This was a belief that had been reiterated in Gerald Fitzgibbon's *Ireland in 1868*, a pamphlet appealing to the 'Roman Catholic gentry' and the common interests of all right-thinking men of property: later itemised by Engels as an archetypal Irish Conservative broadside.
7. Thornley, pp. 195-6. The men in question include figures like Sir John Esmonde (Wicklow), Thomas Tighe (Mayo), Sir George Bowyer (Wexford), and George Morris (Galway).
8. Esmonde was from the first doubtful about the whip. Morris and White supported him. The O'Conor Don, Bowyer, Montagu and King Harman sat on the Conservative side. Sir Colm O'Loghlen provided the classic rationale against tight party discipline (Thornley, pp. 218-19). All the same, Esmonde, Morris and the O'Conor Don supported Butt's proposal to give Home Rule another hearing when parliament opened; and in meetings of the party in 1876-77, only Blennerhasset of the landed element was a regular absentee.
9. See Butt's open letter to Father Murphy of Ferns, *Freeman's Journal*, 7 Sept. 1877. Also Terence McGrath's satirical *Pictures from Ireland* (1880) which profiled a typical Home Ruler thus: 'When Mr Butt's scheme of Home Rule was proposed Mr O'Carroll accepted it, and kept well within constitutional lines in his advocacy of the measure. He was one of the committee that

deliberately chose a Protestant candidate pledged to Mr Butt's principles, in opposition to one of his own faith. Such moderation must, he argued, have its effect in the attempt to induce the British parliament to grant the measure, or the Protestants of the North of Ireland to combine in seeking for it . . .' (p. 81). See also Paul Bew, *C.S. Parnell* (1980).

10. See *Sixty Years' Experience as an Irish Landlord: Memoirs of John Hamilton, DL, of St Ernan's, Donegal*, edited with an introduction by Rev. H.C. White (London, 1894). Hamilton still felt that Irish patriotism had left 'a legacy of vain aspirations of national glory as a *little* independent nation, instead of the truly glorious position of being an independent part of the United Kingdom'.

11. J.S. Donnelly, *The Land and the People of 19th Century Cork* (London, 1974). The best general summary of this controversy is in K.T. Hoppen, *Ireland since 1800: Conflict and Conformity* (London, 1989), chapter 4.

12. 23 May 1856; see Marx and Engels, *On Ireland* (London, 1971).

13. K.T. Hoppen, 'Landlords and electoral politics in Ireland', *Past and Present* 75 (1977), pp. 62-93.

14. McGrath, *Pictures from Ireland*, pp. 185 ff; Lloyd, *Ireland under the Land League* (London, 1892), pp. 218-19; Anna Parnell, *The Tale of a Great Sham*, ed. Dana Hearne (Dublin, 1986).

15. H.M. D'Arcy Irvine, *Letter to the Rt. Hon. W.E. Gladstone on the Irish Land Bill* (1870), p. 8. Another example is Rigby Wason, *A letter to the Rt. Hon. Chichester Fortescue* (1869).

16. Published London, 1870. Also see Henry Dix Hutton, *History, Principle and Fact in Relation to the Irish Land Question* (London, 1870).

17. W.R. Le Fanu, *Seventy years of Irish life* (London, 1893), p. 5.

18. This is the implicit message of K.T. Hoppen's magisterial *Elections, Politics and Society in Ireland, 1832-1885* (Oxford, 1984).

19. 'The late Thos. Conolly, the Hamiltons, the Marquis of Conyngham, Mr Brooke of Lough Eske, and some others', quoted in T. de Vere White, *The Anglo-Irish* (London, 1971),p. 142.

20. See the PhD thesis on it by Andrew Tod (Edinburgh, 1979), and the selections edited by David Thomson and Moyra McGusty (Oxford, 1980).

21. Entries for 18 January 1841, May 1840, 1840 (n.d.).

22. Mr and Mrs S.C. Hall, *Ireland: Its Scenery, Character, etc.* (London, 3 vols. 1841-3), i, pp. iii-iv.

23. Epigrammatically described by W.E. Vaughan as 'rustic statesmen with proconsular functions'; also see *The Real Charlotte*, where the Desart agency conferred 'brevet rank of gentleman' on Roddy Lambert.

24. Introduction to 1872 edition of *Traits and Stories of the Irish Peasantry*, p. 13.

25. Of the authorities cited, see Smith and Hall, *passim*; Hussey, 116; Lloyd, 62; McGrath, 56-7.

26. NLI Mss. 3853, 5776.

27. As reported in *Pall Mall Gazette*, 17 June 1881. On the unpopularity of such ideas, see Solow, pp. 82-5; on the reasons why they were not more generally adopted, W.E. Vaughan in F.S.L. Lyons and R.A.J. Hawkins (eds.), *Ireland under the Union: Varieties of Tension* (Oxford, 1980) and Cormac Ó Gráda,

Ireland Before and After the Famine (Manchester, 1988).

28. *Pall Mall Gazette*, 17 June 1881.
29. See Fitzwilliam Estate Papers, NLI Mss. 4955, 4962, 3983, 3984, 4965.
30. Davitt, visiting Blessington in December 1880, could only find one local outrage to instance: he had to restrict himself to expansive rhetoric, pointing out that 'landlords did not lay the foundations of the Sugar Loaf mountain, or ornament the scenery of Wicklow by making the Vale of Avoca or creating the Meeting of the Waters'. *Pall Mall Gazette*, 14 December 1880.
31. See Brassington and Gale's 1853 report on the estate.
32. T. Jones Hughes, 'Society and settlement in 19th-century Ireland', *Irish Geography* 5.
33. NLI Ms. 5777.
34. See NLI Ms. n 6-8, p. 201-3; his colleague and ally on the local Poor Law Guardians' Board, Andrew Byrne, later became one of the early landlord Home Rulers.
35. See my *Charles Stewart Parnell: the Man and his Family* (Hassocks, 1976), p. xvii.
36. W.J. Fitzpatrick, *Memories of Father Healy of Little Bray* (London, 1894), p. 131.
37. Like J. O'Connor Power, who attacked Parnell on these grounds in *The Anglo-Irish Quarrel: A Plea for Peace* (London, 1880). 'There is no subject about which Mr Parnell is so ignorant as that of Irish history, and his contempt for books is strikingly shown in his reference to Grattan's parliament . . .'
38. Including Henry Labouchere: see *Truth*, 3 November 1881, for a record of a conversation about the landlord position.
39. *Hansard 3*, ccxxxix, 1160.
40. See my 'To the Northern Counties Station' in Lyons and Hawkins, op. cit., pp. 253-4.
41. For instance, his letter to the Dundalk electors about Philip Callan: *Pall Mall Gazette*, 30 March 1880.
42. Described by Captain Nolan, one of its progenitors, as 'not directed against a class', but intended to bring the peers into county administration, and presented by Butt as a measure to integrate gentry and people (*Hansard 3*, ccxxvii, 377, 765; ccxvxii, 87-9). Parnell often used similar language, as when arguing that rents should be fixed in May 1880.
43. 'Home Rulers at home', *University Magazine*, 1876.
44. *An Irishman Looks at His World*, pp. 1, 12, 13.
45. *Ibid.*, p. 208.
46. 'And Mr Parnell's a gentleman too. I wonder how he can ally himself with such blackguards', gently insinuated Mrs Barton, who saw a husband lost in the politician! (Ebury edition, 1915, p. 44).
47. *Ibid.*, p. 253.
48. Found in S.M. Hussey, *Reminiscences*, p. 178, but elsewhere too.
49. T. Maguire, *England's Duty to Ireland, as Plain to a Loyal Irish Roman Catholic* (Dublin, 1886).
50. J.M. Synge, *In Wicklow and West Kerry* (Dublin, 1912), pp. 48-9.

Parnell and the Leadership of Nationalist Ireland

Dr Martin Mansergh

Charles Stewart Parnell's entry into politics in 1874 and election in 1875 certainly owed much to his name. Isaac Butt, the leader of the Home Rule Party, told Barry O'Brien, a Fenian and later Parnell's biographer, 'My dear boy, we have got a splendid recruit, an historic name, my friend, young Parnell of Wicklow', even though on the evidence of his first speech he could hardly string two sentences together. Although Ireland in the meantime has had a democratic revolution, having a name with a tradition behind it is still an asset in Irish politics and in many other walks of life as well. (I suspect that my own invitation to speak to the Parnell Society is in good part a recognition of the contribution that my father has made to Irish historical studies, which has earned him a respect and a reputation which I could not possibly emulate, and which I hope my own political involvement will do nothing to diminish.)

Parnell had some of Swift's 'savage indignation'. It related to two objects, the humiliating treatment of Ireland and of Irish people by England in general and specifically the catastrophe of the Famine. With regard to the first, Parnell relived for himself the experience of the more intelligent and sensitive members of the Ascendancy in 18th-century Ireland. Even the Irish gentry were never treated as equals by the British ruling classes. Their ideals were expressed by Grattan, the reality of their position pointed out brutally by Lord Clare. The Protestant anti-Unionist tradition, which came briefly to the surface again after disestablishment in the 1870s, was allied in Parnell's case to an American ancestry, a grandfather Admiral Stewart of Ulster origins, who had captured two British vessels in the war of 1812.

Most contemporaries, both enemies and friends, described Parnell as anti-British or at least anti-English. That was not of course quite as heinous a charge a century ago as it appears to be today. Barry O'Brien wrote: 'The idea that the Irish were despised was always in Parnell's mind. This arrogance, this assumption of superiority galled Parnell . . . and he resolved to wring justice from England and to humiliate her in the process'. But what does or did the term anti-British mean? It could mean an inherited or acquired antipathy to or dislike of a country, its people and its whole way of life. While it is quite possible that Parnell disliked some things about England, Cambridge University for example, or at least some of the people he met there, the fact is he spent much of his life as a parliamentarian in London, and he eventually married an Englishwoman, with whom he had lived for nearly a decade. His political beliefs were founded on a positive principle stated in his maiden speech when he asked why Ireland, a nation, should be treated as a geographical fragment of England. This was no more than a statement of the position of Grattan and Davis. But since Britain was denying Ireland the political rights of nationhood, Ireland had only two choices, to persuade Britain by sweet reason and saintly patience that she was wrong, or to fight her by every available political means, and in the last resort non-political means, to obtain legitimate national rights. After all, as Liberal politicians were prepared privately to admit by the 1880s, Ireland was held by force not by consent. Anyone engaged in a political battle faces within the framework of that battle an opposing political force, and is obviously anti that force as well as pro its own objectives.

If Parnell was anti-British, then a whole string of British politicians, Disraeli, Gladstone for quite a lot of his career, Chamberlain, Hartington, Harcourt, Forster, Salisbury, Lord Churchill and so on were anti-Irish. To pick a single example, Disraeli's biographer, Lord Blake, says of him: 'Disraeli . . . was at heart wholly out of sympathy with the Irish, and, excepting certain proposals in 1852, made essentially for tactical purposes, he never did or said anything helpful to them'. Britain has been fairly successful over the last century in labelling any vigorous assertion of Ireland's independent political rights as anti-British, while avoiding being confronted itself with the opposite accusation because Irish people are mostly too polite to make it. What in reality is at issue is a difference of opinion, on both sides, as to whether conciliation, or reconciliation as we call it nowadays, is an effective political method for the weak to use vis-à-vis the strong and vice versa. By definition most forms of violence also have limited effectiveness between the weak and the strong. What Parnell and his political allies were engaged in between 1877 and 1882 was creative resistance at its most successful (the civil rights movements of the late 1960s in the North was another example of creative resistance). In many ways this was the most brilliant period of Parnell's life, which created a decisive political momentum, which was never thereafter wholly lost, even though diverted into other channels.

Isaac Butt, the leader of the Home Rule Party when Parnell entered parliament, is an honourable figure in Irish history, but was a hopeless political leader. Starting life as a Tory, he became totally disillusioned by the callousness of Britain towards Ireland during the Famine. He won the respect of the Fenians by defending their actions as political and as President of the Amnesty Association. A very loose Home Government Association of which he was the head grew out of a temporary Protestant backlash against Disestablishment, which was in breach of the promise at the Act of Union that the churches would be perpetually united. It adopted, in place of repeal, federalism (within the UK), that blind alley which crops up with a certain monotonous regularity at different points in Irish history. This ever so mild political movement would not have been complete without clerical condemnation from some quarter. Dr Moriarty, Bishop of Kerry, who it will be remembered had said that 'hell was not hot enough nor eternity long enough' to punish the Fenians, described the Home Rule Association as 'in the circumstances of the country, one of the most mischievous movements to which you have been ever urged or excited', and the Bishop of Cork had gently to point out to him that Home Rule and Fenianism were not quite the same thing. The tensions in the early period between those, including the Church, who favoured support for the Liberal Party and those who favoured an independent movement were not satisfactorily resolved under Butt's leadership.

The Disraeli government of the late 1870s constituted probably the heyday of British imperialism. Butt's disorganised Home Rule party, which imposed no discipline on its members, and allowed nominal 'Home Rulers' to sit on different sides of the House, got no hearing when it put forward private members' bills dealing with issues such as the land, the university question or Home Rule itself. Biggar, Parnell and a small group of MPs systematically obstructed the proceedings of the House, kept ministers and members out of bed at all hours, and eventually forced parliament to change its rules. Parnell sometimes spoke for hours in a deserted House. He said he rather liked an empty House, it gave him more time to think. When later on a young MP asked him what was the best way of learning the rules of the House, he replied: 'By breaking them'.

Butt deplored obstruction, on the grounds that it was the abandonment of constitutional action. He steadfastly maintained that something was being achieved, even when it was obvious that nothing had changed or was going to change. 'They had not obtained Home Rule', Butt said, 'but they had been making a steady progress in the House of Commons and in English public opinion in regard to all their measures'. *The Freeman's Journal* commented in 1878: 'Mr Butt seems to think that his policy of self-effacement on every occasion is the way to win for Ireland her rights'. But in his last years he finally succumbed to the fatal magnetic charm of Westminster, which in one speech he referred to as 'the mother of representative institutions, the seat of intellect, the life, and the power of this great united nation'. He believed that Parnell and his friends were simply antagonising British opinion, and were behaving in a thoroughly counterproductive fashion.

The Irish MP, Mitchell Henry, put it in a rather different perspective: 'I do not hesitate to say that what makes Mr Parnell and some others so hateful to the English press and to most of the English members is that they think them formidable because not likely to be bought by office, or by what is quite as fatal, by personal flattery'.

Parnell's background and upbringing gave him one inestimable advantage. He was not in any sense overawed or intimidated by the venerable aura of British institutions, with which he was thoroughly familiar. He was ready to take them on in their own heartland. Unlike Butt, unlike Redmond, Parnell was not seduced by Westminster. As the radical MP, Dilke, said: 'We could not get at him as at any other man in English public life. He was not one of us in any sense. Dealing with him was like dealing with a foreign power. This gave him an immense advantage'.

Parnell first came to British public notice when, to the shock of the House of Commons, he told the British Home Secretary, Sir Michael Hicks Beach, that he could not regard the Manchester martyrs, who had killed a police guard while trying to rescue prisoners, as murderers. Parnell had already identified himself with the amnesty movement. The British government of the day stated adamantly that Home Rule was 'out'. *The Times* stated: 'Parliament will not, cannot grant Home Rule. The mere demand for it lies beyond the range of practical discussion'. Some flavour of Parnell's attitudes in this period can be gauged from his speeches, as at Manchester in 1877:

Did they get the abolition of tithes by the conciliation of their English taskmasters? No, it was because they adopted different measures. Did O'Connell gain Emancipation for Ireland by conciliation? . . . Catholic Emancipation was gained because an English King and his ministers feared revolution. Why was the English church in Ireland disestablished and disendowed? Why was some measure of protection given the Irish tenant? It was because there was an explosion at Clerkenwell and because a lock was shot off a prison van at Manchester.

In July in the House of Commons, in the process of keeping the House sitting for 45 hours on the South Africa Bill, Parnell said:

I did not think myself called on to refrain from acting on English questions for fear of any annoyance the English might feel, any more than the English have ever felt called on to refrain from interfering in our concerns for fear of any annoyance we might feel.

At the Rotunda in August 1877 he stated:

I care nothing for this English Parliament nor for its outcries. I care nothing for its existence, if that existence is to continue a source of tyranny and destruction to my country.

And he often stated: 'By the judgement of the Irish people only do I and will I, stand or fall'.

The royal family was another British institution for which Parnell showed little affection. In 1880, he engaged in controversy in the columns of the press with Lord Randolph Churchill on the Famine Queen. 'In reference to

Lord Randolph Churchill's contradiction of my statement, that the Queen gave nothing to relieve the Famine in 1847, I find I might have gone still further and said with perfect accuracy that not only did she give nothing, but that she actually intercepted £6,000 of the donation which the Sultan of Turkey desired to contribute to the Famine Fund'. Or take his attitude to a visit by the Prince of Wales in the 1880s:

> I fail to see upon what ground it can be claimed for any lover of constitutional government under a limited monarchy that the Prince is entitled to a reception from the independent and patriotic people of Ireland, or to any recognition save from the garrison of officials and landowners and placehunters who fatten upon the poverty and misfortunes of the country. Would it be tolerated in England for a moment if the Government, for their own party purposes, on the eve of a general election were to use the Prince of Wales as an electioneering agent in any section of the country in order to embarrass their political opponents? The breach of constitutional privilege becomes still graver when we consider that it is the march of a nation which is now sought to be impeded.

Certainly many of the emotional attitudes of Parnell, from his early bid for Fenian support to his late hillside appeal in Navan that royal Meath might one day become republican Meath, were close to what would nowadays be described as republican, even if Home Rule required retention of the monarchical link.

Some, mainly English, historians have argued that Parnell was too self-indulgent, and that there was a price to be paid for his alleged hostility to Britain. Ensor, in his late 19th century volume in the Oxford History of England, claimed 'his whole attitude expressed a deliberate hatred towards their nation, which was not unnaturally returned' and that 'to concede home rule to Parnell seemed like handing over Ireland to a king of the ogres.' But of course whether there would have been any Home Rule Bill to have been defeated but for Parnell's tough political approach must be open to doubt.

In the circumstances of 19th-century Ireland, British resistance to repeal, coercion, evictions and above all the outrage that the Famine constituted, the only surprising thing is how limited was the resort to physical force. Practical experience in 1848 and 1867 showed the difficulties of mounting a militarily significant rising, though doing nothing to diminish the romantic aura of rebellion. Parnell's sister Fanny, still in her teens, was contributing patriotic verse to the *Irish World*. From the very beginning and throughout his career, Parnell sought the support of the Fenians, and never lost touch with 'advanced nationalists' as he usually referred to them, although some of them opposed his political course. Physical rebellion on the open warfare lines of the '98 rebellion, one historical event in which he showed some interest — he was a maker of history not a reader of it — did not seem to him to be a practicable option, and he was fortunate as a politician that the Fenians or many of them were prepared to give political agitation a try, while reserving their other options. He knew better than to mix the role of politician and rebel in the manner of Wolfe Tone or Lord Edward Fitzgerald. He, as a politician, had a certain sphere of action and certain possibilities. If those failed, then the initiative would return to the advocates of physical force. This was not what he desired, it was just political realism. As he said when he was sent to prison, Captain Moonlight would take over. But he sharply repudiated a reported threat by Devoy in 1881 on the lives of British ministers and to burn down cities, if coercion were proceeded with. He was, moreover, appalled at the Phoenix Park murders, and in a moment of rare emotion uncharacteristically offered his resignation to Gladstone both because he regarded Lord Frederick Cavendish as sympathetic to Ireland and because it undermined completely the assurances he had given Gladstone in the so-called Kilmainham Treaty. The Phoenix Park murders certainly did far more damage to the Irish party than to Britain.

While violence did not cease completely during the period of his leadership, he succeeded in harnessing the support of many of those who believed that physical force was in principle justified. Without a vigorous and aggressive policy, he could never have succeeded in obtaining the measure of Fenian and ex-Fenian support that he did obtain for what was basically a constitutional movement. From the mid-1880s to 1912 was one of the most prolonged peaceful periods in modern Irish history. It was when Redmond reverted to the milk and water constitutional nationalism of Butt that the Nationalist Party lost the initiative to the straight separatists.

Nowhere was Parnell's success greater than in harnessing effectively for the first time Irish-American support behind a national movement. Nowadays it is fashionable to denigrate Irish-American views as naïve and ill-informed, because of their more fundamentalist approach to national issues. American support was vital to the success of the Land League and of the Parnellite movement. Parnell, like de Valera after him, proud of his American background, was well-placed to tap that support. British politicians were fully aware that the Irish presence in America had shifted the imbalance of power somewhat more in Ireland's favour. As Gladstone's cabinet minister, Sir William Harcourt, stated, 'In former Irish rebellions the Irish were in Ireland. Now there is an Irish nation in the United States equally hostile, with plenty of money, absolutely beyond our reach and yet within ten days of our shores'. The Irish-American community have made an inestimable contribution over the past hundred years to the attainment and maintenance of Irish independence. Dr Conor Cruise O'Brien, writing 30 years ago, stated, 'America did remain a great resource, in money and encouragement whenever an Irish movement was on a leftward line, a fact that gave Irish politics a greater depth and Irish leaders a much wider range of choice than they would otherwise have had'. Parnell's success also reflected well on Irish-Americans in their own country. The so-called 'New Departure', based on a programme outlined in an open telegram from Devoy to Kickham, President of the IRB, for passing on to Parnell, laid out the conditions for the support of Irish nationalists in America, the pursuit of self-government, vigorous agitation of the land question on the basis of a peasant proprietary and an aggressive and disciplined voting behaviour at Westminster, especially in resistance to coercion. The alliance worked extremely well, while it lasted. The challenge facing Irish politicians of later generations has been to try and reunite Irish-American opinion behind a positive political programme that has some prospect of success, and to re-create if possible the momentum of the New Departure.

The agricultural depression of 1879, the emergence of famine, and the wholesale evictions posed a dilemma both for constitutional and for revolutionary nationalists. What was the proper relationship of the central national issue to a burning social issue like the land question? It is an important question, worth pondering, as it has some relevance to our own time. Professor Oliver MacDonagh, in his brilliant study, *States of Mind*, on Anglo-Irish conflict, has pointed out the political function of simple, easily grasped demands such as Catholic Emancipation, Repeal, Home Rule, and he could easily have added the Irish Republic and later still a united Ireland. The fulfilment of any one of these demands was meant to comprehend with them the solution of all other problems. It was held by some, both Fenians and constitutional politicians, that the solution of all other questions had to await the fulfilment of the central political goal. If social questions could be solved within the framework of the Union, it might serve to weaken the demand for Home Rule or for separation. As against that, the abstract political demand, when it had no immediate prospect of fulfilment because of British opposition, only aroused a limited degree of popular favour and support, presumably because it did not seem to have an immediate relevance to people's lives.

James Fintan Lalor writing in 1848 was of the view that 'the land question contains and the legislative question does not contain the materials from which victory is manufactured. There is, I am convinced, but one way alone; and that is to link Repeal to some other question, like a railway carriage to an engine; some question possessing the intrinsic strength which Repeal wants; and strong enough to carry both itself and Repeal together . . . Repeal had always to be dragged. This I speak of will carry itself — as the cannonball carries itself down the hill'.

To take over the leadership of the land struggle, as was being urged by Michael Davitt, and to relegate Home Rule for the time being to second place, represented an awesome responsibility, and Parnell did not commit himself to it in haste. But as well as a strong political instinct, he had a strong sense of social justice. He played a key role in the abolition of flogging in the navy, for which his likeness has appeared ever since on the packet of Players' cigarettes. He also voted against capital punishment. The scenes that he saw in the West made a deep impression on him. His attendance at the Westport meeting in 1879, despite the condemnation of the aged Archbishop MacHale, when Parnell urged the tenants to keep a firm grip on their homesteads and lands and not to allow them to be dispossessed as they were in 1847, was regarded by Michael Davitt as the most courageous act of his political career. Of course, most of the credit for the setting up of the Land League and for organised resistance meant to stop just short of physical violence belongs to Davitt and several individuals in the West of Ireland. The leadership and prestige of Parnell helped to improve its chances of success. Parnell and Dillon went to America to raise funds for the Land League. He also helped to set a realistic goal of a peasant proprietary of the land.

In America Parnell was the first Irish leader to address the House of Representatives on 2 February 1880, and only one of the very few, including Lafayette and Kossuth, who had yet been given that privilege. He himself described his reception as 'an unprecedented honour to the humble representatives of an oppressed people'. He used his opportunity well and I would like to quote extracts from this speech, which is passed over by all the standard works on Parnell, and which I had to cull from the columns of the *Freeman's Journal*. It has intrinsic political interest, and is an example of a cogent and effective appeal in the context of a fund-raising tour:

> The public opinion of the people of America will be of the utmost importance in enabling us to obtain a just and suitable settlement of the Irish question . . . We do not seek to embroil your Government with the Government of England. But we claim that the public opinion and sentiment of a free country like America is entitled to find expression whenever it is seen that the laws of freedom are not observed. Mr Speaker and gentlemen, the most pressing question in Ireland is at the present the tenure of land. That question is a very old one. The feudal tenure has been tried in many countries and it has been found wanting everywhere, but in no country has it wrought so much destruction and proved so pernicious as in Ireland. We have as a result of that feudal tenure constant and chronic poverty and we have a people discontented and hopeless. Even in the best years the state of the people is one of chronic poverty and when, as on the present occasion, the crops fail and a bad year comes around we see terrific famines sweeping across the face of our land claiming their victims in hundreds of thousands . . . And now that thousands are starving, the singular spectacle is presented by a government which refuses to come to the aid of its own subjects sanctioning appeals to the charity of America. The present famine, as all other famines in Ireland, has been the direct result of the system of land tenure which is maintained there.

Now we have been told by the landlord party, as their defence of this system, that the true cause of Irish poverty and Irish discontent is the crowded state of that country, and I admit to the fullest extent that there are parts of Ireland which are too crowded. The barren lands of the West of Ireland which the people were driven to from the fertile lands after the famine are too crowded, but the fertile portions of Ireland maintain scarcely any population at all, and remain as vast hunting tracts for the landlord class . . . I should like to see the next emigration from the West to the East instead of from the East to the West — from the barren hills of Connemara back to the fertile plains of Meath, and when the resources of my country have been taken full advantage of and fully developed, when the agricultural prosperity of Ireland has been secured, then if we have any surplus population, we shall cheerfully give it to this great country. The emigrants would come to you, as come the Germans, with money in their pockets, education to enable them to obtain a good start in this free country, and sufficient means to enable them to push out to your Western lands instead of hanging about the Eastern cities, doomed to hard manual labour, and many falling a prey to the worst evils of modern city civilisation.

A writer in the London *Times*, giving an account of the island of Guernsey, knows that it supports in marvellous prosperity a population of 30,000 on an area of 16,000 acres while Ireland has a cultivable area of 15.5 m. acres, and would if as densely peopled as Guernsey, support a population of 45m instead of only 5m at present . . . We propose to imitate the example of Prussia and of other continental countries where the feudal tenure has been tried, found wanting and abandoned, and we propose to make or give an opportunity to every tenant occupying a farm in Ireland to become the owner of his own farm.

He then went into John Bright's proposal to set up a Land Commission.

The radical difference between our proposition and that of Mr Bright is that we think that the State should adopt the system of compulsory expropriation of the land whereas Mr Bright thinks that it may be left to self-interest and the forces of public opinion to compel the landlord to sell . . . I ask the House of Representatives of America what would they think of the statesman, who while acknowledging the justness of principle . . . shrinks at the same time from asking the Legislature of his country to sanction that principle, and leaves to an agitation such as is now going on in Ireland, the duty of enforcing that which the Parliament of Great Britain should enforce. I think myself you will agree with me that this attempt on the part of the British Parliament to transfer its obligations and its duties to the helpless, starving peasantry of Connemara is neither a dignified nor a worthy one. It will be a proud boast for America, if after having obtained, secured and ratified her own freedom by sacrifices unexampled in the history of any nation, by the respect with which all countries look upon any sentiment prevailing in America — if she were now to obtain for Ireland without the shedding of one drop of blood, the solution of this great issue.

And Mr Speaker and gentlemen, these Irish famines, now so periodical, which compel us to appear as beggars and mendicants before the world — a humiliating position for any man but a still more humiliating position for a proud nation like ours — these Irish famines will have ceased when the cause has been removed. We shall no longer be compelled to tax your magnificent generosity, and we shall be able to promise you that with your help this shall be the last Irish famine.

Parnell's international appeals were not confined to America. He met the Communard Henri Rochefort, which led to charges of communism being levelled against him. He also wrote to Victor Hugo about landlordism and famine:

We are struggling against the system which produced these horrors. As you, honoured Sir, have so well raised the sympathies of the human race for *les misérables*, we feel that our appeal will go straight to your heart, and we are sure that you will raise your voice in favour of a brave but unfortunate nation.

The rest of the story is well known. The practice of boycotting was endorsed by Parnell as a constructive alternative to assassination. He calculated that each turnip harvested on Captain Boycott's estate cost a shilling to save by farm labourers drafted in from Ulster. It was followed by the introduction of land reform legislation, setting up dual ownership and the land courts but combined with coercion; the public clash between Gladstone and Parnell, Gladstone saying that 'the resources of civilisation were not exhausted', Parnell calling Gladstone 'this masquerading knight errant, this pretending champion of the rights of every other nation except those of the Irish nation', and the imprisonment of the Irish leader in Kilmainham jail. While in jail the agitation continued unabated organised by the Ladies' Land League, in which Anna Parnell played so prominent a part. The struggle ended in a compromise, with acceptance of the land legislation incorporating new provisions covering arrears of rent, and the calling off of the agitation.

I would agree with the late Professor Moody in his life of Davitt in seeing the land struggle of 1879–1882 as the decisive turning-point in the 19th-century struggle towards self-government. Home Secretary Forster, in his resignation speech in protest at Parnell's release from Kilmainham, stated the *realpolitik* of the situation: 'If all England cannot govern the honourable member for Cork, then let us acknowledge he is the greatest power in Ireland'. It represented a major step towards a settlement of the land question, because above all it deprived the landlord of any real profit from being a landlord — this is why over the next twenty years the landlords themselves were to become agreeable to being bought out, admittedly on generous terms. Coercion could not work, if the Irish people united, and without either coercion or consent the effective end of the Union became only a matter of time.

In recent years the land revolution has variously been criticised by historians for promoting the tenant farmer, a force for social conservatism, at the expense of the farm labourer, and regarded as outmoded by some spokesmen for modern farming interests anxious to reintroduce the concept of land-leasing. Nevertheless, Ireland possesses a democratic system of land tenure, with very few large concentrations by foreign standards, which has certainly slowed down the process of rural depopulation. There are those who would say that it has invested ownership of land with excessive importance and prestige. Given the way farm incomes have persistently failed to keep pace with other incomes in recent years, that is perhaps just as well. If one wishes to examine an alternative scenario, one has only to go to Scotland, where vast tracts of land are owned by a single landowner, and the land is largely given over to sheep with much of the countryside denuded of population. Such farming may be efficient, but it supports the smallest percentage of the population of virtually any country in the Community. The other alternative, Davitt's nationalisation of the land, is as unacceptable today as it was a hundred years ago.

But aside from the political aspects, the struggle helped to avert a human and social disaster that might have occurred had the landlords and their agents been given a free hand. In the days before he died Parnell spoke to his wife about the Famine years of the 1840s and remarked: 'There are no means at hand for calculating the people who suffered in silence during these awful years of famine'. He and his generation had seen to it that there would be no more suffering in silence.

Parnell did not subscribe to the view held by the doctrinaire Fenians and in the 1890s by John Dillon and others that land reform would weaken or diminish support among the farmers for self-government. A starving peasant was hardly in a position to be a strong nationalist. Parnell did perceive that by diminishing greatly the power of the landlords he was removing one of the obstructions to self-government. Any unjust regime is supported by a number of bulwarks. It is often difficult to find a way in which such a regime can be set aside, without first removing the bulwarks. Dismantling the power and influence of the Ascendancy, by removing the privileges of the established church and disestablishing it, by removing their influence on elections in the House of Commons and in local government, by reducing to their personal holdings or demesnes the size of their property, and terminating their control over their tenants, turned out to be necessary preliminary steps towards political independence. While particular reforms were never long the central issue, they provided useful intermediary objectives.

Like many contemporaries, and indeed historians, I would have reservations about the so-called Kilmainham Treaty, whereby in return for concessions on rent arrears the agitation was called off and support promised for the Liberal government. Parnell's motives were in good measure personal — a desire to be with Katharine O'Shea again — and a political leader who is wrongfully imprisoned should not need to agree to any conditions for his release. It involved Parnell in the ruthless treatment of the Ladies' Land League, for which his sister never forgave him. While it was hailed as a victory by public opinion in Ireland, it was seen by Davitt and Dillon and by many on the left as a betrayal of principle. Some believed optimistically that if the agitation had continued British rule could have been broken there and then. Though it cannot be proved, there may have been some connection between the Kilmainham Treaty and the Phoenix Park murders — Parnell certainly felt there was. While the Treaty secured the gains of the previous few years, to be more fully realised over the following twenty, the time for negotiation was surely after release from prison, not before.

The next few years were spent mainly consolidating the strength of the party, in order to bring maximum pressure on the British parties to grant Home Rule. In the process, Parnell created a party discipline hitherto unknown in these islands. Apart from developing a machine, with the help of the local clergy, that pushed the right candidates through conventions, the centrepiece was the party pledge, which read as follows: 'I pledge myself that in the event of my election to parliament, I will sit, act and vote with the Irish Parliamentary Party, and if at a meeting of the party convened upon due notice specially to consider the question, it be decided by a resolution supported by a majority of the entire parliamentary party that I have not fulfilled the above pledge, I hereby undertake forthwith to resign my seat'. It is many people's belief to this day that elected representatives should be able to act according to their own lights, and that party should be at best a loose federation. The ineffectiveness of that system can be seen by looking at Butt's party. The best justification for such discipline is once again provided by Dr Conor Cruise O'Brien who wrote: 'A united party was essential if anything practical was to be achieved, and a united party was necessarily a disciplined one and therefore machine-controlled. The sacrifices involved — including often the rejection of individuals of high integrity and ability in favour of pliant henchmen — had to be accepted if political effectiveness was to be secured'. The tight party discipline of the Parnellite party, including the pledge, is a tradition that has been handed on to the political parties of independent Ireland. There was of course a price to be paid for the tight discipline of the Parnellite party. The split when it came in 1890-91 was exceptionally damaging.

Like any effective leader before and after him with a disciplined organisation, Parnell was constantly accused of dictatorship, and of not sufficiently consulting his colleagues. There is of course not the slightest evidence that he ever toyed with the idea of any government other than representative democracy. He occasionally pandered to this image of himself, when tongue in cheek he gave names to his racehorses and hunters such as 'Dictator', 'President' and 'Tory'. He cultivated an aloofness and an air of mystery about him which few other leaders could afford to do. 'Never explain, never apologise' was one of his mottos. His prestige as a leader derived, according to the testimony of his colleagues, above all from his ability to know what to do in a crisis. Indeed, one could argue that that constitutes the very essence of political leadership. He of course took advice. He told John Dillon: 'Get the advice of everybody whose advice is worth having — they are very few — and then do what you think best yourself'. The rest he regarded as lobby fodder. He once said: 'In politics as in war, there are no men, only weapons'. The trouble was that in the crisis of 1890-91, the rank and file suddenly took on a life of their own. Outside of parliament his colleagues, some of whom were very gifted, were allowed to take part in campaigns, the Plan of Campaign being the obvious example, of which Parnell did not really approve. Davitt was given his head to promote his ideas on land nationalisation. On candidates, Parnell did not have strong views of his own, and took the advice of people like Tim Healy and Tim Harrington. He presided over the enormous democratisation of the party, the landowners with their lack of amenability to party discipline being replaced by the sort of representation that would be much more recognisable today. He was careful to do nothing to upset the widest possible extension of the franchise to Ireland, leaving Chamberlain and others under the impression that the artisans and farm labourers would support the propertied interest. Gladstone considered him the most remarkable political figure he had ever met. Parnell, although proud, but modest too, said of Gladstone: 'He knows more moves on the board than I do'.

He travelled round Ireland by hired train, to save time, with a compartment to himself, with different colleagues being summoned to consultations by a secretary. He made a lot of speeches at railway stations. He had a refreshing attitude to the mountains of correspondence which every political leader receives. Katharine O'Shea recalled his advice: 'If you get tired with them, leave them and they'll answer themselves'. As became clear in the divorce crisis, he saw himself not merely as a party leader, but as the leader of a national movement, and he appealed to the country over the head of the party, when it sought to reverse its unanimous vote of confidence in him. Like most politicians, he had not much time to read. Nevertheless his speeches contained quotations from experts of the day. His favourite book was that manual of dialectical debate *Alice in Wonderland*. Certainly it is hard to think of a better book for teaching one to choose one's words carefully. He wrote many of his own speeches in the library of the House of Commons, usually in a last-minute rush, and was apt to lose half of them between the library and the House. But draft speeches and interviews were also prepared for him by a number of different people, Fanny Parnell, Tim Healy, T.P. O'Connor, Katharine O'Shea and no doubt many others. He had a directness of speech and a gift for the memorable phrase. As T.P. O'Connor recalled, 'he had the instinct of genius for the kind of thing that would appeal to his people'. He was not overly concerned with consistency, and was quite happy with the notion that judgements be revised in the light of circumstances and experience. If Professor Lyons' major biography is to be faulted, it is that he seeks and expects too much consistency, and therefore has to explain away statements not consistent with the moderate constitutional nationalist phase of the late 1880s.

The achievement with which Parnell is most associated was, by ruthless opportunistic tactics, persuading one of the great British parties to bring in a Home Rule Bill. He rejected a compromise offered by Chamberlain of greater powers for local government. The fruit of party discipline was gathered when, holding the exact balance of power with 86 seats, he put first the Liberals and then the Tories out of power. That required a lot of self-confidence to do. The first Home Rule Bill, partly modelled on the British North America Act of 1867, would have set up a government responsible to parliament in Dublin with responsibility for domestic affairs, including the police and judiciary, but reserving defence, foreign policy and importantly the regulation of foreign trade, customs and excise to the British parliament. Parnell had publicly stated his interest in using tariff barriers to create Irish domestic industry, rather in the manner of Bismarckian Germany, and this could have been a significant factor in Chamberlain's opposition to Home Rule. There was to be no Irish representation at Westminster. Subsequently, even in the late 1880s there was much backtracking, with Gladstone wanting to reserve control over the police and the judiciary for an interim period, and hedging over a final solution of the land problem by large-scale land purchase. Reduced Irish representation at Westminster was to be reinstated to preserve the link, but the question was naturally whether this would be sufficient leverage to hold the British to their promise of transferring some of the reserved powers.

Assessment of the achievement, by which I mean the recognition of the principle of Home Rule by a British government, depends on the extent to which it could be considered as a final solution. The whole Unionist case against the Home Rule Bill was of course that it was not final, that it paved the way for complete separation. Parnell's assurances that it was final are not to be taken at face value, and they were only personal assurances. He had after all been prepared to call the land settlement of 1882 final at the time. In many speeches and interviews in 1885 he made very clear in advance what he thought of the term final. 'No man has the right to fix the boundary of the march of a nation. No man has the right to say to his country, "Thus far shalt thou go and no further", and we have never attempted to fix the *ne plus ultra* to the progress of Ireland's nationhood, and we never shall'. In a newspaper interview in October 1885, he was asked why he would not give guarantees that legislative independence would not lead to separation. He replied: 'I refuse to give guarantees because I have none of any value to give . . . I have no mandate from the Irish people to dictate a course of action to those who may succeed us'. What he aimed at was self-government such as was enjoyed by Canada and the larger colonies, and he also referred to Hungary as a model, and he clearly saw that it would evolve. His private reaction to the first Home Rule Bill as recorded by Katharine O'Shea was: 'This Bill will do as a beginning; they shall have more presently'. In an interview with Gladstone in opposition in the late 1880s, Gladstone recorded of his meeting with Parnell:

> He thought the turning-point lay in a Dublin Parliament. He did not see what would be given short of this that could be worth taking: whereas if this could be had, even with insufficient powers, it might be accepted. I understood him to mean might be accepted as a beginning.

While Cecil Rhodes tried to interest him in ideas of imperial federation, Parnell remained non-committal. Whether he could ever have become a tame dominion-style prime minister is a moot point.

It is consistently held against Parnell nowadays that like most other nationalist leaders he did not understand Protestant Ulster, which is short-hand for saying he did not accept in full the validity of the Unionist case. Conor Cruise O'Brien, on whose study of Parnell I rely once again, was of the opinion that Parnell alone could have brought in Home Rule for the whole of Ireland: 'He acted as if he believed that the status of Ireland could be decided by negotiation between the representatives of Irish and English majorities'. After all in 1885 he did win a slender majority of the Ulster seats, and he made the most of that argument.

It never occurred to him that counties which did not even have a Protestant majority could be handed over to a separate parliament for the north-east corner, and that meant of course that most Protestants would be left outside its jurisdiction and thus relatively worse off. He did not sympathise with the Orangemen. In one speech he stated:

> This battle is being waged against Ireland by a class of landlords. This loyalty that they boast is loyalty to their own pockets.

But he then went on somewhat rashly to predict:

All I can say is that 1000 men of the Royal Irish Constabulary will be amply sufficient to cope with all the rowdies that the Orangemen of the North of Ireland can produce.

His basic approach was summed up in the famous sentence: 'We cannot afford to give up a single Irishman'. Unfortunately, today, in many quarters the opposite seems to be the motto — 'We cannot afford not to give up a million and a half Irish men and women'. Certainly in 1891 in a tour through the north, he recorded his admiration of the north's industrial prowess, and stressed the importance of conciliating religious fears. But northern Unionist opinion was not interested in having fears conciliated, they only wanted them confirmed, and the divorce case provided useful propaganda material.

Parnell does not appear to have been a particularly religious man. When asked about his religion, he described himself as 'a synodsman of the disestablished church'. His nationalist political attitudes, his uninhibited part in the assault on landlordism, meant of course that politically he did not represent Protestant opinion. Indeed, many of his fellow landlords detested him and regarded him as a traitor to his class. But he sought to serve the nation, not his class or his co-religionists, though conscious of their sensitivities. He recognised, as Wolfe Tone recognised a century before him, without sentimentality, that national progress could only be made with the majority of the people. But for all that he led an overwhelmingly Catholic following, he was not — and here I must differ sharply from Dr O'Brien in *States of Ireland* — an honorary Catholic in his politics and still less of course in his private life. He did believe in an Ireland in which Protestants had a future, as the most significant minority in the country. Going to the opposite extreme, Paul Bew in his brief life of Parnell, while performing a useful service by highlighting Parnell's perspective as a southern Anglo-Irish Protestant landlord, overstresses the point and to my mind greatly exaggerates Parnell's conservative streak and his regard for his own class interest as the key to understanding him. It is true the type of land settlement he envisaged did not involve wholesale expropriation and expulsion of his own class. On the contrary, it facilitated their survival, but it completely undermined their existing position. Certainly by 1890 he had attracted quite a few Protestants, including some from the north, to join the parliamentary ranks. Many of them did not support him during the split.

The relationship between Parnell and the Catholic church is a fascinating subject, well-documented by Professor Emmet Larkin in his brilliant documentary studies of the 19th-century church. Parnell went into politics armed with a letter of recommendation from the parish priest of Rathdrum, and included the demand for denominational education in his personal manifesto. As political agitator and leader he encountered a good deal of clerical opposition at least into the mid-1880s. But equally parish priests, bishops and even archbishops were among his warmest admirers. The clergy were involved with his full approval in the organisation of the party and in particular the selection of candidates at conventions. The parish priest of Clonoulty in Co. Tipperary enthused: 'As Caesar said of old, Parnell might say, "I came, I saw, I conquered". Without attempting to play the Dictator, as he never does, his words were law to the convention'. Archbishop Croke crowed to the Vatican: 'It now comes to pass that the man who was so bitterly assailed by the famous Roman circular is now the recognised leader of the Irish bishops, priests and people'.

Some historians reckon that Parnell's leadership with its political successes raised the self-esteem of the priests as an educated class. Indeed, of course, he raised the whole morale of the Irish nation at home and abroad. Throughout the 1880s Parnell enjoyed the support of a marvellous and forthright churchman, Archbishop Croke, who defended him against charges of communism levelled by some of his episcopal colleagues, who defended the Ladies' Land League against the charge of immodesty and impropriety, and who with another great churchman, Archbishop Walsh, from the mid-1880s gained the upper hand over the less nationalist members of the hierarchy. He successfully deflected the impact of condemnations from Rome that were obtained by the machinations of British diplomacy, in which the then Duke of Norfolk was heavily involved, in the hope of driving a wedge between the church and the party. While keeping a certain formal distance, Parnell worked closely with men like Walsh and Croke, to the point that they felt they could rely on him more than on some of his lieutenants, some of whom adopted a sharply anti-clerical line. He did nothing to antagonise unnecessarily such a powerful social force as the church, and he had regard for their special concerns such as education, but he led and for the most part they followed. One of the factors in the situation in late 1890 was the feeling among the hierarchy that the church had lost too much influence, and the divorce issue represented a golden opportunity of recovering it, as Cardinal Manning urged from the sidelines. Despite ferocious attacks, which were perhaps so emotional precisely because Parnell was a 'fallen idol', Parnell did not blame the Catholic church for what happened. He blamed fairly and squarely English politicians. There is a story that after the divorce case a Protestant clergyman, the Revd. Mr McCree, came and harangued him on his morals and called on him to resign. Parnell replied: 'Mr McCree, I must deny your right to interfere with this matter at all. When I was at college I had opportunities of seeing men of your Church and of your cloth, preparing for their profession, and I must say they were no better than they should be morally or otherwise. But it is altogether different with the Catholic clergy. A Catholic clergyman has to undergo a most severe and searching course of discipline. I do not blame the Catholic clergy for the part they are taking in this disagreeable dispute. But I altogether deny your right to interfere. Good day, Mr McCree'.

Parnell had stormy relations with the press, especially the English press, while having his own paper in Ireland, and giving some of his most important interviews to the American press. Journalists have not much changed their spots. There was a crowd of reporters waiting for Mr and Mrs Parnell after the wedding in June 1891, firmly parked outside the front door. A lady reporter from America, 'being more enterprising than the rest', got into the adjoining house, slipped across the balcony and into Katharine Parnell's bedroom. While Parnell eventually agreed to talk to some of the reporters, the lady from America he utterly refused to see, Mrs Parnell recalled, 'as she had forced herself into my room, but, undaunted, she left warning that she would cable a better interview than any of them to her paper'. Parnell could connive at such practices himself. Tim Healy in 1880 was doing an interview supposed to have taken place between Parnell and the *New York Tribune*. 'He would not even give me five minutes for a real interview, but simply told me to write it, and then only made a slight suggestion after he read it'.

If ever a political leader was the victim of a concerted newspaper campaign against him, it was Parnell. There was a potentially ugly situation early on, when a hostile editor of the *Freeman's Journal* alleged Parnell had, in a speech at Limerick Junction, called some of his colleagues who had failed to support him in parliament 'papist rats'. No such public remark was made. His initial reaction to the London *Times* of 7 March 1887, which printed a letter purporting to be signed by him, condoning the Phoenix Park murders, as part of a series of articles entitled 'Parnellism and Crime', was typically offhand: 'I have never taken any notice of newspapers, nor of anyone. Why should I now?'; and he left home assuring Katharine O'Shea that the London *Times* was a paper of no particular importance, after all. The forged letter, whose author was unmasked by a persistent spelling mistake, provided an excuse for a full-scale inquisition into Parnellism in the early 1880s, particularly during the Land League days, at the instigation of Parnell's mortal enemies, Joseph Chamberlain and Captain O'Shea. A British Secret Service agent, Henri le Caron, was wheeled in to testify against Parnell. There is evidence that the *Times* campaign of articles and letters was concocted at a very high level in the British establishment involving, for example, the constitutional lawyer Dicey who was also strongly Unionist. *The Times*, of course, did not check on the authenticity or source of the documents it was so eager to run. O'Shea testified to the genuineness of the letters. It ended in Parnell's greatest triumph. The Chamberlain-O'Shea combination that had started out by insisting O'Shea be found a seat, which strained but did not split the party, then moved on the divorce issue. To ruin Parnell was to destroy Parnellism.

Before leaving the subject of newspapers, I cannot forbear to mention the role of William Martin Murphy, MP, later newspaper proprietor, and archenemy of Larkin, who campaigned in his newspaper columns for the execution of James Connolly, and who was to be found in the very forefront of the campaign against Parnell, in the final phase, goading the hierarchy to denunciation. He commented on Parnell: 'If we got home rule with his power unimpaired we should only be exchanging British parliamentary rule for the autocracy of a man who has proved himself to be filled with some of the worst passions of human nature'. T.P. O'Connor in after years considered that 'of all the many agencies that finally broke down the Irish party, and led to the rise of Sinn Fein, the daily *Independent* and William Murphy behind it must be regarded as the most potent'.

The divorce crisis and the split in retrospect seems paradoxically the apotheosis of Parnell's career. Yet there was much that was tragic and sordid about the end of a noble career. Parnell himself was not free from blame. His affair, while understandable in human terms, was reckless, but then he had little regard for convention. He thought the storm would blow over. There were times when his private life conflicted with and took precedence over his political duties. He could have shown that O'Shea connived at it, but then there would have been no divorce, and he could not have married Mrs O'Shea. In one of the great love affairs of history, he valued a personal relationship ultimately above a political cause with which he was engaged on behalf of a whole nation. That can be criticised. It can also be admired. If there is any aspect relevant to the continuing divorce debate in Ireland, it is the tenacious and desperate desire of many couples who want to marry or remarry. From the early 1880s Parnell wrote to Katharine as 'wifie'. The ferocity and crudity of the attacks on 'Kitty' O'Shea goaded Parnell into the hyperactivity of his last months.

Matters were very badly mishandled following the disclosure of the uncontested divorce case. The church lay low, as did the Liberals, hoping Parnell would resign. But once the party had voted confidence in him, he would not allow the decision to be reversed. Gladstone's published letter to Morley which stated that Parnell's continuance in the leadership would be 'disastrous in the highest degree to the cause of Ireland', and render his own leadership almost a nullity, was a major blunder. With the full encouragement of the church a majority of the party promptly reversed engines, and sought to remove Parnell from the leadership. Parnell was furious with Gladstone, and regarded him as a hypocrite, because as Prime Minister he had regularly used Mrs O'Shea as an intermediary with Parnell, knowing full well their relationship.

Any political party that allows outside pressure to dictate who shall be its leader suffers such demoralisation as to put at risk its future. But there was a more fundamental issue at stake, the solidity of the Liberal Alliance. It has been assumed by his opponents and by historians that this was an opportunistic diversion. Perhaps it was, but Parnell had genuine grounds for doubts about the political will of the Liberals long before the divorce judgement broke. In 1889 he promised that if constitutional nationalism were to fail, he would not stay for 24 hours in Westminster. 'The most advanced section of Irishmen, as well as the least advanced, have always thoroughly understood that the parliamentary policy was to be a trial and that we did not ourselves believe in the possibility of maintaining for all time, or for any lengthy period, an incorrupt and independent Irish representation at Westminster'. Privately, he told Kettle after his meeting with Gladstone in 1888 that the Liberal Party was thoroughly unsure, and that only three men shared Gladstone's convictions. Without a strong majority, there was no hope of getting it through the House of Lords, and it might be successively watered down by backbenchers. He therefore sought, to set as the price of his departure from the leadership, watertight guarantees that the Irish parliament would have full control over the police and judiciary and the settlement of the land question, and if not, that Irish representation at Westminster could be retained in full. One of the people who had most understanding of the situation was John Devoy, who wrote to Dillon in August 1891 from America:

> Supposing all you say about Parnell's anger against 'poor Mr Gladstone' and the Liberal Party be correct, have you any conception to which that anger is shared by Irish nationalists in America, as it clearly is by large masses of the people of Ireland? Must Parnell alone be perfect while his opponents are free to indulge in all the weaknesses that flesh is heir to? What guarantee have you that any English party will give Ireland what she wants, except the guarantee afforded by a united people and an independent party? How can you ask the Irish in America to have any confidence in the majority after the exhibition they made of their subservience to English politicians and the Irish bishops? Gladstone's letter — or the publication of it — created an entirely new situation. It is simply childish and absurd to talk of your party as independent in face of its yielding to the threat conveyed in that letter.

Parnell criticised not for the first time excessive reliance on a particular English party, and in his final months expressed support for Tory land and congested district bills. He was always dismissive of Davitt's notion that English working class democracy would take up the cause of Ireland.

The fall of Parnell foreshadowed the ultimate failure of constitutionalism. The advanced nationalists received a whole new lease of life. He described himself as 'not a mere parliamentarian'. He declared, as one who had always enjoyed the company of working men and been interested in industry and mining, that 'the future is undoubtedly with the working classes', and expressed interest in and tacit approval for many of the demands of the growing Labour movement: universal suffrage, the eight-hour day, taxes on derelict land, state promotion of industry, and the provision of labourers' cottages.

In his final speech in Listowel in September 1891, he stated:

> If I were dead and gone tomorrow the men who are fighting against English influence in Irish public life would fight on still. They would still be independent nationalists. They would still believe in the future of Ireland as a nation. And they would still protest that it was not by taking orders from English Ministers that Ireland's future could be served, protected or secured.

Back in 1885 he had expressed no surprise that young men were joining the extreme movement, despite the apparent successes of the parliamentary party. Parnell replied: 'Why should they not? All our plans and projects may fail . . . and God only knows but the quarrel may have to be settled that way yet'. He believed self-government was inevitable, and that an important step had been taken.

The fall of Parnell acted as a powerful catalyst for the whole cultural revival, which was the basis of 20th-century independence. But Katharine Tynan was the only member of the literary movement whom he actually met, and whose poetry was read to him by Katharine O'Shea. The ultimate failure of Home Rule undoubtedly reflected even on its initiator. Pearse said of him: 'Parnell was less a political thinker than an embodied flame that seared, a sword that stabbed. He did the thing that lay nearest to his heart . . . His instinct was a separatist instinct'. Parnell was not a consistent moderate nor unequivocally a constitutional nationalist. Neither was he a straightforward separatist. But any time that vigour is felt to be missing from the conduct of our affairs, the career of Parnell will always provide inspiration and encouragement.

Parnell and the Ulster Question

Pauric Travers

'No man has the right to fix the boundary of the march of a nation': despite
the ravages of petrol fumes, smog and acid rain, the words carved on the
Parnell monument at the top of O'Connell Street still survive as a permanent
reminder of Irish nationalist aspirations. For a whole generation of Irish
nationalists Parnell's ringing declaration came to embody the demand for a
thirty-two county Irish republic. Whatever Parnell's intentions, it was understood that the boundary which was not to be set referred not only to the
political status of an independent Ireland but also to its extent: the invocation
was against geographical as well as constitutional boundaries. Parnell's
words seemed to provide an endorsement for both republicanism and anti-
partitionism. However, words out of context, especially when they become
famous in a new setting, have a way of being misinterpreted. Oliver Mac-
Donagh among others has pointed out that Parnell's declaration had been
immediately preceded by a qualification limiting the Irish demand to the
restoration of Grattan's parliament.[1]

Parnell's repeated insistence that the modest Home Rule proposal of 1886
represented a final settlement of the Irish question and would be accepted as
such by the vast majority of the Irish people[2] further illustrates the need for
care in interpreting his views.

As is well known, Parnell after his death assumed a position in the
republican pantheon which might have surprised some of his contemporaries
and indeed Parnell himself. The last two decades have seen the publication
of a number of works which have tended to stress Parnell's moderation, his
limited aims and indeed to an extent his social conservatism.[3]

Parnell's influence and importance are beyond question but his precise
position is still the subject of debate. It is perhaps timely therefore to consider
Parnell's attitude to one important facet of the Irish problem, i.e. the Ulster
question. What was Parnell's position on the Ulster question? How did he
view Ulster Unionism and what did he see as the role of Ulster Protestants
in a Home Rule Ireland? These are the questions which I propose to address
in this paper. I intend to approach these questions by looking first at Parnell's
background and assessing how much he knew about Ulster and tracing his
contacts with the province. Parnell's view of Irish nationality and his attitude
to Ulster Protestants will be explored by focusing on some of his major
speeches on these subjects.

A number of preliminary points need to be made. Implicit in an exercise such as this are a number of obvious and not so obvious difficulties. To begin with, it would be mistaken to assume that a statesman's views or attitudes necessarily remain as fixed as the lines on the Parnell monument. His views may develop, be refined or even change completely. Politicians are not necessarily consistent. In the case of Parnell, the dramatically changing circumstances from the semi-revolutionary days of the land war to the pinnacle of the constitutionalist's career in 1886, and later to the isolation and division of his final years, present peculiar problems in interpreting his statements and divining his real position. As we shall see, there is no doubt that Parnell's views on the Ulster question mature and are refined as his career proceeds.

The difficulty in interpreting the evidence is intensified by the fact that there is so little of it. Parnell's genius was not as a writer and even less as a political philosopher. He has left tantalisingly little in the way of carefully considered written statements of his views. It is easy to share the frustration of Professor Lyons who in wrestling with the economic ideas of Parnell in 1959 commented that 'one is almost driven to conclude that the literary form he favoured most was the telegram'.[4]

For the most part we are dependent on Parnell's political speeches. Speeches written for an audience are notoriously fraught with pitfalls for the would-be analyst: the location, the audience, the circumstances of the time all sway the tone and lay false trails for the historians. For example how does one weigh what Parnell said to an Irish-American audience in Cincinnati in 1880 (even if we can establish what precisely he did say) in comparison with his measured tones on the second reading of the first Home Rule Bill in the House of Commons in 1886 when he is attempting to reassure wavering liberals?[5] Or more relevantly in the present context how does one weigh the studied moderation of Parnell's speech to a mixed audience at the Ulster Hall in 1891, when he exuded concern and sympathy for Unionist fears, with some earlier less conciliatory speeches and actions?

Indeed it is not simply a question of Parnell seeming to give different messages in different speeches. Often he seems to be giving conflicting messages within the same speech. Parnell's approach to public speaking was generally considered and calculated. He was not often given to improvisation or launching into flights of fancy. When he resorted to stirring rallying cries to rouse his audience, he tended to build in qualifications and reservations which, while apparently less interesting, cannot be ignored in assessing his position.

One further preliminary point which needs to be made relates to what one might call the seductiveness of hindsight. Whatever qualifications or denials they may make, historians *do* tend to read history backwards. What they choose to study and in some cases the judgements they make are inevitably influenced both by hindsight and by the circumstances of their own day. In my own case, I freely admit that I might have been less interested in studying Parnell's views on the Ulster question if the Ulster question in a different phase was not, like the poor, still with us. And my perceptions are certainly those of someone living in the late twentieth century. Having said that, I am well aware of the danger of consciously or unconsciously imposing those perceptions on the Ireland or even more the Ulster of the nineteenth century. In analysing and evaluating the views and actions of Parnell it is necessary to try to see them through the eyes of the 1880s, not the 1990s.

Such strictures may seem unnecessary, but they might have been taken more to heart by the authors of some of the more recent published commentaries on the subject. In his 1973 article on the political ideas of Parnell, F.S.L. Lyons speaks of Parnell's 'almost total lack of understanding' of Ulster Protestant fears.[6]

This theme is elaborated on in his 1977 biography of Parnell. While I would not disagree with Conor Cruise O'Brien's contention that that biography will stand as one of the great biographies of modern times, the book occasionally succumbs to the seductiveness of hindsight, not least when Lyons is chastising Parnell's deficiencies vis-à-vis the Ulster question.[7] In arguing that Parnell's 'unfitness to rule' was evident long before the divorce crisis, Professor Lyons cites, among other deficiencies, his failure to respond more positively to the Ulster question. Having argued that Home Rule was unwinnable, he criticises Parnell for concentrating on English rather than Ulster Protestant opinion. Parnell, according to Professor Lyons,

> largely shared Lord Randolph Churchill's unflattering opinion of Ulster Protestantism and never came remotely within reach of developing a constructive approach to the potentially lethal problem it presented, either during the debates on the Home Rule bill or on any of the other recorded occasions when he discussed, publicly or privately, how to deal with the north in the context of a self-governing Ireland.[8]

Lyons goes on to complain that on vital issues Parnell's views were 'non existent'. Parnell's observations on church-state relations and education were 'so perfunctory as to be almost negligible. Worse still, he never seems to have asked himself what he meant by the "Irish nation" or the "Irish race" which he claimed to lead, and the idea that Ireland might possibly contain two nations, not one, apparently never entered his head.'[9]

Lyons' criticisms are echoed both by Paul Bew in his brief but perceptive life of Parnell in the Gill's Irish Lives series, originally published in 1980 and reissued in 1991, and by James Loughlin in his *Gladstone: Home Rule and the Ulster Question*, published in 1986. Loughlin refers to Parnell's 'erroneous analysis of Northern Unionism,' while Bew concludes that Parnell in the crucial years 1885-86 'simply lacked the intelligence, sympathy or vision . . . to produce a political line that would allay the fears of Northern

Protestants'. His views were 'ill-informed and ill-conceptualised'.[10] Conor Cruise O'Brien provides an even starker dismissal: Parnell, he said, 'though a Protestant, was speaking for the Catholics of Ireland, not — as he and his followers appeared to take for granted — for an Irish nation that included Ulster Protestants'.[11]

While the general drift of these comments is similar, there are some interesting differences. Lyons complains of Parnell's failure to make clear what he meant by the Irish nation but O'Brien seems to have no difficulty understanding his position. Lyons complains of lack of analysis whereas for Loughlin there is an analysis but it is erroneous. Bew is probably closest to the mark when he refers to Parnell's lack of knowledge, but he may be placing an undue burden on Parnell in expecting him to be able to produce a political line which would allay Protestant fears and which would not at the same time destroy his own position in the south. Isaac Butt devoted considerable attention to doing just that and made little progress either on Ulster or Home Rule.

While the various criticisms of Parnell have some validity I would argue that they are overstated and that they tend to ignore both the subtleties of his outlook and the realities of the political situation within which he worked. One of those realities was that progress towards the achievement of nationalist demands could only be achieved through persuading English politicians and English public opinion of their merits. The Ulster question was not conceived of as a separate question but merely as an aspect of the wider political issue. The importance of that aspect only gradually became clear.

The increasingly vociferous nationalist demand for Home Rule generated an equally virulent response from those for whom the Act of Union has become a touchstone of their identity. As the nationalist demand grew in intensity, so too did resistance among Unionists, particularly in Ulster. The Unionist community in the rest of Ireland was more dispersed and consequently more vulnerable to the winds of change. In Ulster, however, where the Protestant population was both larger and more broadly based in terms of class, the opposition was more intense. Disestablishment, the land agitation, the 1884 Reform Act and the Redistribution Act of 1885 all created unease in Ulster. This culminated in 1886 with outright opposition to the Home Rule Bill. To some extent this opposition was fomented by English opponents of the Bill like Randolph Churchill, who had no great sympathy for Ulster Protestants but who saw the tactical value of promoting their cause as a bulwark against Home Rule. However, there was nothing tactical about the position of Ulster Unionists, whose opposition to Home Rule was based not simply on the threat to imperial unity but also on economic and religious fears about their fate in a Home Rule Ireland.

Much of the criticism of Parnell vis-à-vis Ulster is based on the fact that at least before 1886 allegiances were more fluid and opinion less polarised than in the later period. A more constructive approach, it is argued, might have produced better results. A solid Ulster Unionist phalanx against Home Rule only emerged slowly. The campaign in 1886, although effective, was not well organised and lacked both coherence and leadership. These only emerged later. Protestant Ulster was not a monolithic community: like the nationalist movement it was a broad church. There were important social, religious and even political differences between the Presbyterians and the members of the Church of Ireland. There was a strong Liberal Unionist tradition in Ulster which was only superseded after the nationalist electoral triumph in Ulster in 1885 when Parnellites won a majority of the seats in Ulster. Significant tensions were evident between landlords and tenants and employers and employees, particularly in Belfast. The Orange Order had long been a predominantly working class organisation looked on with disdain by many unionists for reasons both of religion and class. It had fallen into decline until it was revived by disestablishment, the land war and above all Home Rule. As the Home Rule movement gathered steam so did the popular appeal of the Orange Order. Ironically, the threat of Home Rule helped to mould a more uniform Ulster Protestant identity.

Although his family did own estates in Co. Armagh, by background, education and temperament Parnell was not well equipped to deal with the Ulster question. The liberal Protestant background from which he came had few direct connections with Ulster. There seem to have been no strong family or social ties with the north. Educated as he was largely in England he probably encountered few northern Protestants. Ironically, if he had gone to Trinity College, Dublin, rather than Magdalene College, Cambridge, this might not have been the case. Certainly until about 1880 he would have known much more about England, France and even America, in whose history he was quite interested, than Ulster. An intellectually curious disposition or an appetite for reading might have rectified that deficiency, but Parnell had neither of these. The memoirs written by his friends and colleagues are quite explicit about this. T.P. O'Connor, for example, doubted whether Parnell got any of his inspiration from reading and considered him ill-informed on Irish history.[12]

Katharine O'Shea confirms as much in her account of Parnell's life. 'He was not a man who read', she recalled, 'or who sought to acquire the opinions or knowledge of others, unless he had some peculiar interest in a subject'. He was 'not in the least a well read man . . . he was a maker of history not a reader of it'.[13]

Parnell then was not initially well prepared to deal with the challenge posed by Ulster but this can be overstated. It would be wrong, for example, to write off too easily the fact that he was a Protestant. He was not a religious person and his religious beliefs were not, it would seem, very strong.[14] However he cannot but have been conscious of the fears of Protestants

throughout Ireland regarding their future. It is possible to argue that southern
Protestants had more to fear than their northern counterparts. Parnell would
probably have taken that view. While he did not publicly acknowledge such
fears very often this may be indicative more of what Paul Bew calls a 'self
censorship' than any lack of interest. Parnell strongly advocated the need for
unity within his party and repeatedly urged that anything which might be
divisive should be avoided. Until the divorce crisis, he led by example in this
regard and generally avoided issues which might prove contentious within
the party. Furthermore, at a time when he was trying to persuade English
opinion of the value of Home Rule, it hardly made sense to dwell too long
or too often on the fears of Irish Protestants.

When, in 1886, the issue could not be avoided any longer Parnell repeatedly cited the fact that he was a Protestant himself. At Portsmouth, for
example, in the general election following the defeat of the Home Rule Bill,
he told his audience that as a Protestant he knew Irish Protestants very well
and that while the majority of them would rather not have Home Rule they
did not have strong views. The vocal opposition was coming from the
minority Orange element.[15] It is perhaps significant that it was an English
rather than an Irish Protestant audience which he is trying to convince. Some
months earlier he had gone further:

> I was born a Protestant, I have lived a Protestant and I hope to die a
> Protestant, and if in the future after the concession of the Irish claim any
> danger were to arise to my fellow countrymen, I should be the first to
> stand up for that liberty of speech.[16]

Parnell's personal guarantee did little to placate Ulster Protestant fears.
The *Belfast Newsletter* responded to the words just quoted with a dismissive
but in some ways prophetic editorial:

> Nonsense, Mr Parnell. If you were the first to stand up you would be the
> first to sit down; for your power is gone the moment the flatterers find
> that they can make no more use of you. Instead of protecting others, Mr
> Parnell could not protect himself.[17]

Parnell's ignorance of Ulster can also be overstated. While early in his
career he was ill-informed, he did learn from experience. With some exceptions, such as Henry Campbell who succeeded Timothy Healy as his secretary, he was not close to many of the northern members of his own party.
However, the land war and the spread of the Home Rule party brought him
into much closer contact with Ulster politics. Most of what he knew about
Ulster came from such direct experience. Before the advent of the land war
he had made only one major political visit to the north, during which he spoke
at a meeting in Belfast. Between 1879 and 1883 he visited the province quite

regularly: he addressed meetings at Belfast and Newry in October 1879; at Enniskillen, Belleek and other Fermanagh towns in November 1880; in Co. Down in April 1881; at Derry and in various parts of Co. Tyrone in August and September 1881; and at Clones and Carrickmacross during Healy's by-election contest in Monaghan in June 1883. Thereafter his visits were less frequent. He made only one major speech in Ulster after 1886 — that at Belfast in 1891. In all he made at least eight visits to Ulster during his career, generally speaking at a number of venues on each visit. This is a modest total but it compares favourably with other southern nationalist politicians before and since. It is also more than might have been expected in all the circumstances, bearing in mind that he was never an enthusiastic public speaker and that especially between 1886 and 1890 he addressed few public meetings.

On some of the occasions he did visit Ulster he was accused of stirring up trouble by his very presence and more than once he was at pains to warn Ulster nationalists to avoid gatherings which might provoke assault. For example in his address to Ulster nationalists in March 1886, he appealed to them to consider abandoning open-air proceedings in all localities where they might 'give rise to ill-feeling and excitement'.[18] There was also the related matter of his own safety. Threats were occasionally made and T.P. O'Connor recalled his sleeping with a revolver under his pillow while campaigning in Monaghan.[19]

When in September 1883 it was announced that Parnell would speak in Co. Tyrone it produced an immediate hostile response from Orangemen. One liberal journalist commented:

> What brings Mr Parnell to Tyrone is not clear; what good he can hope to effect we do not know; but it is evident that he has roused the Orange blood of the county.[20]

That these fears were not exaggerated can be seen from one address by a leading Orangeman to his colleagues:

> Are you prepared to allow Parnell, the leader of the enemies of our united empire, the champion of the principle Ireland for the Irish . . . meaning Ireland for the romanists . . . [his] boasted triumphant march through Ulster, commencing with our loyal and peaceful county?[21]

Perhaps not surprisingly, Parnell found himself unable to fulfil the engagement. But during the debate on the Home Rule Bill in 1886 he responded to an interjection from Major Saunderson, the Unionist member for North Armagh, by saying that 'I only wish that I was as safe in going to the north of Ireland as the honourable and gallant member would be in going to the south.'[22]

Parnell's first ventures into Ulster helped to seal the reaction of some

Ulster Protestants towards him. The land agitation of the late 1870s revealed fundamental differences between landlords and tenants, even in Ulster — as is evidenced by the establishment of the Ulster Tenants' Defence Association by T.W. Russell, the Liberal Unionist MP for South Tyrone. Ulster tenants, no less than those in Connacht or Munster, demanded land reform and ultimately land purchase. Parnell and Davitt sought to broaden the basis of Land League support by agitating among tenant farmers in Fermanagh and Tyrone.[23] Although the League attracted some support, it also generated considerable resentment. This was increased when Parnell attempted to promote the Home Rule movement in Ulster. In the autumn of 1881, Tyrone was contested unsuccessfully by a Parnellite candidate, Harold Rylett, an English Unitarian clergyman stationed in the north at the time, as T.P. O'Connor put it, for 'a cure'.[24]

Although the seat was won by Tom Dickson, the Liberal candidate, who was a strong supporter of the tenant cause, Parnell's intervention offended Presbyterian radical sentiment as it had risked giving the seat to Colonel Knox, the Conservative candidate.[25]

Relations between the nationalists and the Liberals had been strained since the passage of the Coercion Act and Dickson was not a supporter of Home Rule, so Parnell felt free to contest the election, but he did so against the advice of some of his colleagues who correctly predicted that it would cause resentment among a section of Ulster Protestant opinion which they should be courting.[26]

Parnell was clearly not well disposed towards an alliance with northern Liberals and moved instead towards extending the sway of his own party. In June 1883, T.M. Healy dramatically won a by-election in Monaghan. The latter success prompted an all-out attempt to win support in Ulster. The so-called 'invasion of Ulster' had mixed results. A series of public meetings were organised which provoked a backlash from the Orange Order. Rival meetings were staged and tensions raised. At a meeting in Rosslea, Co. Fermanagh, serious confrontation between huge nationalist and Orange crowds was only narrowly averted. Lord Rossmore, who had organised the Orange demonstration, was later removed from the Commission of the Peace and political demonstrations were prohibited for a time. While the crisis quickly passed, the scene was set for future confrontation. In 1885 the normally safe Unionist seat of North Fermanagh was lost to a Parnellite after a boisterous campaign because of a split between Unionist landlords and tenants. By the beginning of 1886, the Irish National League was claiming 287 branches in Ulster but its growth was matched by the revival of the Orange Order.[27]

The 1885 general election only served to increase Unionist fears. This first test of the new Reform Act and the revision of the constituency boundaries proved a triumph for Parnell. After a lively and sometimes violent campaign, Home Rulers won 17 of the 33 seats in Ulster, a gain of fourteen. The result seemed to confirm the Parnellite argument that even in Ulster, Unionists were only a vocal minority, and helped to convert Gladstone to Home Rule. However, the nationalist victory was aided considerably by the disunity of the opposition. A common front to oppose Home Rule, such as emerged in the shape of the Irish Loyal and Patriotic Union in the south of Ireland, was more difficult to achieve in Ulster. The main casualties of the 1885 election were the Liberals who failed to gain a seat in Ulster. The middle ground in Ulster politics became and was to remain a precarious position to occupy. The process of polarisation which culminated in partition had begun.

Like most nationalists Parnell was inclined to dismiss most local opposition to Home Rule as the work of the Orange Order and to dismiss the order as an extremist and unrepresentative group. He claimed that the Land League had killed the Orange Order in rural Ulster.[28] When it quickly became clear that the opposite was the case, he reverted to a more abusive approach. He blamed disturbances in rural Ulster on Belfast workers. During the debate on the second reading of the Peace Preservation Act in 1886 he called for the measure which had traditionally been used against nationalists to be used to disarm the Orange population or 'at all events that section of the population which have shown by its frenzy and the frenzy of its leaders, and by its acts that though it is willing to take the open field and fight, yet it is willing to assassinate or attempt to assassinate . . . those who differ from them in political opinion.'[29] He was referring here to a number of violent demonstrations which had taken place against Home Rule earlier in the year. His main concern however was to insist that the Orange element was not a threat. In a strangely ironic speech (given later Irish history), he told the House of Commons:

> To suppose for a moment that any section of the population of Ireland will ever under any circumstances take the field against the British Government is to suppose an absurd impossibility, and that it should be possible to incite the Orangemen of Ulster, numbering certainly not more than 15,000-20,000 men . . . who though they swore and threatened several times to rebel, have never yet rebelled, but who have frequently . . . indulged in the past-time at different periods of the year of murdering and attempting to murder their Catholic fellow countrymen and neighbours . . . to suppose that these people should rebel is the very height of absurdity.

Parnell's conviction that Ulster would not fight Home Rule was partly based on the impossibility of any such rebellion succeeding because of advances in warfare and the strength of the British Army. No Irish rebels, he insisted, could hold out for more than twenty-four hours against the might of the British Army.

Parnell's views on Ulster opposition were similar to those of most southern nationalists. The conventional view was that behind the bluster there was little real substance: Parnell compared it to a scarecrow; Timothy Healy described it more colourfully as 'miserable brag and bluster', a case of 'hold me, Mr Policeman, or I will kill somebody'. The *Freeman's Journal* joked about the regularity with which the Orangemen had come as a 'kind of true-blue symphony or rousing obligato to every great reform proposal for Ireland'. J.J. Clancy, on behalf of the Irish party, published a pamphlet entitled *The Orange Bogey* giving a history of the threats made by the Orange Order over the years, all of which came to nothing. The pamphlet was aimed at explaining what Clancy admitted was 'extreme complacency' on the part of most nationalists regarding Ulster threats to resist Home Rule.[30]

All this is not to say that Parnell completely dismissed Ulster in 1886. Again like most nationalists, he believed that there was a silent majority of Ulster Protestants who, although opposed to Home Rule, might be persuaded as to its merits given time. Interestingly, this divide and rule outlook has also been identified by Richard Davis as part of the Sinn Féin view in his study of the later Sinn Féin movement and the Ulster question.[31] Indeed it probably lies at the heart of the approach of all of the southern constitutional nationalist parties even today.

What was Parnell's attitude to this 'silent majority' of the Ulster community in 1886? He had learned a good deal about Ulster in the previous six years but none of it made him any more inclined to change his fundamental position. At Enniskillen in 1880 he had mistakenly referred to Co. Fermanagh as 'Protestant and loyal'.[32] At that stage he still held the widespread view of the whole province of Ulster as a Protestant monolith. By 1886, he was referring to the 'fiction of Protestant Ulster'. 'It was only recently discovered', he told the House of Commons, 'that there did not exist this Protestant Ulster.' Indeed he made this belated discovery the cornerstone of his case against Ulster. Protestant Ulster consisted only of the three north-eastern counties. If they were excluded from the Home Rule settlement to protect Irish Protestants, seven-twelfths of Irish Protestants would be outside these counties.[33]

Gladstone's Home Rule Bill, introduced in April 1886, was an extremely modest measure. It provided for the establishment of a legislative body in Ireland composed of two 'Orders' which would normally sit together and each of which would have a suspensory veto over measures introduced by the other. The first Order was to consist of the twenty-eight Irish peers who already sat in the House of Lords and seventy-five other representatives elected on a restricted property franchise. The lower Order was to consist of existing Irish MPs and 101 new representatives. Provision was made to protect the interests of the Protestant minority by restricting the assembly's powers relating to religion. Matters relating to foreign policy, defence, trade and policing were also specifically reserved to the Imperial parliament.

Gladstone's advisers and cabinet colleagues shared the nationalist equation of Unionism with Orangeism and bigotry. Ulster Presbyterians could, it was felt, be won over. Only James Bryce, himself a steadfast Presbyterian, sounded a warning note. The Home Rule scheme would, he advised, unite Ulster Protestants and might lead to civil war.[34] The predominant view was more sanguine and it was not felt necessary to make any special provision for Ulster.

As we have seen Parnell did not anticipate civil war even after the riots in Belfast in which more than 50 people were killed — more than in any Irish rising in the nineteenth century and more than the land war. He placed ultimate responsibility for these riots on the shoulders of those English politicians who were opportunistically manipulating Protestant fears. He accepted that the proposed Irish parliament would be a subordinate institution. He also accepted the various restrictions in the Home Rule bill without serious question. He had earlier privately submitted to Gladstone a document entitled 'A Proposed Constitution for Ireland' which was no less modest than Gladstone's later proposal and which included a provision for proportionate representation for the Protestant minority.[35]

Parnell's speech on the second reading of the Home Rule Bill provides the clearest statement of his views on the Ulster question and the role of Ulster Protestants within a Home Rule Ireland. I cannot agree with Lyons' description of the section dealing with Ulster as being an almost frivolous treatment of a potentially murderous theme'.[36] Having dismissed the idea of a monolithic Protestant Ulster and argued the illogicality of trying to protect Protestants by excluding a few counties, he uttered his famous declaration: 'No sir, we cannot give up a single Irishman'. Too often this is quoted in isolation and as a result it seems an uncompromising expression of irredentism. But the words that followed clarified his position:

No sir, we cannot give up a single Irishman. We want the energy, the patriotism, the talent and works of every Irishman to make this great experiment — to ensure that this great experiment shall be successful. The best form of government for a country I believe to be one that requires that that government shall be the resultant of what forces are in that country. We cannot give away to a second legislature for a section of Ireland any portion of the talent or influence of the Irish Protestants. This class — the Protestant class — will form the most valuable element in the Irish Legislature of the future, constituting as they still will a strong minority and exercising, through the 'First Order', a moderating influence on the making of the laws. We have heard of the danger of a first trial of untrained legislators in an Irish Parliament. I regard their presence as vitally necessary to the success of this trial. We want, sir, all creeds and classes in Ireland. We cannot look upon a single Irishman as not belonging to us. However much we recognise their ability, we cannot admit that there is a single one of them too good to take part in this experiment. We do not blame the small proportion of Protestants who feel any real fear. I admit that there is a small proportion who do. We have been doing our best of late to remove this fear and we shall continue to do so. When this bill becomes an Act we shall not cease to try to conciliate such Irishmen.[37]

Parnell, here, I would suggest, is not simply trying to play to the gallery or convert wavering Liberal MPs. He is speaking from the heart because for once he is speaking for his own religious tradition as much as for nationalist Ireland. He saw the inclusion of northern Protestants as a guarantee of the religious liberty of southern Protestants. Without Ulster, they could be isolated and exposed; with Ulster, they would represent a powerful minority.

He is quite explicit about this. In dealing with fears about education and what the Catholic bishops might do, he declared that with Ulster included there was 'not the slightest risk, if there was indeed any such idea on the part of the Catholic hierarchy to use their power unfairly against the Protestants . . . we would be able to settle this and other questions together very satisfactorily'. The corollary is, of course, that with Ulster excluded, things might not be quite so satisfactory. Remember, as Bew argues convincingly, Parnell's vision of a self-governing Ireland was not one where a Catholic nationalist peasantry had completely supplanted the Protestant landowner. Landlordism might have vanished but the country gentleman was still to have his social and political role. Exclusion of Ulster could make that vision a pipe-dream.

What Parnell envisaged then was a constitution so framed as to prevent domination of one side by the other. He may perhaps have been unduly optimistic in his view that 'when we are all assembled in one chamber, different sections of Irishmen threshing out a subject . . . great questions will be settled on the basis of compromise, and more or less to the satisfaction of both parties', but the restrictive property qualification for the First Order and its powers were specifically designed to prevent one party dominating.

A second feature of Parnell's speech is his emphasis on the talents of northern Protestants. He was particularly interested in the development of Irish industry and although he denied that economic development was confined only to the north, he was conscious of the contribution northern Protestants could make to a self-governing Ireland. Again, the corollary was that if Ulster was excluded, future progress in the south of Ireland would be severely hampered. The Ulster Protestant fear that Home Rule, by tying Ulster to a backward rural economy, would result in the destruction of her industry had been given some credence by Parnell's declaration in 1882 that an Irish parliament would be likely to introduce protection.[38] However, the 1886 bill explicitly reserved customs and excise duties to Whitehall, thus effectively precluding any resort to protection. In accepting Gladstone's bill as a final settlement, Parnell specifically agreed that protection was ruled out. While this was partly a step down enforced by the Liberals, it was also designed to placate Ulster Protestant opinion.

Such concessions, if concessions they were, became academic with the defeat of the Home Rule Bill. In the subsequent election, Parnell campaigned largely in England. In so doing he repeated the basic message which he had been rehearsing for some time. It might be argued that he would have been better occupied campaigning in Ireland or even in Ulster. But the fate of Home Rule was decided by English MPs and Parnell's approach was quite pragmatic.

The Liberal defeat made Home Rule and Ulster a less pressing matter. In the remaining years of his life, Parnell devoted only one major speech to the Ulster question. At the Ulster Hall in May 1891 his message was unusually conciliatory. Having praised Ulster industry and enterprise, he declared that

> it is the duty of the majority to leave no stone unturned, no means unused, to conciliate the reasonable and unreasonable prejudices of the minority . . . Ireland can never enjoy perfect freedom, Ireland can never be united, so long as there is a . . . [minority] who consider, rightly or wrongly — I believe and feel sure wrongly — that the concession of legitimate freedom to Ireland means harm or damage to them, either to their spiritual or their temporal interests, the work of building up an independent Ireland will have upon it a fatal clog and a fatal drag.[39]

The speech ended with an appeal to both sides to avoid attaching to their fight 'any more than is legitimate of a sectarian or a religious aspect'.

Paul Bew interprets this speech as a new departure for Parnell and he attributes the change to Parnell's own personal and political trauma. The divorce split and the opposition of the bishops had, he thinks, freed him from his dependence on Catholic nationalism and from his self censorship. Parnell is no longer the 'tame Protestant leader of the Home Rule movement'.[40] This argument is plausible but there is no new departure. While the speech is slightly more explicit than any of Parnell's previous comments, there is nothing in its spirit which is not in the 1886 speech. It is a return to the language of conciliation rather than a first venture.

Parnell in his early years was ill-informed about Ulster and tended to underestimate the importance of the Ulster question. During the 1880s his understanding of Ulster increased. He might still be criticised for not devoting more time and energy to conciliating Ulster opinion, but whether that would have achieved anything is another matter. English opinion had yet to be persuaded of the value of Home Rule and it was a reasonable tactic to set about doing that. To have too publicly accepted the merits of Ulster fears might well have destroyed the case for Home Rule completely. That was, after all, what Randolph Churchill and others hoped would happen.

As to Parnell's view of Irish nationality, it is simply not correct to say that there is any doubt or confusion about what he meant by the Irish nation. He may not often have defined what he meant but that may simply be a case of never feeling the need to define what he took for granted. While Parnell was occasionally abusive about Orange bigotry and on at least one occasion referred to Unionists as the English party, he also more than once referred to Orangemen as 'my fellow countrymen'. It is implicit in many of his public utterances that he considered the Irish nation to consist of all of the people inhabiting the island of Ireland, Protestant and Catholic, nationalist and Unionist. That is crystal clear from the extract from his speech in the second reading of the Home Rule bill which I have quoted. He believed that Ulster Protestants would make a major contribution to religious toleration and economic development in a Home Rule Ireland.

Pace Lyons, Parnell specifically rejected the notion of two nations put forward by Lord Salisbury in 1886. If economic development was the putative basis for identifying two nations, then he pointed out that the line on the map should be drawn down the length of Ireland dividing west and east, not north and south. And if it was religious, Parnell would not accept that there was such a difference between Ulster and southern Protestants.[41]

Finally, Conor Cruise O'Brien has speculated that if partition had been offered as a 'quid pro quo' for Home Rule, it is probable that Parnell would have 'swallowed partition and have got his followers, both in parliament and in the country, to swallow it'.[42] I consider that highly unlikely because of Parnell's views on the importance of northern Protestants in a Home Rule Ireland. He was much more likely to, and did, compromise on the question of sovereignty and the status of an Irish parliament. Which brings me back to the words on the Parnell statue about setting the boundary to the march of a nation. In the sense that they refer to the geographical boundaries of the nation, they seem to me to be an entirely appropriate epitaph for Parnell.

Notes

1. Oliver MacDonagh, *States of Mind* (1983), p. 60.
2. See, for example, *Freeman's Journal*, 9 June 1886.
3. Paul Bew, *C.S. Parnell*, Gill's Irish Lives (Dublin, 1980); F.S.L. Lyons, *Charles Stewart Parnell* (1977).
4. F.S.L. Lyons, 'The Economic Ideas of Parnell', in M. Roberts (ed.), *Historical Studies* II (1959), p.61.
5. For the Cincinnati speech, see Lyons, *Parnell*, pp. 110-11.
6. F.S.L. Lyons,'The Political Ideas of Parnell', *Historical Journal*, XVI, 4 (1973), pp. 768-9.
7. Review, *Irish Historical Studies*, XX, No. 80 (Autumn 1977), p. 516.
8. Lyons, *Parnell*, p. 619.
9. Ibid., p. 623.
10. Bew, *Parnell*, pp. 140 and 142.

11. Review, *IHS*, XX, No. 80 (1977), p.518.
12. T.P. O'Connor, *Memoirs of an Old Parliamentarian* (1929), I, p. 99.
13. Katharine O'Shea, *Charles Stewart Parnell: His Love Story and Political Life* (1914), II, pp. 244 and 247.
14. Ibid., p. 247.
15. *Freeman's Journal*, 26 June 1886.
16. *Belfast Newsletter*, 23 Jan. 1886.
17. Ibid.
18. *The Times*, 16 Mar. 1886.
19. O'Connor, *Memoirs*, I, p. 237.
20. *Impartial Reporter*, 27 Sept. 1883. Quoted in Paul Bew & F.Wright,'The Agrarian Opposition in Ulster Politics 1848-87', in S. Clarke & J.S. Donnelly Jr., *Irish Peasants: Violence and Political Unrest 1780-1914* (1983), p. 219.
21. Ibid.
22. *Freeman's Journal*, 9 June 1886.
23 T.W. Moody, *Davitt and Irish Revolution* (Oxford, 1981), p. 424.
24. O'Connor, *Memoirs*, I, pp. 236-7.
25. B.M. Walker, The Land Question and Elections in Ulster, 1868-86', in S. Clarke & J.S. Donnelly Jr, *Irish Peasants: Violence and Political Unrest 1780-1914* (1983), pp. 248-9.
26. *Devoy's Postbag* (1953), W. O'Brien & Desmond Ryan (eds.), II, pp. 142-3.
27. Loughlin, *Gladstone*, p. 31.
28. Ibid., p. 126.
29. *Freeman's Journal*, 20 May 1886.
30. Ibid., 25, 27, 28 May 1886; J.J. Clancy, *The Orange Bogey* (1886).
31. R. Davis, 'Ulster protestants and the Sinn Féin Press, 1914-22', *Éire-Ireland*, XV, 1980, pp. 60-84.
32. Loughlin, *Gladstone*, p. 127.
33. *Freeman's Journal*, 9 June 1886.
34. 'The Case of the Ulster Protestants', memorandum by Bryce, 12 Mar. 1886, Gladstone papers, BL Add. Ms. 56447, ff 1-10.
35. *Freeman's Journal*, 9 June 1886; K. O'Shea, *Parnell*, II, p. 18-19.
36. Lyons, 'The Political Ideas of Parnell', *Historical Journal*, XVI, 4 (1973), p. 769.
37. *Freeman's Journal*, 9 June 1886.
38. Lyons, 'The Economic Ideas of Parnell', in M. Roberts (ed.), *Historical Studies* II, p. 70.
39. Quoted in Bew, *Parnell*, pp. 129-30.
40. Ibid., pp. 128-9.
41. *Freeman's Journal*, 18 May and 9 June 1886.
42. Review, *Irish Historical Studies*, XX, No. 80 (1977), p. 518.

The Rivals of C.S. Parnell

Alvin Jackson

(i)

Like Trotsky with Stalin, or Röhm with Hitler, Edward Saunderson and the Irish Unionists have been etched out of the images of Parnell's career. They scarcely intrude in the biographies of the Uncrowned King, playing a sub-textual role in the narrative as once in Parnell's own vision of Ireland. Not least among those Irish influenced by Parnell, Unionists have themselves been coy in acknowledging the broader forces shaping their origins.[1] Each tradition, Parnellite and Unionist, has placed its faith in a barricaded history; each tradition lies content within the corrals of its own past. An historiographical apartheid has served everyone's interests, with nationalist and Unionist zones matching, but not quite overlapping. 'The integrity of their quarrel', the profound interdependence of their histories, have proved to be less simple and less satisfying postulates.

Unionism in Ireland was a central influence on Parnellism in its years of glory and decline. The formal organisation of the Unionist movement in 1885-86 was an essential prelude to the defeat of the first Home Rule Bill (in June 1886). Organised Unionism supplied lobby fodder, popular speakers, and — above all — credibility to British Conservative policy on Ireland. British governments could not, and did not, pursue strategies in Ireland in the absence of all forms of indigenous support; and in the later 1880s they cultivated Irish loyalists with much the same zeal that Katharine O'Shea applied to Mrs Wood at Eltham. Like Aunt Ben, Irish loyalists could be eccentric and inconvenient; like Aunt Ben they represented a necessary source of capital for exploitation.

Irish Unionists were a crucial element of the Anglo-Irish alliance against Home Rule — and they contributed scarcely less effectively than Gladstone or Healy or Archbishop Walsh to the shattering of Parnell's ambitions. They were, individually, implicated in some of the more bizarre and unsavoury efforts to subvert the Parnellite movement. Saunderson, the Irish Unionist leader, recorded a twilight meeting in January 1886 with the disaffected and indiscreet Philip Callan, the displaced MP for North Louth, at which a pistol was flourished, oaths delivered, and Callan's revenge against his autocratic former leader plotted in detail.[2] Irish Unionists, in particular E.C. Houston of the Irish Loyal and Patriotic Union, were at the centre of the web spun by Richard Pigott.[3] Irish Unionist abstention at the key North Sligo contest in

March–April 1891 was judged to be fatal to the Parnellite counter-offensive.[4]

Yet the Unionists were also *dependent* upon their adversary. Irish Unionism developed and defined itself partly through exploring the relationship with Parnell and his movement. Irish Unionist institutions aped those of Parnellism. The parliamentary party, which evolved in 1885-86, was to some extent entranced by the model of its older, Irish sister. Like the Irish parliamentary party, the loyalist body was designed as a liberation from English politics. Like the Irish parliamentary party, the loyalist body was designed as an Irish pressure group which might act in alliance with one or other of the great parties of the British state. The organisational structure of the Irish parliamentary party was mimicked by Irish Unionists. Edward Saunderson, as chairman of the Irish Unionist parliamentary party, was the chief Irish opponent of Parnell before 1890, whether in the House of Commons or on the campaign trail. The members of the Irish Unionist parliamentary party were the chief opponents of Parnellism, whether in the Commons or in Ireland.

Here then were two Irish parties, bound in a paradoxical relationship — at once symbiotic and confrontational. Here were two Irish leaders, Parnell and Saunderson, bound by their antagonisms. Their histories should surely be as complementary as the struggle which entwined them in the years before the Uncrowned King's death.

(ii)

Who were the Irish Unionists whom Parnell and his party faced in the House of Commons?[5] Their parliamentary presence, measured either by their political influence or by their impact on fellow members, was always more significant than their bald numerical strength — a mere fraction of the Parnellite total — might suggest. The number of Unionist MPs returned by Irish constituencies never exceeded 23 during the period 1885 to 1918, though, equally, it never fell below nineteen. This stability, even at a low level of representation, provided strength and cohesion to the group. It reflected the absence of any seriously disruptive and sustained threat within the Unionist heartland; and it meant that British Tories and Irish nationalists were each faced with a more or less permanent loyalist ginger group. Loyalist numbers held with a dreary consistency, only matched by the nature and permanence of their complaints.

Yet, even with a core of around twenty members, Irish Unionists could still exercise numerical punch. Though nineteen Irish Unionists in 1886 might be overwhelmed in a tide of British or Parnellite MPs, by 1906, for example, almost the same number (20) represented a substantial fragment of the total — British and Irish — Unionist parliamentary contingent. With rather more than one in eight members of the Unionist parliamentary party of that year an Irishman or an Ulsterman, the British Unionist leadership had to recognise their strengths and susceptibilities.

Moreover, Unionists sitting for Irish seats were strengthened, in theory, by a number of compatriots representing British constituencies. Their numbers were never large, generally hovering around 4% of the Conservative and Unionist parliamentary total, but their individual importance as spokesmen and string-pullers far exceeded their corporate vulnerability. Edward Saunderson recorded in January 1886 that 26 members had attended a preliminary meeting of his evolving party; and since only eighteen Irish Conservatives and no Irish Liberals had been returned at the general election, the remaining eight almost certainly came from the sixteen Tories of Irish background sitting for English constituencies in the Home Rule parliament.[6] A small number of these English MPs were consistently associated with the Ulster party — men like Arthur Smith-Barry, J.G. Butcher, and R.U. Penrose-Fitzgerald, all prominent antagonists of Parnell and of the Plan of Campaign.[7]

Categorised according to occupation, the membership of the Irish Unionist parliamentary party developed rapidly in the Parnellite era. The landlord element within the party was decimated, claiming 60% of members in 1880 and only 4% in 1918. The mercantile, industrial, and professional classes, especially lawyers, were the chief beneficiaries of this demise. Few lower professionals and wage earners were returned before the watershed election of December 1918.

This fall in the representation of landlords, mirrored in the experience of the Parnellite party, is associated both with measures of franchise reform and constituency redistribution — important drops occurring in 1885 and again in 1918 — and also with the reorganisation of Unionist machinery in 1904-05. The generally upward trend in lawyer numbers was also interrupted conspicuously at the election of 1906. The land campaign of T.W. Russell, conducted during this period, directed attention at inefficient landlord and lawyer representation, and the subsequent fall in their respective numbers may well reflect a shift in local Unionist attitudes.[8]

The general trend, however, was towards a growth in lawyer representation, and there was a sound parliamentary rationale for this. The increasing complexity of Irish legislation, particularly land legislation, demanded technical legal skills which the old squire-politicians did not possess. Lawyers like Dunbar Plunket Barton, MP for Mid-Armagh (1891-1900), or William Moore of North Antrim (1899-1906), or William Ellison-Macartney of South Antrim (1885-1903), or Edward Carson, dominated the Unionist contribution to debate on Irish legislation: Edward Saunderson, on the other hand, lacking technical mastery of land law, struggled with the details of legislation, and preferred general indictment to specific and reasoned criticism. Such an approach may have made for lively (if uninfor-

mative) debate, but Irish Unionism, to survive in the teeth of intractable
Parnellite opposition, needed a more heavyweight defence than Saunderson
and his kind could provide. Lawyers became the new knights errant of
Unionism, and were rewarded with a large share of the limited number of
parliamentary seats available to the cause.

Lawyers, therefore, were scarcely losers by their usefulness to Unionism.
Parliament provided a catalyst for the careers of the ambitious, accelerating
promotion to the judicial bench. Not all were as fortunate as John Ross
(member for Londonderry City, 1892-95) who in 1896, at the age of 43, was
appointed a judge of the Irish High Court.[9] But most lawyer-MPs of reasonable abliity could look forward to promotion to one of the Irish law offices
and thence to the judiciary. The Irish Attorney General and Solicitor General
in Unionist governments were always recruited from the seven or eight
lawyers of the Irish Unionist party in the Commons. With a one-in-four
chance of winning office, these members were peculiarly favoured in the
parliamentary promotion stakes.

Unlike the Parnellites, the Ulster party was able to win new commercial
wealth to its ranks. Great employers, like the linen manufacturer William
Ewart, and the shipbuilders Edward Harland and G.W. Wolff, might sit for
their home constituencies in Belfast. Wolff represented the eastern division
of the city (where his yards were situated and his labour recruited) for
eighteen years. Successful merchants like Sir Daniel Dixon, who owned a
timber and shipping business, or Sir James Haslett, a retail chemist, also held
Belfast constituencies. Businessmen with smaller, local firms, or rural family
connections might represent one of the county seats. John Brownlee Lonsdale, a wealthy merchant and banker, had roots in Mid-Armagh, which seat
he held between 1900 and 1918.[10]

The decline in the landed group, and the rise of middle class representation, are associated with a fall in the number of Oxford and Cambridge
graduates among members of the Party. Oxbridge was a desirable component
of an ambitious and able young (Unionist) Irishman's political training. For
landlords, with a greater ease of access to the English social elite, and with
perhaps a greater sense of supra-national class solidarity than local lawyers
or businessmen, Oxbridge provided a useful badge of rank, and cemented
social and class bonds. But with the popularisation of Irish politics came
localisation: Irish Unionist members needed to stay in close contact with
their constituencies, and with the development of local opinion. Against the
background of Russellism, Labour politicking, and Presbyterian agitation at
the end of the nineteenth century, constituency knowledge was at a premium.
And in this context, Oxbridge — or any tertiary education in England — was
a liability.

Professional men regarded education in a more functional light than the
landlord class: the intangible advantages of a liberal arts education at

Oxbridge paled beside the more solid merits of the law and medical schools at Trinity College, Dublin, or of a vocational apprenticeship. For aspirant lawyers, Trinity suffered no rival: Oxbridge offered a training for the English legal system, but few Irishmen took advantage of it, preferring a less competitive career in their home country. Some (William Ellison-Macartney, for example) *did* graduate in law from (in his case) Exeter College, Oxford; some (Carson, J.H.M. Campbell) *did* pursue successful careers at the English bar. But both categories were exceptional.

All forms of Irish education were increasingly patronised by Unionist representatives during the period. More Irish Unionist members were recruited from Trinity and Queen's College, Belfast, and more claimed a wholly Irish secondary education. These increases mirror, again, developments in the occupational backgrounds of the members: more representatives of the professions, more merchants and industrialists, were being elected, filling the vacuum created by the departure of the landlords. Unionist professionals — certainly lawyers — were almost by definition Trinity graduates for the first half of the period under consideration; though Queen's, Belfast, claimed an increasing number of graduates, especially in the sciences — men who took their skills into industry and commerce, and thence into parliament.

A fall in the educational attainments of party members seems, like the retreat of landlord representatives, to be associated both with measures of parliamentary reform and with the party reorganisation of 1904-05. Significant falls in the numbers of Oxford and Cambridge graduates and of old boys of the elite Clarendon schools occur in 1885, 1891 and also at the election of 1906, following the creation of the Ulster Unionist Council in 1904-05. This may simply reflect the preferences of an expanded electorate (or perhaps the party's conception of popular preferences); but in 1891, with a growth in the number of winnable constituencies, there was also a need to recruit — and speedily — more candidates.

The popularisation of the 1906 party, revealed by the figures for occupation, is confirmed by a breakdown of its educational background. Fewer graduates than ever were elected, and for the first time a Unionist was returned who had received only primary education (T.H. Sloan, member for South Belfast, 1902-10). With the restoration of a Liberal government and the challenge of Home Rule, loyalist constituency dissent weakened: the balance between occupational and educational attainments, temporarily upset in 1906, was restored (though long-term trends continued apace).

A portrait emerges of an Ulster party moving, in the last years of the nineteenth century, from landlord to business and lawyer domination; of a party with high, but weakening, educational attainments. Its members were ageing, and acquiring a fund of parliamentary experience. They suffered comparatively little constituency opposition: they represented a stable bloc within a British Unionist party whose fortunes were more fluid.

Juxtaposing these bald characteristics with those of the Parnellite and later Irish parliamentary parties not only provides a comparative perspective on the Ulster party: it also illuminates the parties' relationship at Westminster. In fact, the Ulster party emerges as quite different in occupational composition from Parnell's party. The number of landowners sitting as nationalist members dropped dramatically at the general election of 1885 — and never rose subsequently above 9% of the total membership. Tenant farmers, on the other hand, though a negligible force in the party of 1880, greatly increased their representation in 1885, and grew thereafter from strength to strength.[11]

Within the Ulster party landlord numbers were also falling off — but from a much greater initial strength, and as late as 1900 they still accounted for a quarter of the membership. This decline was also symptomatic of a readjustment in the ratio of rural to urban members. Landlords were not, as in the Parnellite party, replaced by farmers. Indeed, though the party included a few prominent farmer spokesmen — T.W. Russell, Thomas Lea — farmers themselves were not returned during the period under discussion.

Lawyers and businessmen instead filled the gap in the ranks of the Ulster party. Parnell's party had a much weaker legal contingent, though even then lawyers were overrepresented in relation to businessmen. Lawyers were, of course, necessary to nationalist parliamentary success; but they lacked the opportunities for promotion possessed by their colleagues in the Ulster party. A parliamentary seat, therefore, was a much more equivocal career asset.

The Irish parliamentary party failed singularly to attract big business into its ranks. In 1892, of eighty Parnellite and anti-Parnellite members elected, only nine (in the calculation of F.S.L. Lyons) were businessmen of substance; by 1910, when 83 nationalists of varying descriptions were returned, a single MP represented the major business interests of Ireland.[12] The feebleness of the party's business lobby deprived it of social cachet and wealth, and weakened its claim to embrace all sections of Irish society.

Irish Unionists, on the other hand, *were* able, with negligible effort, to recruit the linen barons and shipbuilders who together dominated Ulster industry. Business representation, moreover, grew progressively stronger, accounting for half the Ulster Unionist seats won at the general election of 1906.

Journalists, from local hacks to figures of national importance (like T.P. O'Connor) constituted a significant element within the Parnellite party. Its leaders were keenly alive to the value of a sympathetic press, and even owners of comparatively minor provincial papers were recruited to serve in the Commons. Irish Unionist members, like Horace Plunkett and Walter Long, were also aware of the value of press backing: both were involved in negotiating the purchase of established papers.[13] Yet, journalists and proprietors did not feature significantly in the Irish Unionist parliamentary party, at least before 1918. Three local press magnates were returned at the Coupon Election: R.J. Lynn, editor and managing director of the *Northern Whig*, Peter Kerr-Smiley, chairman of the *Whig*, and Thomas Moles, the editor of the *Belfast Telegraph*. Kerr-Smiley had held his seat since January 1910; hitherto the only Irish Unionist member connected with the newspaper industry had been H.O. Arnold-Forster — and even he, by 1900, had become effectively a career politician.[14]

In part the absence of journalists (if not of proprietors) may be connected with the extreme social conservatism of Parnell's opponents in the 1880s and 1890s — a party dominated by wealthy landowners, lawyers and businessmen, though with a smattering of tame and token populists (like William Johnston of Ballykilbeg). In the 1880s the Unionist party included very few lower professionals, wage earners or small farmers. Later, mavericks of doubtful social standing (like Tom Sloan) might slip into the party ranks, but Unionist selectors consistently preferred wealthy candidates to those with more democratic and more costly credentials.

The Irish parliamentary party had always a broader social base, and indeed between Parnell's death and 1910 the numbers of working and lower middle class MPs grew. By January 1910, where no Irish Unionist member was recruited from the lower professional and wage-earning ranks, these classes provided 46% of the Irish parliamentary party's membership.[15] Yet, if this made for accessibility and popularity in the constituency, then a party dominated by small shopkeepers and farmers was an alien and unnatural component of a still gentrified House of Commons. The Parnellites' parliamentary effectiveness, based upon numbers and the skills of the leadership, was undoubtedly impaired by both their strange nationality and their strange class origins. Loyalist MPs could not always overcome the barriers of nationality — but, crucially, they were *not* separated from their English allies by class.

In sum, the ideological distinctions between the Irish Unionist parliamentary party and the Parnellites were compounded by more personal distinctions between the make-up of each body. Irish Unionists were separated from the Parnellites not simply by political conviction, or, for the most part, by religion, but also by educational and professional experience and — further — by the extent of their respective assimilation within the British political elite. Given these differences, it might readily be expected that there was little scope for the growth of any constructive personal or political relationship between members of the two parties. This expectation is tested next in the light of the particular attitudes of Edward Saunderson, and of the bond between him and his more conspicuous Irish rival, Charles Stewart Parnell.

(iii)

The parallels are intriguing. Both Saunderson and Parnell were scions of the Church of Ireland gentry class. Their respective ancestors, Francis Saunderson and Sir John Parnell, had, despite the lure of the peerage, remained staunchly anti-Unionist: both Saunderson and Parnell were shaped by a colonial nationalist inheritance from the late eighteenth century. Each had an overbearing mother. Each was educated out of Ireland, and each to some extent acquired the mentality of the exile. They each schooled themselves to politics, rather than exhibiting any immediate flair. They led from the margins of their respective movements, Parnell as a landlord and as a Protestant, Saunderson as a landlord and as a Cavanman — as an outsider to the heartland of Ulster Unionism. Each had a strain of anti-clericalism and anglophobia. Their respective political styles could be aloof and disdainful.[16]

But the coincidences supplied by nature and nurture were not embodied in any public harmony between the two men. Saunderson, born in 1837, followed his father, Alexander, into the House of Commons as Liberal MP for Co. Cavan. Like his father, Edward Saunderson was initially sensitive to the political and social claims of Catholic Ireland; like the early Parnell he was less patient with Catholic clerical dignity, and with Catholic doctrine. His fiery denunciation of transubstantiation at the General Synod of the Church of Ireland (reminiscent of Ian Paisley at the Oxford Union in 1967) confirmed the Catholic voters of Cavan in their shift towards Home Rule, and cost Saunderson his seat at the general election of 1874.[17] The demise of Liberalism, popular electoral rejection, and the land agitation of 1879-81, encouraged Saunderson to redefine his politics; and by 1882-83 he had taken refuge behind a more embattled and exclusivist creed. A spokesman for resurgent Orangeism, increasingly sceptical of the English party structure, Saunderson was by 1885 promoting a distinctive and separate Unionist movement. Rejecting Parnellism, he was enormously impressed by its parliamentary influence. Rejecting Parnell, Saunderson was yet impressed by the nationalist leader's qualities of leadership, and profoundly dismayed by the standard of loyalist opposition which was offered in the House of Commons.[18]

Saunderson created a separate Irish Unionist parliamentary party in 1885-86, and helped to formulate a broader Unionist movement. He fought Parnell in the Commons through 1886, and — out of the Commons — as a platform speaker in the later 1880s. Parnellism was the focal point of his political existence: Unionism, as led by Edward Saunderson, emerged as a negative creed, the political expression of what most Irish Protestants chose to reject, rather than a positive expression of what they sought or represented. Parnell and Parnellism were therefore central both to the organisational forms and rhetorical style of the Unionism which Saunderson promoted in the later 1880s.

Yet, within the House of Commons Saunderson played an important role in opposing the Uncrowned King and his courtiers. Indeed in many sessions his chief contribution as chairman of the Irish Unionists lay in responding to the Parnellite amendments to the Motion for a Loyal Address. These amendments fell along similar lines, all generally relating to Home Rule or to lesser grievances perceived by the minority community: Saunderson's responses certainly varied little from year to year. Armed with references and quotations (almost certainly supplied by the Irish Loyal and Patriotic Union), he aimed to portray Parnell and the nationalist members — the prospective rulers of Ireland under a Home Rule parliament — in the worst possible light.

Discrediting his opponents was Saunderson's chief aim, and to this end he sacrificed both equanimity and relevance (he was frequently cautioned by the Speaker for wandering off the subject of debate onto more familiar rhodomontades). He was choleric and provocative: many illustrations of this time portray him with an ill-natured facial expression and extravagant declamatory gestures of hands and arms.[19] But, if he was sincerely impassioned, he may also have consciously desired to goad his opponents into a compromising and damaging reponse; and when the parties of Ireland were most bitterly divided — under Arthur Balfour's Chief Secretaryship — the Parnellites frequently reacted as Saunderson would have wished.

Saunderson's accusations attempted to link the Irish party either individually or collectively with crime. He drew attention to allegedly provocative speeches by the Irish members, coupling his quotations with statistics of violence, which he claimed represented the direct aftermath of his opponents' oratory: for their part the Irish members were prepared to make similar accusations against Saunderson (in 1883-84, 1886 and 1893).[20] His own language was certainly violent, though he only occasionally transgressed the formal bounds of parliamentary propriety. Like the Parnellites he was acquainted with the eccentricities of the parliamentary Manual of Procedure, and could gauge with increasingly greater precision what he could get away with, and what would provoke the intervention of the Speaker. Even when he was asked to withdraw a damning phrase, he could contrive to win some advantage. In February 1893, speaking on the Address, he referred to Father McFadden, the controversial parish priest of Gweedore, Co. Donegal, as 'this murderous ruffian'. Asked to amend his language (not by the Speaker, by Gladstone and Arthur Balfour) Saunderson substituted 'excited politician' for the offending reference: he thereby gained a laugh, scored a point off his opponents, and ensured that the slur, even though now swathed in good humour, would remain in the minds of his opponents.[21]

Saunderson's Unionism was therefore frequently expressed in negative and antagonistic terms, and it was only comparatively late in his career that he began to develop a wider dimension to his political faith, and to curb his earlier stridency of tone. Before Parnell's death Saunderson was febrile and acerbic, driven by a despair, both at his perception of the condition of Ireland, and by the suspicion that he was fighting a foredoomed cause. It was rumoured in the late 1880s that he had resigned himself to the inevitability of Home Rule for Ireland, and indeed some of his speeches during the debate on the second Home Rule Bill seem to confirm this suggestion.[22] His belligerence was therefore that of the 'last-ditcher', and he sustained an at times self-defeating defiance of the Parnellites.

He was selectively pained by violence, affected by his own, long statistics of crime. But the turmoil of the land war had a more direct and personal impact: at the beginning of the Plan of Campaign, when unrest in Ireland was beginning to escalate, Johnston of Ballykilbeg found that his leader's London home had been placed under police guard.[23] Gradually and unsurprisingly, Saunderson began to cast his faith in apocalyptic terms: 'the war between us', he told Dillon in July 1890, 'is war to the death'.[24] This was a rare admission, evidently inspired by a genuine, uncontrollable rage (as opposed to the ritualistic anger which he more frequently deployed). Cautioned by the Speaker, Saunderson explained his violent language in a passage which revealed the intensity of feeling underlying his more formal indictments of the Parnellites:

> I regret, Sir, if my warmth has betrayed me beyond the rules of debate. It is not easy for hon. Members who do not understand the condition of affairs in Ireland, and who do not know what boycotting means to realise the misery that has been brought by the action of the League, but it makes my blood boil to think that these things should be supported by a great Party in the State . . . it would be a great satisfaction if some of the most eloquent of Ireland's sons would forget this policy, which must end in nothing, and join with me, as I am ready to join with any man, in promoting the good of the country.[25]

Before the defeat of the second Home Rule Bill the polarity between Saunderson and his Irish opponents was perceived by him as virtually absolute. They were the 'heathen' of his correspondence with his wife — a malign force, susceptible only to brute strength, whether in terms of rhetoric, or of coercive legislation. Indeed, Saunderson's own bitter stand had a physical dimension which confirms the nature of his relationship with the Parnellites. Thus, in March 1893, when T.W. Russell moved the adjournment of the House, and after a characteristic accusation of incitement, Saunderson was challenged by Willie Redmond to repeat his imputations outside the House. Reginald Lucas, Saunderson's biographer, described the ensuing scene in terms of farce and of the ridiculous — but at least one press report suggested that the two men nearly came to blows and were only prevented from doing so by the intervention of fellow-MPs, and (possibly) by the presence of a police officer.[26]

The potential for violence accelerated into reality on 27 July 1893. On the completion of the Committee Stage of the Home Rule Bill, a fight developed in the Commons in which Saunderson and several of the Irish members were involved. Descriptions of the 'scene' entered a host of parliamentary memoirs, many observers or participants dismissing it as being little more than a temporary aberration, caused by the peculiar parliamentary circumstances. Saunderson suggested that relations between himself and the nationalist members would be quickly healed. Indeed Reginald Lucas reported that Saunderson had gone to T.P. O'Connor, saying that 'he was indebted to him for ten minutes of the best fun that he ever had'.[27] But this is an ambiguous anecdote — for it contains not only a suggestion of rough good humour, but also an implied accusation of responsibility — that O'Connor had been responsible for the fight. It seems more probable that the 'scene' of July 1893 should be regarded in the context of years of bitterness, the repeated exchange of damning accusations and earlier prospects of violence. The sad reality was that, before 1893, even basic civility between Saunderson and the Irish party was abnormal; and despite his facile references to a supposedly typical Irish ability to reject rancour, Saunderson's own quarrel with Parnellism proved to be too deeply felt to permit the growth of any worthwhile personal relationships.

Nevertheless, within this spectrum of distrust there were perceptible gradations. Saunderson never softened his attitude towards Parnell during the latter's lifetime. His speeches were uniformly antagonistic — and it is probable that he regarded Parnell as, in effect, a traitor to class and creed. Dillon and O'Brien were similar objects of Saunderson's ire. Conversely, even when Saunderson was at his most belligerent, he preserved a grudging respect for Michael Davitt — for his directness of purpose, and for his courage. This limited tolerance is first perceptible in a pamphlet, written by Saunderson in 1884 — *Two Irelands: Loyalty versus Treason* — but it was expressed later, even at the height of the Plan of Campaign.[28] And, up to a point, Davitt reciprocated. After Saunderson's death a nationalist journalist recalled a conversation with Davitt and others in which the Colonel was referred to derisively as 'a bigot': 'A bigot he may be', Davitt retorted, 'yet I like the man. He can say hard things about an opponent, and he does say them quite fearlessly. In politics he is an open, fearless fighter. He loves his God and he loves his country — but his country is Ulster'.[29]

After the Parnellite split John Redmond was also favoured with some comparatively laudatory allusions from the loyalist leader. Redmond was tolerated because he was perceived to be a gentleman and because, as the head of the Parnellites after the schism, Saunderson judged him to be less under clerical sway than T.M. Healy. Redmond can scarcely have welcomed such expressions of approval; and indeed if Saunderson had been more sensitive to the difficulties of his opponent's position, he might have grasped that statements such as the following could only be counterproductive: 'I venture to assert', Saunderson told the House in 1893, 'that there is only one Gentleman below the Gangway that has the right to speak in the name of the Nationalist electors in Ireland, and that is the member for Waterford . . .'[30]

Affection such as this had a somewhat shallow foundation. Indeed, such statements are possibly better evidence for Saunderson's unrelenting opposition to Home Rule than for any effective qualification of this attitude. At any rate they testify to a naïve directness in expressing his own sympathies, which would become more fully apparent in Saunderson's heavy-handed mockery of nationalist divisions. Mockery, rather than sustained approval for Redmond, was more characteristic of Saunderson's statements after 1891 — and thus one is driven back to the blunt truth that, whatever his wavering, Saunderson held a hearty contempt for his political opponents.

On the other hand, there is little unambiguous evidence to suggest that most nationalist members in the 1880s other than disliked Saunderson. There was certainly a development within their attitudes over the years — a development linked indeed to Saunderson's own shifting mood ('It is *you* who have changed', William O'Brien once taunted Saunderson).[31] But it would be quite wrong to suggest, as Lucas did in 1908, that private camaraderie complemented the public antipathy which existed between Saunderson and the nationalists.[32] In the last decade of his life Saunderson mellowed, and his opponents reciprocated — but there is little evidence of any close personal or professional relationship behind the scenes. Saunderson and the nationalists certainly referred to each other occasionally in pacific terms. Thus in 1896, when he denied harbouring any personal rancour for *individual* members of the Irish parliamentary party, Healy called out 'no more have we for you'.[33] And in 1899 Justin McCarthy could refer affectionately in his *Reminiscences* to his old opponent.[34] But before the mid-1890s even this superficial banter was rare. A more typical display of their relationship was given when Saunderson interjected a brief remark into a speech delivered by Thomas Sexton in August 1889. Sexton delivered a coruscating rejoinder: 'I trust that the hon. and gallant gentleman will remember that he is the one member of this House whose interruptions I cannot tolerate'.[35]

(iv)

Why were Saunderson and Parnell locked into such a peculiarly vicious combat? Sharing a similar political ancestry, united by certain formative experiences, by class and by religion, one might have predicted a less marked division between the two men. There are a variety of possible perspectives on their superficially paradoxical relationship. The experience of Ulster since 1969 has encouraged many to resolve northern community relationships into simple polarities — British and Irish, settler and indigenous, Protestant and Catholic. This reductionism diverts, however, from the volatile nature of Anglo-Irish and northern Protestant self-perception, certainly in their difficult nineteenth-century forms. To some extent, Protestant identity was in flux in the nineteenth century, shifting from the confident 'Irishness' of the 1780s and 1790s to the scarcely less confident 'Ulster' or 'British' identity of the mid and late twentieth century.[36]

Saunderson and Parnell exemplify this transition, each responding differently to the contemporary reformulation of Irish identity along more popular, Catholic and Gaelic lines. They shared the same background, and confronted the same communal dilemma, but ultimately they supplied different retorts. Parnell chose to work within and to harness the new Irishness, while Saunderson worked outside, contributing instead to an alternative form of identity, exclusivist, northern and Protestant.

Parnell and Saunderson were therefore divided by the unstable nature of their own tradition; but they were also divided by their approach to their shared religion, and divided by their sense of place. Saunderson hailed from Belturbet, Co. Cavan, at the outer edge of Ulster and of intensive Protestant settlement in Ireland. Parnell was, of course, a Wicklow man. Living in the 'cultural corridor' of Ulster, Saunderson's political options were, perhaps, rather wider than those of Parnell.[37] He had access to the heartland of rural, Gaelic Ireland, to northern Connacht and western Leinster, and he was certainly informed about the social and political development of Catholic nationalism. Yet he was also on the geographical fringes of an alternative Ireland, in the loyalist north-east. His own career was an uneasy perambulation around this cultural marchland, passing from a liberal and paternalist territory in the 1860s towards a more narrowly and defensively class-based political creed by the early 1900s.

Parnell, like O'Connell, knew little of Ulster, and demonstrated only the most superficial acquaintance with the character of northern politics. Domiciled in Wicklow, he lacked the variety of political bases and strategies available to Saunderson. Socially and religiously on the margins, Parnell baulked at the political isolation which increasingly contaminated much of the Anglo-Irish gentry in the mid and late nineteenth century. There was of course no demotic loyalism in south Leinster to compensate for rejection by Catholic Ireland, and to provide the temporary continuation of political and social norms. Like many anti-Treatyites in 1922, Parnell's creed had much to do with his location at the periphery of the Catholic nation.[38] Like Saunderson and the Unionists, Parnell's creed had much to do with the role of the Protestant minority in Irish society. But Saunderson's Protestantism was not merely the faith of the lords and gentry on the Ulster-Connacht frontier, it was the creed of the Orange labourers in North Armagh, and of the mill workers in Lurgan and Portadown. Parnell's experience and definition of popular politics were wholly different, and his view of Protestantism was confined to his knowledge of the gentry in his home county. So, if both Saunderson and Parnell carried the legacy of colonial nationalism, then they interpreted and exploited this legacy in very different ways. Parnell's nationalism, like Saunderson's Unionism, was at least partly the response of an Anglo-Irish and Protestant gentleman to the threat of utter supersession in a new Ireland.[39]

Saunderson and Parnell were not merely divided by geography, they were divided too by their shared Protestantism. Saunderson inherited from his mother (herself the daughter of a prominent clerical family) an intense evangelicalism which governed his politics throughout his varied career.[40] Saunderson was actively religious, preaching in the church on his estate, proselytising among his friends, and patronising some of the leading evangelists of the day. He was a conscientious synodsman of the Church of Ireland. His was a low, unadorned episcopalianism, focusing on the inerrancy of Scripture and upon an intense conversion experience. It provided him with a rigid morality which he freely transferred into the arena of party politics. Evangelicalism drove a doctrinal and electoral wedge between Saunderson and his Catholic tenants and constituents in Cavan; equally, evangelicalism helped to unite Saunderson, an outsider and a landowner, to North Armagh, a constituency which had shown a repeated susceptibility to Protestant religious revival.[41] Saunderson's fierce, manichaean morality helped to form his critique of Parnellism and of its perceived crimes: his moral sense distanced him from Parnell.

Evangelical zeal was the motor of Saunderson's Unionism. Parnell's Protestantism was, by way of contrast, latitudinarian to the point of incoherence: the creed of a gentleman, rather than that of Athanasius or of Nicaea. His well-documented sympathy for the Plymouth Brethren clearly never developed into active profession.[42] This flexibility simultaneously separated him from his more zealous co-religionists in the North and enabled him to lead a primarily Catholic movement without apparently sacrificing any personal principle (at any rate until the O'Shea divorce). Protestant religious fervour was as alien and intolerable to Parnell as Catholic fervour — but he was physically and socially remote from the heartland of the former, where he had experience of the latter at the end of his driveway, in Rathdrum. Combining gentlemanly status with energetic piety, Saunderson was much more alien to Parnell than the devout Catholic tradesmen and farmers of his own home town.

But the individual tensions between Parnell and Saunderson merely epitomised the relationship between their parties. Here, too, religion and geography played their part: the Irish Unionist parliamentary party in the 1880s was a wholly Protestant grouping confronting an overwhelmingly Catholic Parnellite party. Those few Protestants in the ranks of the Irish parliamentary party tended to be Presbyterian (in contradistinction to the dominant Anglican ethos of their loyalist counterparts); others, like Parnell or J.G. Biggar, were either lapsed or apostate. The Irish Unionist parliamentary party was a largely, though not exclusively, northern party; Ulster was the only province which the Irish parliamentary party did net wholly infiltrate and capture.

Aside from the familiar religious, territorial and cultural distinctions, it will now be clear that the Irish parliamentary parties of the 1880s were divided by class and by occupation: there proved to be little opportunity to overturn communal and historical tensions through personal relationships. At a time when nationalism reflected the strategic priorities of Lalor and Davitt, landlords still dominated the Irish Unionist parliamentary body. Although this was not *always* reflected in the grouping's approach to land legislation — concern for Liberal Unionist sensitivities dictated a certain caution after 1886 — it was nonetheless true that the particular targets of Nationalist campaigning throughout the 1880s were also among the chief components of loyalist representation. In this way the social and economic tensions of rural Ireland in the 1880s were complemented, even exacerbated, by the parliamentary process.

Lawyers and the business classes of Belfast were scarcely less well represented in the Irish Unionist parliamentary party — once again in contradistinction to the occupational composition of Parnell's following. As late nineteenth century nationalism hurtled along a neo-romantic and anti-urban trajectory, organised Unionism emerged as a Belfast-dominated and economically pragmatic creed. The gradual mobilisation of Ulster Unionism, culminating in 1905 with the Ulster Unionist Council, focused largely on Belfast. As has been observed, the shipbuilders Edward Harland, G.W. Wolff and George Clark all sat for Belfast constituencies before 1910; the crucial freighting interest was represented in parliament by Sir Daniel Dixon and Sir James Porter Corry. The only disruption to the propertied Conservative monopoly of Belfast politics before 1910 was caused by Protestant populist candidates, whose faith and enthusiasms were equally inaccessible to the Irish parliamentary party.[43] Here, again, embodied on the Irish Unionist benches was the ideological antithesis of late nineteenth century nationalism.

In theory the opportunities for fruitful communication, for mutual comprehension, were good. Saunderson and Parnell identified themselves with different cultural traditions in Ireland, but personally and emotionally they had much in common. Their respective parties, representing different perspectives on Irish history and on Anglo-Irish relations, nonetheless shared the same parliamentary arena. They were *all* Irish exiles at Westminster; they *all* had to learn the painfully intricate rules of the English parliamentary club. The House of Commons, across whose floor they glared at one another, had historically served to divert violent conviction, to blunt the edge of ideological passion. But Saunderson and Parnell did not exploit the British parliament to elucidate their differences. And their respective parties sustained a highly ritualised combat which offered little scope for any more subtle mutual interrogation. Saunderson and Parnell were divided by their Protestantism, and by their perspectives on Ulster; they were distinguished by their separate regional bases. Parnell's party consciously resisted incorporation within a predominantly English parliament; Parnell's party was to some extent separated culturally and socially from the rest of the Commons. But, above all else, the men of the Irish Unionist parliamentary party embodied much that late nineteenth-century nationalism chose to reject: landlordism, big business, Anglo-centricity. There *were* pressures for mutual assimilation. But culturally and personally, Saunderson and his party appeared as alien as those Englishmen whose blandishments the Parnellites so stoutly resisted.

Notes

1. For some comments on the Unionist sense of the past see: Terence Brown, 'Remembering who we are' in *Ireland's Literature: Selected Essays* (Mullingar, 1988), pp. 223-42; Marianne Elliott, *Watchmen in Sion: The Protestant Idea of Liberty* (Derry, 1984); Alvin Jackson, 'Unionist Myths, 1912-85' in *Past & Present* (forthcoming).
2. Public Record Office of Northern Ireland (hereafter PRONI), Edward Saunderson Papers, T.2996/1/61: Saunderson to his wife, 15 Jan. 1886.
3. F.S.L. Lyons, *Charles Stewart Parnell* (London, 1977), pp. 368-71.
4. Ibid, p. 583.
5. This section of the essay depends heavily on Alvin Jackson, *The Ulster Party: Irish Unionists in the House of Commons, 1884-1911* (Oxford, 1989), pp. 53-113.
6. Saunderson Papers, T.2996/1/66: Saunderson to his wife, 23 Jan. 1886.
7. Laurence M. Geary, *The Plan of Campaign, 1886-91* (Cork, 1986), pp. 52, 111-13.
8. Russell has begun at last to receive adequate scholarly attention. See Paul Bew, *Conflict and Conciliation: Parnellites and Agrarian Radicals, 1890-1910* (Oxford, 1987), pp. 86-95; Alvin Jackson, 'Irish Unionism and the Russellite Threat, 1894-1906' in *Irish Historical Studies*, XXV, 100 (Nov. 1987); Elizabeth Malcolm, *'Ireland Sober, Ireland Free': Drink and Temperance in Nineteenth Century Ireland* (Dublin, 1986), pp. 171-77; and an excellent recent article by James Loughlin, 'T.W. Russell, the Tenant Farmer Interest and Progressive Unionism in Ulster, 1886-1900' in *Éire-Ireland*, XXV, 1 (Spring 1990), pp. 44-63.
9. John Ross, *The Years of my Pilgrimage* (London, 1924), pp. 120-23.
10. Lonsdale, though of central importance, remains the victim of neglect. The best primary source for his career is PRONI, H.B. Armstrong Papers, D.3727/E/46. I am grateful to Anthony Malcomson for originally drawing my

attention to this collection.

11. Conor Cruise O'Brien, *Parnell and his Party, 1880-1890* (Oxford, 1964), pp. 18, 152.

12. F.S.L. Lyons, *The Irish Parliamentary Party, 1890-1910* (London, 1951), p. 175.

13. A.M. Gollin, *The Observer and J.L. Garvin, 1908-14: A Study in a Great Editorship* (Oxford, 1960), p. 15. Trevor West, *Horace Plunkett, Cooperation and Politics: An Irish Biography* (Gerrards Cross and Washington, 1986), pp. 90-94.

14. For Arnold-Forster's career see Mary Arnold-Forster, *The Right Honourable Hugh Oakeley Arnold-Forster: A Memoir* (London, 1910).

15. Lyons, *Irish Parliamentary Party*, p. 169.

16. For Edward Saunderson see: Jackson, *The Ulster Party*; Henry Saunderson, *The Saundersons of Castle Saunderson* (London, 1936); Reginald Lucas, *Colonel Saunderson MP: A Memoir* (London, 1908). For Parnell's background see R.F. Foster, *Parnell: The Man and his Family* (Hassocks, 1976).

17. *The Anglo-Celt*, 26 April 1873, 3 May 1873; Lyons, *Parnell*, pp. 118-22.

18. *The Portadown News*, 2 Dec. 1905; *Lurgan Mail*, 2 Dec. 1905 (Saunderson reflecting on his career).

19. See, for example, the portrait by H. Harris Brown reproduced as a frontispiece to the Lucas volume and in Henry Patton, *Fifty Years of Disestablishment* (Dublin, 1922), p. 230. See also the sketch by Begg in Lucas, *Saunderson*, p. 276. Even the *Vanity Fair* caricature depicts Saunderson in truculent mood (28 February 1887).

20. Saunderson Papers, T.2996/1/100: Saunderson to Mrs Saunderson, 25 Aug. 1886. *Hansard*, series 3, cccviii, 715 (25 Aug. 1886). Lucas, *Saunderson*, pp. 110-11.

21. *Hansard*, fourth series, viii, 256 (2 Feb. 1893). Lucas, *Saunderson*, p. 190.

22. PRONI, Montgomery Papers, D.627/428/50: Richard Bagwell to Montgomery, 12 Aug. 1888. *Hansard*, fourth series, xii, 486 (20 April 1893).

23. PRONI, William Johnston Diaries, D.880/2/39: 28 April 1887.

24. *Hansard*, third series, cccxlvi, 1011 (7 July 1890).

25. *Ibid.*

26. Lucas, *Saunderson*, p. 193. *Hansard*, series 4, ix, 840 (2 Mar. 1893). Saunderson Papers, T.2996/12/5: scrapbook containing, *inter alia*, Redmond's challenge. *Belfast News Letter*, 7 Mar. 1893 (London letter).

27. Lucas, *Saunderson*, pp. 199-202. *Hansard*, fourth series, xv, 732 (27 July 1892). Other observers were genuinely shocked. Arthur Griffith-Boscawen, writing fourteen years after the event, recalled that it was 'the most disgraceful [scene] I ever witnessed in the House': *Fourteen Years in Parliament* (London, 1907), pp. 33-34.

28. E.J. Saunderson, *Two Irelands: Loyalty versus Treason* (Dublin and London, 1884), p. 26.

29. *Irish Independent*, 22 May 1908: review by 'Jacques' of Lucas, *Saunderson*.

30. *Hansard*, fourth series, viii, 1328.

31. *Hansard*, fourth series, iv, 1606 (23 May 1892).

33. Lucas, *Saunderson*, p. 133.
34. Justin McCarthy, *Reminiscences*, two volumes (London, 1899), ii, p. 395: 'I do not think there is a more popular man in the House of Commons than Colonel Saunderson'.
35. *Hansard*, third series, cccxl, 16 (21 Aug. 1889).
36. For some thoughts on the issue of Protestant identity see: Elliott, *Watchmen in Sion*; D.W. Miller, *Queen's Rebels: Ulster Loyalism in Historical Perspective* (Dublin, 1978); James Loughlin, *Gladstone, Home Rule and the Ulster Question, 1882-1893* (Dublin, 1986).
37. Edna Longley, *From Cathleen to Anorexia: The Breakdown of Irelands* (Dublin, 1990), p. 24. Louis MacNeice distinguished sharply between the Ulster gentry — 'an inferior species' — and the superior southern variant. MacNeice, 'A Personal Digression' in Alan Heuser (ed.), *The Selected Prose of Louis MacNeice* (Oxford, 1990), pp. 60-66.
38. Tom Garvin, *Nationalist Revolutionaries in Ireland, 1858-1928* (Oxford, 1987), pp. 146-7.
39. Paul Bew, *C.S. Parnell* (Dublin, 1980), pp. 138, 142.
40. Saunderson, *The Saundersons of Castle Saunderson*, pp. 57-8; Lucas, *Saunderson*, pp. 34-6. For a flavour of Saunderson's spirituality see Edward Saunderson, *Present and Everlasting Salvation: Three Addresses with a Preface by the Bishop of Ossory* (Dublin, 1907).
41. See, for example, the report of a revival in Lurgan and Portadown in 1905: *Lurgan Mail*, 14 April 1905.
42. Lyons, *Parnell*, p. 20.
43. For a fuller exploration of this theme see: Henry Patterson, *Class Conflict and Sectarianism: The Protestant Working Class and the Belfast Labour Movement, 1868-1920* (Belfast, 1980).

LEFT: Michael Davitt on Land League Flag. RIGHT: Land League Poster. (*National Museum of Ireland*).

Parnell and the Irish Land Question

Laurence M. Geary

'We are all revisionists now', one of Parnell's biographers, Roy Foster, claimed in the first issue of the *Irish Review* in 1986. Nowhere has the revisionist surgical knife been more deftly applied than to the corpus of writing on the Irish land question. The post-Famine land system, as conventionally portrayed, by Pomfret in 1930, for instance, and by Palmer a decade later, was intolerable and rapacious, with rack-renting, wholesale evictions and endemic agrarian crime as the norms. A severe agricultural depression in the late 1870s exacerbated the situation, both factors coalescing to unleash an intense period of rural upheaval between 1879 and 1882. This traditional interpretation of the land war as a spontaneous, mass uprising of a homogeneous, rural population against predatory landlordism has been challenged and re-evaluated by revisionist historians and sociologists over the past three decades.

According to the new orthodoxy, the quarter of a century following the Famine was a period of rapid and generally progressive rural change, during which agriculture, despite the occasional set-back, flourished. By the mid-1870s, output had increased by forty-seven per cent over the 1850s average, and was disposed of for substantially higher returns. Price and production increases far outstripped the rise in agricultural rents, which are thought to have appreciated on average by about twenty per cent in the thirty years after the Famine. Far from being rackrented, the general body of tenants in post-Famine Ireland were thus in the relatively privileged position of holding their lands at what in real terms were falling rents.

Evictions were not as widespread as suggested hitherto. In most years they rarely exceeded one for every one thousand agricultural holdings. In addition, tenant right, or the Ulster Custom, as it came to be called, was a reality on most Irish estates. The practice defied definition. There were as many variations and interpretations of the custom as there were landlords and tenants. But its essence was the acknowledged right of the tenant to sell his interest in his holding, which was defined as the value of the occupancy right. Thus, the three Fs — fair rent, fixity of tenure and free sale — were enjoyed on a practical and fairly widespread basis long before they were formally conceded under the Land Act of 1881.

In the post-Famine period, the quality of rural life improved immeasurably and agricultural prosperity was largely responsible for the significant advances in housing, diet, education and general living standards that evolved. During this period there occurred what the historian James Donnelly has termed 'a revolution in rising expectations'.

This situation changed dramatically in the late 1870s. Commenting on the meteorological returns for 1879, the Registrar-General for Ireland, Dr T.W. Grimshaw, observed: 'The weather . . . is likely to be remembered by everyone, but especially by agriculturalists, whose interests have so materially suffered during the year owing to the inclemency of all the seasons.' This was the third successive year in which wet, cold and cloudy conditions predominated. Rain fell on 208 of the 365 days. In the autumn, inspectors of the Local Government Board for Ireland reported that the cutting and drying of turf had been seriously disrupted by the incessant rain, while the harvest generally was significantly below average. Ominously, potatoes were described as 'deficient in quantity, inferior in quality and affected by blight'. The crop had declined from 4.2 million tons in 1876 to 1.1 million tons in 1879. All root and grain crops, as well as livestock production, suffered during these inclement years. The Board mistakenly assessed oats as being universally 'good and plentiful'. In fact, they shared in the general decline of all root and grain crops during these inclement years, falling from 1.1 million tons to 0.8 million tons between 1876 and 1879. Livestock production also suffered. In addition, agricultural prices were extremely depressed. Falling prices were accompanied by a general restriction of credit on the part of banks, moneylenders and shopkeepers. Agricultural competition from America and Canada and contracting labour markets in Ireland and Britain exacerbated the situation further. The subsistence tenant farmers of the western part of Ireland were most seriously affected. In mid-November 1879, the Local Government Board concluded that the entire province of Connacht, together with counties Donegal, Clare, Kerry and the West Riding of Cork, were in 'an exceptionally distressed condition'.

With the onset of winter the situation deteriorated alarmingly. Early in January 1880, the Bishop of Elphin, Laurence Gillooly, stated that distress prevailed throughout Co. Roscommon. 'The majority of our peasantry have neither money nor credit', he wrote, 'and a large proportion of them not even the necessaries of life', an observation that applied with equal validity to virtually all of the western half of Ireland. According to the parish priest of Dungloe, Co. Donegal, the labourers and small farmers were 'on the very verge of famine'. They were reduced to eating 'black seaweed' at Glencolumbkille. At Ardcarne and Tumna, Co. Roscommon, the peasantry were said to be 'in a state of starvation'. A dearth of food, firing, clothing and credit was reported from Kilgarvan, Co. Mayo, where some 200 families had been forced to pawn their clothes, leaving their children semi-naked. Indeed, an inundation of reports from all parts of the country testified to the wretchedness of the poor and the ubiquity of distress.

The rising tide that had lifted all economic boats for a quarter of a century was now on the ebb and a prolonged period of prosperity was transformed by the severe agricultural crisis of the late 1870s into one of near famine conditions. Many Irish farmers, particularly along the Atlantic seaboard, were once again threatened with bankruptcy, eviction and starvation. The failure of landlords and their agents to grant voluntary rent reductions and their insistence on the payment of customary rents reactivated feelings of dissatisfaction and disaffection that had long lain dormant in the hearts of the western tenantry.

Against this background, Michael Davitt, recently paroled after spending several years in prison for trafficking in arms as a member of the Irish Republican Brotherhood or Fenian organisation, drew up resolutions for a huge demonstration at Irishtown, in his native Co. Mayo, on 20 April 1879, to demand justice for the tenant farmers. From this beginning the agitation spread rapidly throughout the west of Ireland, culminating, in mid-August 1879, in the establishment of the rather oddly named National Land League of Mayo, which was transformed by Davitt, two months later, into the Irish National Land League, with two declared objectives: To protect the Irish tenant farmers against their landlords in the short term and ultimately to convert them into owners of their holdings.

Davitt secured Fenian support for his initiative and completed a novel alignment of political forces by persuading Charles Stewart Parnell, whose political star was in the ascendant and whose appeal at this time was all things to all shades of nationalist opinion, to accept the presidency of the new organisation. But, along with most observers, Parnell, too, had been caught off balance by the rapidity and unexpectedness of the deteriorating economic situation. His response was vague, indecisive and full of generalities. At Ballinasloe, on 3 November 1878, he told the assembled tenant farmers that he was in favour of land purchase as it had been carried out in France and Prussia:

> There were five and a half millions of people in this country, enough people to win their own freedom, and if they were determined they would win it; they would win the land and the right of living on the soil under the landlords by paying rent, or by purchasing from the landlords and becoming possessors of their own farms (*applause*). He himself was in favour of the latter system, which prevailed in France and Prussia, and would prevail in Ireland (*hear, hear*).

'In the meantime', he continued, 'they must stop eviction, they must keep the people in the country by keeping the landlords from raising rents', an observation that must have seemed strange to an audience confronted with destitution and starvation and for whom even the payment of existing rents was an impossibility. There is probably a good deal of truth in Davitt's subsequent observation that Parnell's views on the land question at this time were evolving, and while he advocated peasant proprietorship he never viewed it with any great enthusiasm. Nonetheless, 'the land of Ireland for the people of Ireland' remained a powerful and emotive clarion call.

What Parnell did grasp from the beginning was the political significance of the new situation, the re-emergence of the perennial Irish nexus, land and politics. He believed that the agrarian issue was the key to the national question, the engine that would drag home rule in its wake, in Fintan Lalor's apposite phrase. 'I would not have taken off my coat and gone to this work', Parnell said at Galway, on 20 October 1880, 'if I had not known that we were laying the foundation in this movement for the regeneration of our legislative independence'. His attitude to the land question differed politically from that of the Fenians, who believed that the British government, 'a parliament of British landlords', in John Devoy's words, would not concede peasant proprietorship to Ireland. The Fenians were prepared to support the Land League and land agitation on the basis that they provided the raw material for revolutionary activity. In short, such activities were seen as the best means of severing the link with Britain. In contrast, Parnell believed that it was possible to settle the land question within the constitutional framework, provided sufficient pressure was brought to bear on the government. The basis of conflict between landlord and tenant would thus be removed and the former could then take his rightful place in the vanguard of the Home Rule movement. At the very least, landowners would discontinue using their influence negatively against Home Rule. The movement for legislative independence would thus gain sufficient credibility to ensure its ultimate success. This assessment of the Irish political situation was naïve and overly optimistic, ignoring, for instance, Irish landlord intransigence and the role of English political parties, especially the Conservatives. Nonetheless, Parnell adhered steadfastly to these beliefs for the remainder of his political career.

As a constitutionalist, Parnell was slow to commit himself to agrarian agitation, realising how difficult it would be to keep it under control, but it was a risk he had to take if he were to achieve his political ends. Accordingly, at Westport on Sunday 8 June 1879, more than two months before the Mayo Land League came into existence, Davitt and Parnell appeared together on a political platform for the first time. In Professor T.W. Moody's words, Parnell's speech was 'a characteristic mixture of realism, sincerity, political acumen, understatement and rousing defiance'. The ultimate solution to the land question, he said, was tenant proprietorship, but the immediate problem was the payment of rent. Whereas at Ballinasloe some seven months earlier he had insisted that landlords must be prevented from raising rents, he now argued that the tenant must be allowed to remain on his holding and enjoy the fruit of his labour so long as he paid a fair rent. What was a fair rent?

A fair rent is a rent the tenant can reasonably pay according to the times, but in bad times a tenant cannot be expected to pay as much as he did in good times three or four years ago. If such rents are insisted upon a repetition of the scenes of 1847 and 1848 will be witnessed. Now what must we do in order to induce the landlords to see the position? You must show the landlords that you intend to keep a firm grip of your homesteads and lands. You must not allow yourselves to be dispossessed as you were dispossessed in 1847.

He hoped that the landlords would see reason and that they would reduce the present rents which in his opinion were 'out of all proportion to the times'. Parnell again stressed the fundamental connection, as he saw it, between the land question and the national question. 'If we had the farmers the owners of the soil tomorrow, we would not be long without getting an Irish parliament', he concluded.

Parnell's platform advice to the Irish tenants became more sharply focused as his understanding of the agrarian and the economic situation deepened. At Tipperary in September 1879, he told his 20,000 strong audience that if they were not given reasonable rent reductions it was their duty not to pay any rent at all, a message he was to repeat at Tullow and Cork in the succeeding weeks. At Navan on 12 October 1879, he told them practically:

Go to your landlord and if he disagrees with your estimate of what the fair rent should be, ask him to appoint one man and say that you will appoint another, and they will settle it between them. If he refuses this arrangement, offer him what you consider you can fairly be called on to pay in these times and ask him for a clear receipt. If he refuses to give you a clear receipt put the money in your pocket and hold it until he comes to his senses. If the tenants on each property join together and do this the cause of the tenant farmer in Ireland is won. No landlord can prevail against you.

The mainstay of the Land League programme was its opposition to evictions and the mobilisation of public opinion against landgrabbers. While he was not the first to do so, Parnell spelled out his policy very explicitly at Ennis on 7 September 1880. Having advised his listeners not to pay unjust rents and to keep a firm grip on their homesteads, he exhorted them 'not to bid for farms from which others have been evicted, and to use the strong force of public opinion to deter any unjust men . . . from bidding for such farms'. At this point several members of the audience observed interjectionally that those who transgressed this code deserved to be shot. The platform speaker disagreed, suggesting instead a less violent but equally effective method. He advocated that the landgrabber be placed in a 'moral Coventry' and be shunned by his neighbours 'as if he were a leper of old'. This policy of social ostracism, or boycotting as it came to be called, was employed on a prodigious scale, not alone against landgrabbers, but ultimately against landlords and their agents, process servers, solicitors or anyone, indeed, who supported them in any way. Boycotting depended for its effectiveness on the complete disruption of the business and social life of its victims and proved to be a devastating weapon.

The Land League was a movement based primarily on moral force, with Parnell and other leaders constantly urging the methods of peaceful persuasion. Nonetheless, a penumbra of outrage surrounded the League from the very beginning. There was in fact more rural violence during this period than at any other time in the second half of the nineteenth century. All the ruthlessness of agrarian vendettas reappeared; intimidation, cattle-maiming, burnings and shootings became an integral part of the Irish rural landscape. This upsurge in agrarian violence increased with the arrest of Parnell and several of his lieutenants in October 1881. The response of the imprisoned leaders was a manifesto which called for a general strike against rents. It is unlikely that Parnell would have agreed wholeheartedly with the no-rent doctrine, given its radical nature and his own role as national leader. But it suited his purposes to go along with it. It also suited him politically to be imprisoned at this time. 'The movement is breaking fast', he informed Katharine O'Shea on the day of his arrest, 'and all will be quiet in a few months, when I shall be released.'

Parnell had forecast that if incarcerated his place would be taken by 'Captain Moonlight', one of the many synonyms for Irish agrarian societies. The prevailing anarchy of the next few months compelled Gladstone, the British premier, to conclude 'The Kilmainham Treaty' with Parnell at the beginning of May 1882. The government agreed to release the imprisoned leaders and to amend the Land Act of 1881, in return for which Parnell pledged himself to end outrages and intimidation and promised the future cooperation of the Irish party 'in forwarding Liberal principles and measures of general reform'.

The Land Act of 1881, which conceded the long-cherished three Fs, was a major reform. Rents were fixed by judicial arbitration for periods of fifteen years; a tenant could not be evicted as long as these rents were paid; additionally, he was entitled to sell his interest in his holding for the best price he could obtain. By legalising the three Fs, the Land Act of 1881 established a system of dual ownership in the soil between landlord and tenant, a development which made peasant proprietorship inevitable in the long term. For the present, the rent provisions of the act had the effect of reducing the average rental by about twenty per cent, and this went a long way towards satisfying the immediate demands of many Irish tenants.

The activities of Captain Moonlight in the autumn and winter of 1881 and the Phoenix Park atrocities within days of his own release from prison in

May 1882 convinced Parnell that the time had come to dissociate himself once and for all from agrarian agitation and to steer nationalist energies onto the track of parliamentary politics. In October 1882, the Irish National League, with national rather than agrarian primary objectives, superseded the Land League and during the next few years Parnell condemned extra-parliamentary tactics on the grounds that they retarded political progress towards Home Rule.

The Irish economy, following a slow recovery from the catastrophic depression of the late 1870s, plummeted once again in the mid-1880s, and gave rise to a new wave of agrarian agitation. On 21 January 1886, in the troughs of a winter of considerable discontent, Parnell drew the attention of the members of the House of Commons to the seriousness of affairs in Ireland. He admitted that tenants were combining to resist the payment of customary rents, but claimed that these movements were spontaneous and had received neither encouragement nor financial assistance from the National League. He declared that both he and his party were doing all in their power to stamp out boycotting and to curb anti-rent combinations.

In the wake of Gladstone's conversion to the Home Rule cause, Parnell was determined that nothing should impede progress towards its realisation, least of all agrarian agitation, with all its concomitant hazards. Consequently, striking tenants were refused aid by the National League and were told bluntly to pay their rents. This refusal of financial assistance precipitated the collapse of the majority of anti-rent combinations on Irish estates, as Parnell no doubt intended. He was at the apogee of his power at this time and his control of the National League and the parliamentary party were absolute. In his single-minded pursuit of legislative independence from the summer of 1882 onwards, Parnell, by withholding financial and moral support, emasculated agrarian agitation in Ireland.

The refusal of the parliamentary party and the National League to countenance anti-rent combinations during the period of the Home Rule debates in 1885 and 1886 was greatly resented by many hard-pressed Irish farmers. To them, the prospect of legislative independence was secondary to the more pressing problem of rent and falling prices. Despite the best efforts of Parnell and his fellow constitutionalists the countryside remained seriously disturbed, with agrarian violence and outrage prevailing extensively.

The rejection of Gladstone's Home Rule Bill in the summer of 1886 and the continuing deterioration in the economy brought the agrarian question into much sharper focus. Parnell and the parliamentary party could no longer ignore the issue. At a party meeting in Dublin on 4 August 1886, the government was warned that the payment of judicial rents had become impossible and a call was made for the immediate revision of all such rents, the cancellation of arrears, the suspension of evictions, and the alteration of the rent-fixing clauses of the 1881 Land Act.

A fortnight later, on his arrival in London for the new parliamentary session, Parnell informed John Morley that Irish rents could not be paid and that agrarian agitation was inevitable in Ireland unless the government took positive action. For his own part, Parnell was converted to the belief that, for the immediate future, the parliamentary party should concentrate on land reform in order to help the tenants through the current crisis. In this way he hoped not alone to prevent large-scale disturbance in Ireland but to project both himself and his movement as constitutional and law-abiding.

In late August, Parnell warned the members of the House of Commons that there existed in Ireland 'a state of affairs more intensified in their probable evil effects than existed even in 1880' and, unless remedial legislation was introduced, neither he nor the Irish members would be able to control the passions of the tenants during the coming winter. He proposed a Tenants' Relief Bill and, in moving its second reading on 20 September 1886, said the tenants could not be left to the mercy of the landlords. 'The history of Irish landlords is a history of which they cannot be proud . . . These men whom you have put in as stewards have been false to their trust and have oppressed, ill-treated and rack-rented their tenants'. The Bill contained three clauses: the Land Commission should be empowered to reduce judicial rents fixed before 31 December 1884, on condition that the tenants paid half the rent due in the current year and half their previous arrears; leaseholders should be admitted to the benefits of the 1881 Land Act; the courts should be empowered to suspend all eviction proceedings on payment of half the rent and arrears. The Bill, which was regarded as very moderate by the Irish members, was intended, in John Dillon's words, to ensure 'peace and quiet' in Ireland during the winter. Both he and Parnell were anxious to cement the liberal alliance and were apprehensive lest it be undermined by trouble in Ireland.

Any tampering with judicial rents, regarded as sacrosanct by the Tories, was bound to be resisted. But, if the Bill's defeat was inevitable, its unceremonious rejection also marked a turning point. The insensitivity of the newly elected Conservative government to Irish distress and their refusal to countenance the possibility of introducing any remedial legislation made a renewed agrarian agitation in Ireland inevitable.

The Plan of Campaign was the response. The Plan, which may be defined as a device for collective bargaining on individual estates, was promulgated in the Parnellite weekly, *United Ireland*, on 23 October 1886. It was not the official policy of either the National League or the parliamentary party. But its leadership and principal exponents were drawn from the agrarian wing of the party and the secretary of the National League, who drafted the Plan's manifesto, pledged the League's full support.

Parnell's attitude was equally unambiguous; it was one of undisguised antipathy and he disavowed the agitation publicly on several occasions, notably in a press release in December 1886 and, more comprehensively, in a major address to the Liberal hierarchy at the Eighty Club in London on 8 May 1888. Parnell's press statement was issued in the wake of a great public meeting at Castlerea on 5 December 1886, at which John Dillon delivered a violent fulmination against landlordism and the Irish land system, perorating, 'We call on the people this winter . . . to fight for free farms and freedom and to fight in order to destroy a system which has eaten into the manhood of our race like a corroding ulcer'. John Morley felt compelled to complain to the Irish leader that the Plan of Campaign was not alone having an adverse effect on English public opinion but was threatening the very basis of the Liberal-nationalist alliance. Parnell was stung into action. He had taken no part in the formulation of the agitation, he attempted to reassure Morley, and the fixed point in his tactics was the maintenance of the alliance with the English Liberals. He agreed to send to Ireland at once for one of his lieutenants and to press for an immediate end to violent speeches. William O'Brien, whose pyrotechnical speechifying was matched only by his literary flamboyance, has left a highly colourful, if suspect, description of his fog-shrouded meeting with Parnell behind Greenwich Observatory in December 1886. It seems likely that O'Brien managed to reassure Parnell by some vague promise or other to moderate the agitation in Ireland. In effect, Parnell was fobbed off, his attempted interference in the operation of the Plan of Campaign ignored and the agitation continued to be promoted with no less vigour and commitment than heretofore.

The Eighty Club provided a prestigious platform for Parnell to air his current political concerns. Having effortlessly, almost contemptuously, dismissed the recent Papal rescript condemning boycotting and the Plan of Campaign, he devoted most of his address to the Plan itself. He claimed that when the agitation was started in October 1886 he was dangerously ill — an illness which was 'both genuine and serious' according to F.S.L. Lyons — and so unable to express any opinion on the Plan. 'I was so ill that I was unable to put pen to paper or even to read a paper and I knew nothing about the Plan of Campaign until weeks after it had started.' He acknowledged the success of the agitation from the agrarian standpoint. 'It has prevented enormous suffering in Ireland', he said. 'It has in fact pacified the country.' But, he continued, he was opposed to it on political grounds. From the beginning, he feared that certain elements in the Plan would have an adverse effect on English public opinion and on the political situation generally. 'Therefore', he said, 'I should have advised the Irish tenants to suffer a little while, to bear their evictions in the firm confidence that although their troubles might last for a year or two, yet in a short time they might be put an end to forever by the concession of self government to their country.' He had hoped in the course of events to replace the Plan with 'a method of agrarian organisation' which he had been maturing for some time, one which he claimed would be 'free from . . . those political defects, incidental to the Plan of Campaign . . . But we shall now have to wait', he concluded.

Parnell's speech contained several factual inaccuracies. His concluding statement is uncorroborable and must remain questionable. In fact, the whole address was deeply flawed because its thesis was fallacious. The implication that the problems and hardships of the tenant farmers would have been remedied 'in a year or two' by a Home Rule parliament was sophistical and mischievous. The events surrounding the rejection of Gladstone's Home Rule Bill in June 1886 had clearly indicated that there was not the remotest possibility of Irish legislative independence being granted in the foreseeable future.

Parnell's Eighty Club address was a cynical attempt to reassert his authority, which two years of seclusion, political inactivity and, particularly, his failure to lead the agrarian struggle, had done much to undermine. It was an attempt to wrest the initiative from John Dillon and William O'Brien, the leading exponents of the Plan of Campaign, and to indicate that the political struggle took precedence over the agrarian one.

By the summer of 1889, the Plan's leaders were faced with considerable difficulties, not least increasing evictions, an acute shortage of funds, and a more organised and better coordinated government and landlord response. William O'Brien proposed the formation of a new organisation, the Tenants' Defence Association, with the twin aims of raising money to sustain tenants evicted from Plan of Campaign estates and of preventing further evictions, especially on the beleaguered Ponsonby property in East Cork. Parnell appeared to give his imprimatur and gave O'Brien to understand that he would launch the new movement formally at Thurles in the near future. On 11 July 1889, the *Freeman's Journal* announced, on Parnell's authority, the immediate formation of the Tenants' Defence Association and stated that it would be 'the official act of the whole Irish party'. At an informal meeting in the House of Commons four days later, Parnell called upon the members of the parliamentary party to share with him the responsibility for the new body and impressed upon them the absolute necessity for united action on their part. Parnell was one of the committee of seven appointed to draft a constitution for the proposed organisation.

Within a few weeks, Parnell had informed O'Brien that he would not attend the Thurles convention, a decision to which he adhered steadfastly during the succeeding months. His action in committing himself and the parliamentary party publicly to the Tenants' Defence Association and subsequently refusing to attend the formal launch of the movement, thereby depriving it of his great prestige, disenchanted several of his closest followers, John Redmond, T.P. Gill, Thomas Sexton, O'Brien and Dillon, among others, and so disillusioned one, W.J. Lane, MP for East Cork, that he threatened to resign from politics altogether. Finally, on 4 October 1889, Parnell despatched an open letter to Sexton, informing him that the state of his health prevented him from attending the Thurles convention and requesting Sexton to deputise for him. This was treated with a great deal of scepticism, one iconoclast suggesting that Parnell preferred 'fornication in Hastings . . . to a little effort at politics in Ireland'.

Such sexual congress, or, more precisely, Parnell's long-lasting, deeply cherished and widely-known relationship with Katharine O'Shea, was responsible for the final collapse of the Plan of Campaign, a development which led *The Tablet*, the English Catholic weekly, to reflect: 'It is surely a curious instance of the irony of human affairs that this immoral conspiracy which has so withstood even the express condemnation of the Holy See should now receive its death blow from the hand of Mrs O'Shea'. The agitation disintegrated in the wake of the O'Shea divorce case and the subsequent rending of nationalist Ireland into pro- and anti-Parnellite camps. The split in the parliamentary party was reflected in the ranks of the campaigners, several leading advocates siding with Parnell, although the majority lined up against him. The tribulations in the nationalist camp demoralised the tenants, and by mid-1891 many of them had made extremely unfavourable settlements with their landlords, accepting terms which contemporaries regarded as ruinous. Although a small number of disputes dragged on for several years, to all intents and purposes the Plan of Campaign was moribund by the time of Parnell's death in October 1891.

For Parnell, agrarian agitation was primarily a political weapon. He used the situation of the late 1870s to build up his own power base in Ireland. The consequences of the Land League years were momentous, not least the catapulting of Parnell to the forefront of nationalist politics and the emergence under his charismatic leadership of a new form of militant constitutional nationalism. His statesmanship helped to bring to an end the first phase of the land war on terms highly advantageous to the tenants, and to forge an alliance between Irish nationalists and English Liberals, the raison d'etre of which was the restoration of Ireland's legislative independence. However, agrarianism was too elemental a force for Parnell, one for which, both by background and inclination, he felt little sympathy. He was a constitutionalist, driven by the obsession of Home Rule for Ireland. His failure to recognise the unreality of this aspiration, certainly in the immediate aftermath of the rejection of Gladstone's Bill in the summer of 1886, suggests a blind-spot in his own political make-up. But it does explain his subsequent unrelenting hostility to the Plan of Campaign and agrarian agitation generally.

References

The following works have been used in the preparation of this paper:

The Irish Crisis of 1879-80: Proceedings of the Dublin Mansion House Relief Committee. Dublin, 1881.

Bew, Paul. *Land and the National Question in Ireland*, 1858-1882, Dublin, 1978.

— *C.S. Parnell*, Dublin, 1980.

Clark, Samuel and Donnelly, James S. Jr. (eds.). *Irish Peasants: Violence and Political Unrest*, Manchester, 1983.

Donnelly, James S. Jr. *The Land and People of Nineteenth Century Cork: the Rural Economy and the Land Question,* London and Boston, 1975.

Geary, Laurence M. *The Plan of Campaign, 1886-1891*, Cork, 1986.

Lyons, F.S.L. *Charles Stewart Parnell*, London, 1977.

Moody, T.W. *Davitt and Irish Revolution, 1846-1882*, Oxford, 1981.

Vaughan, W.E. 'Landlords and tenants in Ireland, 1848-1904', *Economic and Social History Society of Ireland, 1984.*

Landlord v Tenant in the Land War.

Parnellism and Crime: Constructing a Conservative Strategy of Containment 1887-91

Margaret O'Callaghan

Cleared in the face of all mankind beneath the winking skies,
Like phoenixes from Phoenix Park (and what lay there) they rise!
Go shout it to the emerald seas — give word to Erin now,
Her honourable gentlemen are cleared — and this is how:

They only paid the Moonlighter his cattle-hocking price,
They only helped the murderer with counsel's best advice,
But — sure it keeps their honour white — the learned Court believes
They never give a piece of plate to murderer and thieves.

Their sin it was that fed the fire — small blame to them that heard —
The 'bhoys' get drunk on rhetoric, and madden at a word —
They knew whom they were talking at, if they were Irish too,
The gentlemen that lied in Court, they knew, and well they knew.

'Less black than we were painted'? — Faith , no word of black was said;
The lightest touch was human blood, and that, you know, runs red.
It's sticking to your fist today for all your sneer and scoff,
And by the Judge's well-weighed word you cannot wipe it off.

Hold up those hands of innocence — go, scare your sheep together,
The blundering, tripping tups that bleat behind the old bell-wether;
And if they snuff the taint and break to find another pen,
Tell them it's tar that glistens so, and daub them yours again!

If black is black or white is white, in black and white it's down,
You're only traitors to the Queen and rebels to the Crown.
If print is print or words are words, the learned Court perpends:
We are not ruled by murderers, but only — by their friends.

Cleared (In memory of a Commission)
Rudyard Kipling.

It is not the first time that you have poisoned the bowl and used the dagger
against your political opponents in that country (Ireland) where you could

not overcome them in fair fight.

Charles Stewart Parnell,
July 1888

Analyses of English policy towards Ireland in the years from 1879 are both detailed and fragmented. The proliferation of contemporary accounts and the publication of a large number of biographies and surveys in the past twenty years has lent to the historiography a quality of finality. The publication in the past decade of studies that seek to explore the 'land question' in terms of peasant mobilisation have answered the questions deemed to be important by those who pose them. Questions of policy are seen to be answered separately, or to be explored through the magnifying and distorting mirror of the Cooke and Vincent school. Liberal policy towards Ireland is seen to be understood and resolved and the *Coercion and Conciliation* thesis of L.P. Curtis, that Conservatism began 'killing home rule by kindness' after the defeat of murder by Arthur Balfour's calming coercion measures, provides a neat conclusion to a period of disorder.

Because of the drama of the Home Rule Bill, 1886 is considered to be *the* important year in the evolution of Liberal and Conservative policy towards Ireland: the Liberal intent to pursue a policy of Home Rule, the defection of the Whigs and the adoption by the Conservatives of the high imperial ground through their public rhetoric on the issue of Ireland. By undermining the significance of Ireland in that year and proclaiming it to be merely an issue around which political groupings reconstituted themselves, Cooke and Vincent have concluded that the issue of Ireland was never important as a 'thing in itself' in English politics. Attempts to refute this view invariably enter into the 'facts' as presented by Cooke and Vincent. This is history written as detective novel with multiple choice endings — each new letter shifts the story, producing a different optional ending, but the plot, the characters and the decisions as to what was important remain in the control of the minds of the original authors.

In writing about the Special Commission on Parnellism and crime most historians have adopted a consensus verdict: that the Commission was an error of judgement on the part of Salisbury's government. But as Sir Joseph West Ridgeway wrote to Balfour in 1890, commenting with amusement on the depression of the uninitiated, 'He [the Irish Attorney General] is utterly demoralised by the present phase of the Parnell Commission and regards a change of government as a certainty . . . The curious thing is that all along we have anticipated a collapse of *this part* of the case with equanimity. I do not therefore understand this panic'.

The significance of the Special Commission has been distorted by the extent to which historians have viewed it as a sprawling anomaly that represents a failure of judgement on the part of the otherwise astute Conservative administration of Ireland after 1886. This analysis conforms to the judgement of Randolph Churchill at the time: a view that emphasises the embarrassment of Conservative politicians and the extent to which by their association with *The Times* they compromised their case. As a corollary to this historians have accepted the view of the Conservative administration after 1887 that was posited by Conservatives at the time — the view that Arthur Balfour's role in 1887 was to bring Ireland back from a state of chronic lawlessness into which Land and National League violence had plunged it. According to this view Balfour succeeded where Hicks-Beach and Liberal predecessors had failed — in redeeming Ireland from League-orchestrated chaos.

The accepted view of the Conservative administration of Ireland after 1886 is that, having attempted reasonable measures under Hicks-Beach, the Conservatives were finally forced to recognise the essentially intractable nature of Irish violence and to defeat it by force before embarking upon a constructive policy of ameliorative social reform. This interpretation is facilitated by the apparent disjuncture between the 'high' politics of Westminster in 1886 and the realities of Irish administration before and after that date. Thus in the historiography there is an apparent lacuna for the years 1883 to 1886 in Ireland. The historiography has particular emphases: the violence of the Land War of 1879 to 1881, the 1881 Land Bill, the Kilmainham Treaty, the Phoenix Park murders and the necessary Crimes Act followed by an Arrears Bill. Studies of the Liberal Irish administration after 1882 are few.

The Chief Secretaryships of Trevelyan and Campbell-Bannerman are rarely written about: it is as if for those years from 1882 to June 1885 the domestic condition of Ireland is an irrelevance. With the singular and significant exception of Maamtrasna, politics are conducted in the rarefied atmosphere of Westminster. But these are the years of the politicisation of the Irish nationalist party, years during which that party's leaders endeavoured to distance themselves from violence and forge a constitutional political identity committed to the achievement of Home Rule. Their language was of political change and their tactics were devoted to fighting their cause at Westminster. On going to Ireland as Lord Lieutenant in June 1885 Carnarvon, acting on the advice of the Permanent Under Secretary, advised an end to the Crimes Act and an abandonment of coercion. The crimes figures for these years would seem to confirm the correctness of such an analysis.

L.P. Curtis, in the standard work on Conservatives and Ireland, while acknowledging the significance of Ireland in imperial terms, essentially writes a history of these years on the assumption that the Conservatives were doing what they said they were doing — necessarily defeating crime in Ireland before proceeding to ameliorative social measures. Thus the state of Ireland is said to be what Conservative rhetoric proclaimed it to be in 1887

— one of anarchy and near disintegration.

The Cooke and Vincent thesis on 1886 is tenable if it is accepted that significant political activity took place where they see it as having taken place — in the private correspondence and conversational exchanges of politicians. Like literary critics of a discredited generation they see political rhetoric as a thin and obfuscatory patina behind the screen of which 'real' political action takes place. Thus the political rhetoric of 1886 can be dismissed as irrelevant. The public language of politics is subverted by nudging reminders of the infinity of private intrigues that contribute to the truth behind its foundation. Public language then is barren and meaningless — essentially a lie — and history, the search for 'truth', is concerned with what *really* happened behind the scenes. Not merely is that view philosophically naïve — in that it posits a recoverable 'truth' behind a smoke-screen — but it also involves a fundamental failure to recognise the salient and essential characteristic of the political - the degree to which its meaning is defined only when it becomes a public act through language. By definition the focus of such analysis is microscopic and necessarily static. Process or change cannot be accommodated by an analysis that is exclusively concerned with unravelling private motivations, one that considers 'real' politics to be over at the moment that its labyrinthine hinterland gives way to public language or public action.

The Conservative Party in 1886 carefully orchestrated a rhetorical onslaught on the notion of Home Rule for Ireland. Having committed themselves to a public expression of the Irish incapacity for self-government they were no longer in possession of the political choices that preceded the language of 1886. Public political language is not a redeemable temporary expedient — it is an irrevocable political act that changes the nature of political reality.

Goschen had made the definitive point when he said: 'Is the imperial parliament bound to listen to the voice of the majority of any particular portion of the Empire, and to come to a conclusion in accordance with that voice!'

Moreover Ireland presented an even more complex problem:

> . . . the views of the majority of the Irish people with regard to some of the chief principles of legislation are different to those of the inhabitants of England and Scotland . . . the attitude of the Irish people, partly from history, perhaps partly from the misgovernment of their country, for which we are paying so heavy a price, towards laws which are recognised in other countries is a hostile attitude and different from the attitude of most of the nations of Europe.

To Gladstone agrarian crime was: 'a symptom of a yet deeper mischief of which it is only the external manifestation!'

Moreover:

> if we, the English or the Scotch were under the conviction that we had
> such grave cause to warrant . . . action as is the conviction entertained by
> a large part of the population in Ireland I am not at all sure that we should
> not, like that part of the population in Ireland, resort to the rude and
> unjustifiable remedy of intimidation!

In 1886 the Home Rule debate placed the question of Irish self-government in what Victorian politicians called the 'realm of practical politics'.
The Irish nationalist party at Westminster, organised on the structure of the
National League, was a democratic, constitutional reality in English political
life. The democratic process ensured that the Irish party was perceived to be
electorally *bona fide*, a group worthy of political cultivation. The defeat of
Home Rule in the Lords was politically irrefutable, but the Home Rule party
was sufficiently committed to the process to see its future role as defined
within parliament.

Within two years, in an action constitutionally unprecedented, this
perception was utterly changed. All of the leading members of the Irish
parliamentary party were in effect 'tried' before a Special Commission
constituted by Act of Parliament on the following charges:

> (i) That the respondents were members of a conspiracy and organisation
> having for its ultimate object to establish the absolute independence of
> Ireland.

> (ii) That the immediate object of their conspiracy was, by a system of
> coercion and intimidation, to promote an agrarian agitation against the
> payment of agricultural rents, for the purpose of impoverishing and
> expelling from the country the Irish landlords, who were styled the
> English garrison.

> (iii) That when on certain occasions they thought it politic to denounce
> certain crimes in public, they afterwards led their supporters to believe
> that such denunciation was not sincere (a charge chiefly based on the
> 'facsimile' letter of 15 May 1882, alleged to be signed by Mr Parnell).

> (iv) That they disseminated the *Irish World* and other newspapers tending
> to incite to sedition and the commission of other crime.

> (v) That they, by their speeches and by payments for that purpose, incited
> persons to the commission of crime, including murder.

> (vi) That they did nothing to prevent crime, and expressed no *bona fide*
> disapproval of it.

(vii) That they subscribed to testimonials for and were intimately associated with notorious criminals, defended persons supposed to be guilty of agrarian crime, supported their families and made payments to secure the escape of criminals from justice.

(viii) That they made payments to persons who had been injured in the commission of crime.

(ix) That the respondents invited the assistance and accepted subscriptions of money from known advocates of crime and dynamite.

The contention of this work is that such a transformation reveals the central meaning of Conservative strategy in Ireland after 1887, and that without an awareness of its implications no satisfactory understanding of the development of Irish nationalism or the emerging imperial strategy of Conservatism is possible. More particularly it contends that the real aims of Arthur Balfour's Chief Secretaryship can only be understood in the light of such an awareness.

The National League, as had been noted in Royal Irish Constabulary District Inspectors' Reports for late 1885, was anxious to emphasise its essentially political status. During the election of 1885 National League officials 'drilled their supporters as to the procedure for voting so that they should make no mistake. Their zeal and devotion to the national cause are quite remarkable.'

After Kilmainham and the formation of the National League the aim of the parliamentary party had been to set a distance between themselves and the worst excesses of rural agrarian discontent. Indeed as the machinery of the Land Commission substantially revised rents, and as the Arrears Bill took effect, the political significance of the land question receded, at least until the bad harvest and falling prices of 1885 to 1886. The tensions in the Conservative cabinet of January to June 1886 on the issue of coercion were shelved by the compromise of the Queen's speech which suggested that special powers could be invoked legislatively if the ordinary law did not suffice. Salisbury was continuing to hold the balance between Hicks-Beach and Churchill on the one hand — with Carnarvon as a grim reminder of the potential dangers of such ambiguity — and on the other his own strongest sentiments as expressed in the *Disintegration* article of 1883 and parodied in the wounded passages of Cranbrook's diary.

The post-Home Rule Conservative administration was however significantly different. Despite Churchill's self-aggrandising role as mediator between Hicks-Beach and Salisbury it is difficult not to see a certain distancing in Salisbury's reserved and wry 'appreciations'. Beach in Ireland still clung to the assumption that the game was the same as previously: that coercion would be used if and when serious crime seemed to warrant it, and that simultaneously the legitimate grievances of an oppressed tenantry would be appeased. Parnell too, by immediately proceeding with a Tenants' Relief Bill, was seeking to treat the agricultural depression as a functional issue that required resolution lest it erupt in violence which the National League could not control.

Ironically, it was to be the trump card of earlier dealings with Gladstone — 'deal with me or Captain Moonlight will take my place' — that was to undo the nationalist strategy. For in dealing with Salisbury, Parnell was confronted by the reality of which his own public image was merely a mask — a man of infinite coolness, caution and patience. Parnell gave the appearance of control, of a long-term strategy — it was this quality that gave him his uncontested if galling superiority over excitable and unstable peasants like Healy. In Irish terms he was the urbane, unruffled aristocrat and indeed so he appeared on the Westminster stage. But confronted by the reality he was merely a simulacrum.

Hicks-Beach grew frustrated and irate in Dublin as the cabinet refused to listen to the force of his position when he warned that economic conditions would lead to a renewal of violence outside even nationalist control. The Irish committee of the cabinet was effectively a cypher: Salisbury, Beach, Churchill, Matthew and W.H. Smith. Beach was effectively negated, Churchill was fully occupied in feeling important as a superannuated intermediary, Matthews, presumably included to give Churchill an even more reassuring sense of control, was meaningless and W.H. Smith was absolutely 'sound'. The institution of the Cowper commission, the only concession to Beach's demands, was designed — in the long term — to investigate agrarian grievances, despite Hicks-Beach's view that its real role was to prop up the landlord interest. According to Ashbourne, despite the existence of 'crime figures' it was impossible to make any firm statements about the state of Ireland.

> Some parts are bad, others indifferent and others again in a fairly good state. Kerry is the worst. Clare possibly is next in badness, Limerick is bad and in parts nearly bankrupt. Other counties are some degree better. Rents in some districts will be paid fairly; in others with substantial reductions; in others not at all.

The contention of the parliamentary party was that unless measures were taken to reduce rents judicially, violence would erupt among the tenants in the most distressed areas. While the parliamentary party had been organised upon the structured grievances of an oppressed tenantry in 1879-81 they had no desire to become the hostages of 'Captain Moonlight' in 1886-87. Hence their desire to have agrarian grievances swiftly resolved.

To Beach the Irish land problem was an economic one. The landlords were being crushed by an irrefutable economic imperative. Rents required to be reduced because, particularly in the south-west, tenants could not afford to pay them. Rooted in Dublin Castle and deluged as he was by a documentary avalanche of police reports on every aspect of the life of 'crime' in the country, he nonetheless declined to take up the high ground of the rights of property and enforcement of the law. The appointment of Sir Redvers Buller to 'pacify' the south-west was a triumph for Salisbury, but as Buller's letters to Hicks-Beach and evidence to the Cowper Commission revealed, his first-hand experience of conditions there undermined his efficacy. He saw violence as springing from the intolerable economic condition of tenants in the counties of Clare and Kerry particularly: instead of merely putting down 'disorder' as instructed, he assumed the role of tenants' apologist.

He saw the weapon of the boycott as rooted in the private sanctions of an impenetrable community. Though politicised and 'named' by the Boycott case of 1881 it essentially sprang from age-old regulatory rituals. Its politicisation and organisation from 1879 to 1881 had however transformed its potency. Despite the language of Dublin Castle reports which spoke of a primeval and incomprehensible peasantry — the nationalists' 'dupes' — local newspapers, intercepted letters and National League communications present a different view. Literacy was high, newspapers like *United Ireland* and the *Kerry Sentinel* were widely read. The machinery of the Land Commission since 1881 had ensured that most tenant farmers could analyse valuation, rental and prices with considerable skill. In short if the Irish peasantry were distinguished in any sense it was in the degree to which they were highly politicised and litigious. Land Commission and Land Court litigation had effectively created not merely a career circuit for aspiring barristers but also a form of unwitting public education.

Balfour was appointed Chief Secretary for Ireland on 7 March 1887. On that day *The Times* published the first of the articles that were to be known as *Parnellism and Crime*, in which allegations of criminality were made against Parnell, the Land and National Leagues and the Irish party. A debate which had been apparently resolved before 1886 was suddenly reopened. On 18 April, on the second reading of the Bill, *The Times* published a facsimile letter signed by Parnell and linking him with the Phoenix Park murders. Balfour immediately called for an enquiry into these allegations.

Balfour's 'campaign' in Ireland began with the passing of the Crimes Act. It was to be over a year before the Special Commission was constituted to investigate allegations made in the course of the O'Donnell libel case. This has led historians to mention the publication of the articles and letters as an aside in March 1887, indicating that they may have helped to swing wavering Liberal Unionist support behind the Bill. Balfour's Irish policy, his commitment to ordering chaos, is then examined. When the intractable twelve-volume report of the commission is mentioned on its publication, it is accepted as an embarrassment to the Conservative government. The vindication of Parnell on the single issue of the Pigott forgeries is presented as the 'failure' of *The Times*' case. In short, Parnell's brief hour of glory and triumph on the issue of approval of the Phoenix Park murders is treated as the salient reality, Sir Charles Russell's devastation of Pigott as the apotheosis of the Irish nation.

The question then posed is how the Conservative government could have ill-judged such an issue; whether *The Times* was in fact 'tipped' by the Conservatives to print the articles and letters on the crucial Crimes Bill dates; whether Joyce was telling the truth when he alleged that he was responsible for directing a Castle operation to cull from the police reports of a decade earlier incriminating evidence on nationalists to substantiate *The Times*' case. Doubts will always be cast on Joyce's story: he was a bitter and disappointed man. A careful reading of the extensive Balfour papers does however reveal his considerable importance to the Irish administration at the time. But a debate around imponderables cannot be conclusive. It can perhaps be said that the absence of any written record in the private correspondence of those responsible for Irish government on so important a question is surprising.

A debate on what *is* known may however prove more useful. The Attorney General appeared on behalf of *The Times* at the insistence of his colleagues. In an unprecedented legislative departure a Special Commission was constituted by Act of Parliament. In defiance of all legal practice 'incidental' incriminating evidence produced by *The Times* in the libel action brought by O'Donnell was transposed into the charges which the 'Irish nationalist conspiracy' was to face. Elected members of parliament were 'tried' on criminal conspiracy charges for events that had taken place almost a decade earlier. The Commission, constituted by the Conservative government, was structured to enable 'evidence' to be given by selected members of the Royal Irish Constabulary. Even if Soames of *The Times* received no direct assistance from Dublin Castle the fact that *The Times* was given powers to subpoena, complete with relevant 'records', any member of the constabulary and hence have indirect access to all of the crimes papers of government is remarkable in itself. The sheer quantity of material supplied to *The Times* and the rambling and interminable nature of the Attorney General's case contrived to ensure that the investigation would be as long, as extensive and as comprehensive as possible.

To see such a monumental exercise as a 'mistake' on the part of the Conservative government is strange. Moreover, the delight with which the Conservatives treated the Report's publication scarcely indicates any regret at its progress or conclusions. Substantially it had succeeded in establishing precisely what it had been constituted to establish — that nationalism and crime were one and the same thing.

The constitutional achievement of the parliamentary party between 1882 and 1886 was effectively negated. Interminable details of horrific barbarity, particularly in the south-west, were neatly juxtaposed with information that branches of the Land or National League had been set up, or had met, near the scene of the crime. Sir Charles Russell's skill in breaking down a man already on the point of collapse appears to have masked his forensic incompetence for the remainder of the proceedings. In short, nationalists felt pleased because a letter that nobody — not even Salisbury — believed Parnell to have written, was demonstrated not to have been written by Parnell and, perhaps more characteristically, they relished the cathartic thrill of hearing seven hundred years of Irish history unfolded by Russell. More understandably perhaps the temptation retrospectively to view Parnell as having been triumphantly vindicated immediately before his catastrophic fall is irresistible. Thus the Special Commission can be seen as Parnell's finest hour, in stark contrast to his subsequent defeat.

But the enquiry was only incidentally about Parnell. It was about the nature of the movement of which he was leader and about the focus through which its development since 1879 was to be seen. It recast the terms of the debate about Ireland and was a vital ideological underpinning to Balfour's declared mission in Ireland. The National League, which in 1886 had been the political organisation of the Home Rule movement, was transformed in two years into a suppressed criminal conspiracy. The role of the Commission was to demonstrate systematically that a criminal conspiracy was in fact precisely what the National League had always been. In this it succeeded.

It showed the Land and National Leagues as contiguous conspiracies uninterrupted since 1879 except for those periods during which a Crimes Act was vigorously enforced in Ireland. That the Liberals and the Irish poured scorn upon its findings was irrelevant. It was intended — secondarily — for public consumption but primarily as an irrefutable, judicially sanctioned 'legal' document which demonstrated to the Conservatives themselves the rightness of their adopted position. It provided an ideological justification for their chosen analysis of the nature of Irish agitation and made coercion a demonstrable ideological necessity and not merely a governmental expedient. But above all it effectively stymied the future political evolution of 'nationalism'.

The tension within the nationalist party from the time of Kilmainham onwards had been between those who viewed compromise with the English government as the 'great betrayal' and those who believed, particularly after the passing of the Arrears Bill, that the 'land struggle' which they had availed of, organised and monitored was an uncertain weapon. Parnell's strategy was, while continuing to evoke the spectre of 'Captain Moonlight' as a bargaining counter, to battle constitutionally for Home Rule. He never fully carried his party with him in this, as the Plan of Campaign demonstrated. Nor indeed was it in the interests of his conception of the constitutional struggle to have the 'land issue' at boiling point. Hence his immediate, reasonable requests to the Conservatives for a Tenants' Relief Bill in late 1886. But Salisbury was a very clever man. Manifestly, the way to defeat the nationalist party was by exposing the tensions within its position. Hicks-Beach's agitation about what 'ought' to be done in Ireland was the hectoring of an ingenue — he did not recognise the extent to which the necessary corollary to the anti-Home Rule rhetoric of 1886 was the utter discrediting of 'nationalism' in Ireland. The land question and Captain Moonlight could potentially hoist the nationalists with their own petard. The verbal battle of 1886 had taunted the Irish with criminality, duplicity, murder and savagery. That language had created a reality in which future constitutional bargaining with nationalists was ideologically impossible for any Conservative and Liberal Unionist government. The Special Commission was constructed to render the Irish parliamentary party constitutionally impotent, since it established them all as criminals:

One hand stuck out, behind the back,
to signal 'strike again',
The other in your dress-shirt-front
to show your heart is clane.

What distinguished Conservative coercion after 1887 from the coercion that preceded it was *not* its greater success or the fact that it was followed by ameliorative measures, but rather that it refused to distinguish between different kinds of nationalists — the constitutional party, the cattle hougher, the back street assassin, the boycotter: they were all the same — criminal because they were nationalist.

Balfour's coercion measures were no more or less successful than earlier coercion. Their single success was in defeating boycotting. On any other level his talk of defeating crime was dubious. When Balfour came to Ireland it was peaceful with two exceptions: the south-western counties where 'crime' — mostly intimidation and boycotting and moonlight murder — had been outside the control of the nationalist party for years, and the Plan of Campaign which was always confined to particular estates and which would never have reached its dramatic crescendos but for the nature of the terms of the Crimes Act which, by suppressing the National League, provoked a confrontation between 'all' of nationalist Ireland and the 'forces of law and order' in precisely the kind of setpiece calculated to underline the equation of crime and nationalism. This equivalence was simultaneously demonstrated in all of the daily newspapers through the reports on the transactions of the Special Commission. Dillon and O'Brien, with characteristic short-sightedness, played their allotted roles. Parnell was constitutionally impotent as he hovered beneath charges of the approval of murder. The debate was recast.

The extraordinary nature of the Irish administration facilitated that political recasting. The Reports of the Royal Irish Constabulary are remarkable documents. With the possible exception of France, no European country was so intimately documented. Not merely were all agrarian returns made through the RIC but on the basis of county inspectors' confidential reports, Divisional Commissioners appointed under the Crimes Act sent detailed monthly accounts to Dublin Castle monitoring the level of agrarian discontent, of violence and local dissatisfaction. These, together with figures of evictions, crimes and outrages, were studied by the Under Secretary and Chief Secretary, were quoted in debates in the Commons and the Lords and formed the basis on which the state of the country was assessed and policy justified.

This was very far removed from the primitive machinery of solicited resident magistrates' reports on which Forster had relied in 1880. The structure had grown up during the Land War and was refined by the creation of 'areas' under Spencer. Instituted by the Liberals to provide 'solid information' to substantiate garbled reports, the system itself became a weapon of propaganda. Crimes figures had always been thrown back and forth indiscriminately during coercion debates and had provided party political ammunition, but the form and content of reports under Balfour substantially altered. Returns headed *Fifteen years of agrarian crime — the effects of agitation and the result of the Crimes Acts* provided the format through which 'crime' was assessed. The negation of all variables in the statistics of crime other than the presence or absence of a Crimes Act posited a view in which, since the foundation of the Land League and the beginnings of the Irish nationalist conspiracy, violence was seen to be the constant norm — held at bay only by the firm lid of coercion.

Criminality was then the corollary to nationalism, its essence and effect. The intricate reports of the period before 1886 gave way to litanies that invariably concluded with statements to the effect that 'the demeanour of the people is much improved'. Undoubtedly intimidation and boycotting figures dropped dramatically when it was appreciated that non-jury trials would not result in automatic acquittal. Davitt's *Charter of the Land League* of December 1880 had stipulated that those who 'betrayed' the policy of the League by bidding for a farm from which a tenant had been evicted for non-payment of rent 'should be looked upon and shunned as a traitor to the interests of his fellow tenant farmers and an enemy to the welfare of his country.'

Any Land Leaguer who participated in serving ejectment processes, assisting at evictions or who purchased stock or produce at sheriffs' execution sales was to be ostracised. But by August 1882 nationalist journals had recognised that such exhortations had taken on their own dynamic:

It is difficult to believe that any section of our fellow countrymen would be so blind to reason and to common sense as to believe their interests could be advanced by the commission of so heinous a crime as that which we record today, and yet all the circumstances of the cruel deed force upon us the conclusion that it was inspired less by private malice than by a misguided wicked belief that it could advance a public principle. It is sad to reflect for a moment that such a feeling could obtain in Ireland, and it is particularly discouraging at a time when bold efforts are being made to teach the people the virtue of self-reliance, and point out to them the road to liberty by means which heaven can approve of.

William O'Brien's *United Ireland*, the most valuable source for an understanding of the emerging tensions within the nationalist position from 1882, continues to be ignored by historians, yet it reveals the ambiguities of that position in a perspective utterly at variance with the 'high' view. It is the disintegrating control of nationalism from 1881 that emerges most clearly. It was those cases which the National League executive had felt most uneasy about that provided *The Times* with the wealth of their case. Since *The Times'* case was that boycotting and intimidation were brutal, inhuman and League-orchestrated, Soames chose the 'worst' cases from the copious crimes records of these years.

The Curtin murder case at Castle Farm in the midst of the Tralee-Castleisland-Killarney triangle, where moonlighting had a sound wren-boy tradition on which to build, was one of the most barbarous and complex stories of these years. The Curtins were substantial, 'respectable', educated tenants on a 160 acre farm held from Lord Kenmare. On 13 November 1885 two killings took place on the farm that were eventually to drive the family from the neighbourhood. They were also to create considerable anxiety in the League headquarters in Dublin and to arouse a level of interest perhaps only equalled by the Maamtrasna murders. From the point of view of *The Times* no more ideal case could have been chosen to illustrate the brutality of the boycott as an instrument. The extent to which ostracism was relentless and compassionless, and the degree to which, despite the summary powers of the law, information was something that the community was skilled at keeping to itself, were manifest. To *The Times* this demonstrated the tightness of the grip of fear in which the National League held the people. But the evidence of Sergeant Francis Meehan of Farranfore, who replied to the question about whether or not he obtained help from the local community with an unequivocal 'none whatever', is perhaps more revealing in demonstrating the extent to which the Royal Irish Constabulary lived civilly among people who revealed little or nothing to them.

Four or five men called to Curtin's house on the night of 20 November 1885. The family heard the arrival of the men 'from the parlour'. The National League Branch in Firies was started in March or April of 1885.

Curtin was a vice-president of the League and both of his sons were members. At the time of his death, though he himself had paid his rent to Lord Kenmare, he was apparently negotiating on behalf of the tenants for an abatement. The 'boys' who called on the night of 20 November were on a mission for arms, though it is clear that there were other matters at issue which are unlikely ever to come to light. Quite what happened within the house that night is unclear. Curtin was shot dead and a young man in his early twenties — one of the raiders — was also shot dead.

Sir Charles Russell, speaking from an 'official' briefing, emphasised that the murder of John Curtin had never been classified by the police as an agrarian crime. Russell claimed that the dispute was not about land. The 'boys' raiding for firearms were neighbours' sons. John Curtin fired the first shot, killing Timothy Sullivan, the son of a local widow. He was then shot himself. One of the Curtin daughters, Lizzie, gave evidence before the tribunal. After the shootings four servants in the house refused to fetch the police, though they did 'go for a priest'. The only people who witnessed the killings were the family and the moonlighters, one of whom died.

What *is* clear is the treatment that the family received after the event. John Curtin's funeral was sparsely attended. After the funeral the family was rigidly boycotted. Though they had always bought their supplies from Cork they had purchased smaller items locally. That became impossible. Their workmen left the farm. Their horses could be shod only in Tralee or Killarney. On the roads and in the village the family were 'hooted and shouted at, called informers and murderers'. Even the local parish priest, Father O'Connor, displayed more sympathy for the widowed mother of Timothy Sullivan. Stones were placed on the road before them and groups stood by the side of the road to watch 'to see us pass them, and kept hooting and shouting the whole time'. Ballads were composed about the family and publicly posted. Two Sundays after the trial in December 1885 the family's pew in the chapel at Firies was smashed. The attempt to replace it was greeted by a further assault when the carrier was beaten while the new pew was smashed at the chapel gate. Two men were sentenced to fourteen years' penal servitude at the trial for Curtin's murder. It was after this verdict that the intense boycotting and persecution of the family began. On the day that the pew was smashed the Curtins' herdsman for thirty-two years came and handed over the key of his cottage. He claimed to be afraid to stay.

In January 1886 the National League headquarters in Dublin became seriously alarmed about the Curtin case. John O'Connor, the MP for Tipperary, who knew the family, had attended Curtin's funeral. Davitt came to the area but visited the family of Sullivan, while not coming to the Curtins. His alleged purpose was to end the intimidation which was providing the League with highly unfortunate publicity at a time when its activities were politically concentrated on constitutional politics. Finally Alfred Webb, the Treasurer of the National League, intervened.

His letter, headed with the League's Abbey Street address in Dublin, was circulated to local League branches:

Private. To some of my nationalist friends.

My dear Sir,

Can nothing be done to save Mrs Curtin and her family from outrage . . . I spent last Sunday with the family. I never will forget my experiences. Were I now to relate them they might be used as arguments for coercion . . . It is the duty of all Nationalists openly, unequivocally and effectually to stand by the family.

In February 1887 the farm was put up for auction. There were no bidders. It was later purchased for a quarter of its value by a man in the neighbour-hood.

What this demonstrates is that the offences for which Irish nationalist politicians were held to be answerable encompassed every private vendetta of a peasant society. The nature of the intense observation to which Irish rural communities were subject together with the practice of constant monthly scrutiny of 'crime figures' facilitated the mergence of all rural crime into the murky, all-encompassing fold of 'nationalist conspiracy'. If the role of police in a society is indicative of the nature of that society then Ireland was, from 1880, a society in which the permanent scrutiny of the civilian population was the paramount reality.

From 1879 to 1886 Irish nationalism had evolved from a crude agrarian base to a sophisticated political strategy. The achievement of Arthur Balfour's Irish Chief Secretaryship was to negate that development and remould the nature of the Irish challenge to a parody of the confused agrarian conspiracy of 1879-81. In this he was facilitated by the personal enmities that existed within the parliamentary party. For Dillon and O'Brien were men with fixed goals but no strategy.

Balfour presented to the cabinet in April 1889 a memorandum prepared by Jenkinson in 1883, to which he attached considerable importance:

I have always held that our policy in Ireland during the last three years could only make matters grow worse and worse and was not an honest one towards the people of Ireland. Our government of the country was neither one thing nor the other. It had the pretence of being a constitutional government and we were not honest enough because while we set our faces against Home Rule we gave free licence to the press and allowed it to vilify and abuse our administration and to educate the people to believe that Ireland never can be prosperous unless it has a parliament of its own. We also allowed the National League to rise up on the ashes of the Land

15/5/82.

Dear Sir,

I am not surprised at your friends anger but he and you should know that to denounce the murders was the only course open to us. To do that promptly was plainly the... was our best policy.

But you can tell him and all others concerned that though I regret the accident of Lord F Cavendish's death I cannot refuse to admit that Burke got no more than his deserts

You are at liberty to show him this and others whom you can trust also but let not my address be known. He can write to House of Commons

Yours very truly
Chas S Parnell

On 11 March 1889 *The Graphic* published its 'Special Commission Number' — an illustrated and descriptive record of the proceedings of the Special Commission appointed to inquire into the charges and allegations made by the "Times" newspaper against Irish MPs and others. The illustrations were sketches made in court by artist, Mr. Sydney P. Hall. On the following pages are reproduced some of these sketches.

ABOVE: Facsimile letter published by "The Times", and alleged to be signed by Mr. Parnell. Subsequently admitted to be a forgery by Richard Pigott. BELOW: The opening day. The attack — the opening speech by the Attorney-General (Sir Richard Webster), with INSET: Pigott, the forger.

General View of the Court. See key on facing page.

KEY TO THE GENERAL VIEW OF THE COURT

1. Mr. Justice Day. **2.** Sir James Hannen (President of the Court). **3.** Mr. Justice Smith. **4.** Mr. T. D. Sullivan M.P. **5.** Mr. H. Campbell, M.P. (Private Secretary to Mr. Parnell). **6.** Archbishop Walsh. **7.** Archbishop Walsh's Chaplain. **8.** The *Standard* Reporter. **9.** Mr. Henry Cunynghame. (Secretary of the Commission). **10.** Mr. T. Harrington. (Secretary to the National League). **11.** Mr. H. Labouchere, M.P. **12.** Mr. Justin McCarthy, M.P. **13.** The *Pall Mall Gazette* Reporter. **14.** The Usher of the Court. **15.** Central News Messenger. **16.** Mr. G. E. Buckle (Editor of the *Times*). **17.** Mr. Macdonald (Manager of the *Times*). **18.** Mr. Soames (Solicitor of the *Times*). **19.** Mr. Walter, jun. **20.** Mr. George Lewis (Solicitor for the Irish Members). **21.** Mr. C. S. Parnell, M.P. **22.** Mr. Michael Davitt. **23.** Mr. J. G. Biggar, M.P. **24.** Mr. Lockwood, Q.C., M.P. (Counsel for some of the Irish Members). **25.** Mr. Reid, Q.C., M.P. (Counsel for some of the Irish Members). **26.** Sir Charles Russell, Q.C., M.P. (Counsel for Mr. Parnell). **27.** Sir Henry James, Q.C., M.P. (Counsel for the *Times*). **28.** Sir Richard Webster, M.P., the Attorney-General (Counsel for the *Times*). **29.** Mr. Ronan (Counsel for the *Times*). **30.** Mr. H. H. Asquith, M.P. (Counsel for Mr. Parnell). **31.** Mr. Arthur Russell (Counsel for some of the Irish Members). **32.** Mr. A. O'Connor, M.P. (Counsel for some of the Irish Members).

Viscount Castlerosse,
eldest son of
Lord Kenmare
(an interested spectator)

Sir Robert Peel
(a former Chief Secretary
for Ireland)

The Right Hon.
H. Childers M.P.

Lady Jessel

Mr. Oscar Wilde

SOME WITNESSES TO OUTRAGES

David Freely, farmer, and
member of the Land League.
After he had paid his rent
Moonlighters called for the
"— rent-payer". His son
was pulled out of the house
and shot dead.

Pat Walsh,
a Kerry labourer who
declined to answer
questions about
secret societies.

Mrs. Caroline Blake, a witness
from Connemara.

Bridget Barrett, whose
husband, Thomas Barrett,
took grazing land from
Mr. Bingham. He was shot
dead through the window as
he was going to bed.

Pat Sloyne,
a "Gombeen" man beaten
for paying his rent.

Pat Gannon (who had been shot
in the jaw in the Crimea) was wounded
in the knee by Moonlighters for the
crime of paying his rent.

Jeremiah Buckley,
a deaf witness, examined
by Mr. Graham. He paid
his rent, and Moonlighters
cut off the lobe of his right
ear. "What sort of scissors
did they use?" "I don't
think they were good ones."

Norah Fitzmaurice, whose
father was murdered at
Lixnaw.

ABOVE: Mr. Parnell and his solicitor (Mr. George Lewis) on the way
to a consultation — a chance meeting with Major Le Caron.

BELOW: Mr. Parnell annotating photographs of newspapers:
Mr. H. Campbell takes charge of them.

League and to cover Ireland with its branches and its organisation. Depend upon it the time has now come when the present state of things can no longer continue, when we must make up our minds to the adoption of one of two courses. We must have recourse to what is called the 'strong arm' policy or we must boldly acknowledge the principle of Home Rule and give Ireland gradually if possible a separate parliament.

Jenkinson, in 1885, reported on the low level of violence. His comments of 1885 were also circulated at the same April 1889 cabinet by Balfour, with emphasis on the role of Parnell. Though violence was low in September 1885 Jenkinson said that:

> at the same time the feeling against the English government and the landlords was never worse than it is now. I do not hesitate to say that were it not for the faith which the people have in Mr Parnell and for the influence which he and his party exercise over them, there would be an outbreak of serious outrages in all the worst and most distressed parts of Ireland . . . It is a most serious consideration that the peace of Ireland depends upon the influence and position of Mr Parnell and upon the forbearance of the Extremists . . . Any words which may lessen Mr Parnell's influence or dash the hopes which at the present time fill the hearts of the Irish people . . . We may be quite sure of this: that unless Mr Parnell succeeds in obtaining during this next year Home Rule or a promise of Home Rule he will either fall from power and lose all control or he will have to place himself at the head of a revolutionary movement.

In May 1889, a month after the discussion of these memoranda in cabinet, Balfour wrote to Ridgeway:

> There is a curious lull in politics both here and in Ireland . . . I hope it is not a lull that precedes a storm but there are rumours about (more or less well authenticated) that if the Judges find against the Parnellites they will give up during the remainder of the Parliament the constitutional game altogether and will return to Ireland and promote a recrudescence of crime and outrage. If there is any truth whatever in these rumours they are partly satisfactory and partly disquieting.

The reasons for the end of Parnellism as a political movement have been sought in the confusion and bitterness of the Parnellite split of 1891. It is in Committee Room 15 or at the hands of Gladstone that the causes of the defeat of Parnell and hence Parnellism have been analysed. But Parnellism was not merely the movement led by Parnell. It was the term used to describe the slow evolution of Irish constitutional nationalism.

Parnell's reluctance to involve himself in the Plan of Campaign was due to his unwillingness to move retrogressively in his political tactics. In contrast to this William O'Brien placed the material concerns of the tenants above political ends. Dillon however — choleric, dyspeptic and devoid of judgement — relished the politics of unreality on which he began to lead in 1887. Tim Healy was the petit-bourgeois opportunist par excellence, delighted to be at Westminster, retaining his distilled vitriol for the election circuit of 1891.

The investigations of the Special Commission had effectively destroyed Parnellism. The crude tactic of equating Parnellism with crime worked. By bringing every residual cattle hougher and informer to the same level as the parliamentary party, the sophisticated, loose and undefined network that Parnell held together effectively collapsed. By recasting the debate in terms of defeating crime — which was of course synonymous with Parnellism — the viability of the parliamentary party as a political force at Westminster was at an end. The respect with which Gladstone, and indeed Hicks-Beach and Churchill, had treated the Irish at Westminster before 1887 gave way to a Conservative view whereby their status as politicians was treated as a manifest joke. Balfour in correspondence with Ridgeway displays certain fundamental beliefs: that Irish politicians always lie, that their antics are amusing, that structures like New Tipperary are a fitting monument to their absurdity. In the police intelligence this perspective was mirrored by the reports on their 'dupes' whose fluctuating propensity for 'breaking out' was monitored on graphs of crime figures. Balfour changed personnel where he could. District inspectors soon learnt the type of report that was expected from them. Extracts from speeches from prominent nationalists became a euphemism for the ranting of any townland activist. The rhetoric that came up from the level of the sans-culottes 'groaners' and 'hooters' was certainly alarming: 'Keep the snake from amongst you . . . put a brand on him . . . the sign of the cross between you as you would with the very devil from hell.'

The achievement of the Conservative administration was effectively to undermine the constitutional pretensions of Irish nationalism, to claw back ground conceded politically in the past. 'Parnellism and crime' was the text around which this mission was accomplished. Arthur Balfour confessed to thinking that his years in Ireland had been the most important of his life. He was right. In these years all of the central strategic necessities of the retention of power in the face of emerging nationalism were developed: the absolute equation of nationalism with crime, the removal of political effectiveness from constitutional nationalists, the deployment of 'new' personnel to tighten up the regime, the ridicule of existing officers seen to be corrupted by their environment. But most important was the recasting of the debate in terms of defeating crime, a perspective into which historians have been more than willing to enter.

Parnellism was dead because it was politically bankrupted by the Conservative strategy of containment after 1887. The Special Commission dismantled the nationalist alliance by publicly examining its entrails. By seeking to prove that they were not 'criminals' the parliamentary party had already lost the game. The drama of the battering ram was diversionary.

On a letter from West Ridgeway to Balfour in December 1890 is scribbled: 'We want P. to win because his success will break up the Gladstonian alliance and be a smashing blow for the priests.'

The letter itself was circulated to the cabinet, annotated by Balfour:

Parnell is falling entirely I fear into the hands of the extremists. Last night P.N. Fitzgerald ('the leading IRB organiser', Arthur J. Balfour) was on the platform and Clancy, the sub-sheriff ('a physical force man', Arthur J. Balfour) and Holland, the Invincible have been his lieutenants. The moderate men will hold aloof and I fear he will fall. He made a very telling speech last night but he was very excited, jumping about the platform and thumping the table. But this was nothing to his excitement at the *United Ireland* office today when he found he had been outwitted. He was in a terrible state of excitement and showed it to everyone.

Parnell's fall into the hands of the hillside men in 1891 is commonly represented as evidence of the desperate mental confusion into which his personal dilemma had forced him. His rejection of constitutionalism, his repudiation of Home Rule — all are seen as the follies of a sick man. This is of course part of a view of Parnell's last years that posits adultery as a degenerating malaise. Parnell's lack of apparent political activity after 1887 may have in part been due to his personal circumstances. It is more likely to have come from his horrified and powerless observation of the dismantling of his achievement. He was sufficiently shrewd not to be deluded by the significance of his Pigott vindication. It is perhaps valid to suggest that his final rejection of constitutionalism sprang not from hysteria but from lucidity. For constitutional nationalism was effectively dead before Parnell's fall. The irony is that the minutiae of that tragedy have diverted attention from the real triumph of Conservatism.

Editor's note: Due to pressure of space, it has not been possible to include the extensive footnotes to this article. Readers interested in these footnotes should consult Margaret O'Callaghan's unpublished PhD thesis, 'Crime, Nationality and the Law: the politics of land in late-Victorian Ireland' (University of Cambridge, 1989).

Parnell and the South African Connection

Dr Donal McCracken

During the last quarter of the nineteenth century the two regions which caused persistent trouble for Britain were Ireland and South Africa. For many British and Irish politicians there gradually developed the idea that the Irish and South African questions were running in harness and analogous. In 1884 Lord Derby warned, 'The question is do you want to create another Ireland in South Africa?'[1] This linking of the two regions in the minds of politicians was cemented by the periodic interest taken in events unfolding in South Africa by Irish nationalists and by the occasional contacts made between them and prominent leaders in South Africa. Though the numbers of Irish immigrants in the Boer republics of the Transvaal and the Orange Free State and the British colonies of the Cape of Good Hope and Natal never appear to have exceeded 20,000, the impact of the Irish in the subcontinent was not negligible. The Irish impact on South African retailing, the railways, police, professions and to a certain extent politics helped to emphasise the concept of 'another Ireland'.[2] Events came to a head in the second Anglo-Boer war (1899-1902) when nationalist Ireland was engulfed in pro-Boer fever, but the foundations of that extraordinary phenomenon were laid a generation before by a handful of Irish MPs at Westminster, the most prominent of whom was Charles Stewart Parnell.[3]

When the Boer war was at its height a rumour circulated in Ireland, eventually finding its way into James Joyce's *Ulysses*, that Parnell had not died. His suspiciously heavy coffin had contained only rocks. Parnell had followed the path of the Fenian Alfred Aylward 23 years before and had forsaken Ireland for South Africa to fight for the Boers, whose hatred of the English was only matched by the Irish. Parnell had changed his name and was now none other than the legendary Boer commando leader, de Wet.[4] In fact, Parnell never visited South Africa, though no more suitable a setting could there have been for the 'sunny land' which the dying Chief and Katharine O'Shea used to dream of retiring to. Parnell's lieutenants, such as Swift MacNeill and John Redmond, made occasional sorties out to South Africa. In 1894, three years after Parnell's death, Patrick O'Hea, his former private secretary and MP for West Donegal from 1885 to 1891, came to Durban and was admitted to the Natal bar.[5] But Parnell himself never crossed the equator.

Parnell's association with South Africa arose quite fortuitously in the summer of 1877 when the Conservative government of Disraeli introduced a South African Confederation Bill. This followed upon the annexation in April of the Boer-run Transvaal republic. Seven Irish MPs, including the 31-year-old Parnell, decided to obstruct the passage of the Bill through the House of Commons.[6] Their reasons for this were various. Parnell confessed he was deliberately breaking an unwritten law that Irish MPs did not interfere in English or imperial concerns.[7] This in itself enraged English members and was a warning sign to Isaac Butt, the cautious and conservative leader of the Irish party at Westminster. With the possible exception of the eccentric Frank Hugh O'Donnell, it is doubtful if the seven Irish rebels had much genuine concern for the old Transvaal republic. Parnell's grandiose statement, 'As it was with Ireland, so it was with the South African colonies,' convinced few of his sincerity.[8] *The Times* certainly was not convinced and caustically noted, 'Mr Parnell's pious wrath would deserve more attention if it appeared that he had exact knowledge of the facts of the case'.[9]

The leader-writer had cause for anger. The seven spoke in relays, one after another, culminating in a piece of obstruction which lasted from 5.15 p.m. on 31 July to 2.10 p.m. on 1 August 1877, a marathon unparalleled in the history of parliament.[10] One of the filibusterers, O'Donnell, was especially jealous of Parnell's role in this epic. In his autobiography, O'Donnell later wrote, 'I believe Parnell hardly knew that South Africa was outside Europe'. This was possibly not far from the truth, but Parnell emerged from this adventure as *the* threat to Butt's leadership. O'Donnell fumed, 'In plain words, Mr Parnell began to achieve his fame and notoriety in supporting my arrangement with President Kruger for making the annexation of the Transvaal Republic the occasion for the utmost possible opposition to the confederation measure which professed to ratify the annexation'.[11] Be this as it may, Parnell's performance in the South African debates was outstanding. On one occasion he outwitted the chancellor of the exchequer, who tried to have him ejected from the chamber. MPs also saw the oratory which was soon to rally nationalist Ireland behind him. In the early hours of the morning of 1 August the chancellor asked the Irish to give way as they were 'suffering considerable physical inconvenience'. Parnell retorted:

> The government are bringing up their reserve forces, but the first mail-boat will bring ours from Ireland; and even in London the member for Cavan [Joseph Biggar], though now peacefully asleep, will soon return like a giant refreshed.[12]

The immediate consequence of this obstruction was a modification of the rules of debate in the Commons and the instant creation of Parnell as an ogre in the English public mind. Shortly afterwards Parnell had to endure a train ride with 'an Englishman from South Africa' who, unconscious of the identity of his travelling companion, lectured Parnell on the villainous Irish leader.

The long-term consequences were more profound. The event created an interest in South African affairs not only with Parnell, but also in nationalist Ireland. Years later Paul-Dubois observed, 'The Irish are always proud to remember that they resisted the annexation of the Transvaal in 1877'.[13] The following year when John Devoy sketched out his proposals of what he considered the 'new departure' should be, he added a clause advocating support for all struggling nationalities in the British empire or elsewhere.[14]

Though the South African Bill was eventually passed, events dictated that the story did not end there. The Anglo-Zulu war erupted in January 1879. The practice of using blacks as auxiliary troops in South Africa was condemned by Parnell as a 'disgrace to humanity and civilisation'.[15] Meanwhile events in Ireland were also unfolding fast. Agricultural depression, evictions, boycotts, the growing influence of the Land League and the beginning of the land war drew the attention of Parnell, who from May 1880 was the leader of the Irish parliamentary party. Thus for the British, crises loomed in Ireland and in South Africa. Unbeknown to all but a few in Britain contact was renewed between the Boers and the Irish. In 1880 the chairman of the Transvaal committee in Amsterdam visited Parnell and the Fenian, Patrick Egan; it was agreed that three well-trained Dutch army officers should be despatched to the Transvaal at the expense of the Irish Land League.[16] How far this clandestine contact went is not known. Sir Owen Lanyon, the Irish-born administrator of the Transvaal, had no doubts that the undercurrent of unrest in the Transvaal was fomented by 'Fenians, Dutch carpet-baggers and unscrupulous leaders like Kruger and Joubert'.[17]

The climax to events in South Africa came rapidly in early 1881 with the outbreak of the first Anglo-Boer war. On Sunday 27 February a British force under the Dubliner, Major-General George Colley, was routed by Boer commandos at the battle of Majuba Hill in northern Natal. Attached to the Boer forces was Alfred Aylward, a fact quickly seized upon by the ecstatic Irish press. Interestingly, the chief British peace negotiator in O'Neil's cottage at the foot of Majuba was Sir Evelyn Wood, the brother of Katharine O'Shea.[18]

The Boer victory elated Irish nationalists. The prospect of a subjugated people the size of the population of Dublin winning their independence from the British by force of arms was not lost on the Irish. Parnell's sister, Fanny, who had not long to live, was so delighted at the Boers' success that she composed a 12-stanza poem, the first verse of which ran:

Now Christ thee save Paul Kruger!
Now Christ thee save from harm,
And may the God of Joshua
Bear up thy strong right arm.[19]

To what extent the Boer victory at Majuba exacerbated the Irish crisis is a matter for speculation. At this time Parnell was flirting with the extreme wing of Irish nationalism and his public utterances often verged on the subversive. On 9 October 1881 while speaking in Wexford, in reply to Gladstone's assertion that law and order would be maintained in Ireland, Parnell proclaimed:

> At the beginning of the session he [Gladstone] said something of this kind with regard to the Boers. He said that he was going to put them down, and as soon as he had discovered that they were able to shoot straighter than his own soldiers he allowed these few men to put him and his Government down.

Four days later Parnell was incarcerated in Kilmainham jail. Suitably enough the cabinet meeting which took this decision had been called originally to discuss the Transvaalers' delay in ratifying the Pretoria peace convention.

The South African connection might well have been broken at this point as the two regions moved off along separate paths: the Transvaal to peace and an economic boom after gold was discovered on the Rand in 1886, and Ireland to the horrors of 1881, with mounting agrarian outrages, the Phoenix Park murders in May and renewed coercion. This divergence, in all likelihood, would have lasted until the second Anglo-Boer war broke out in October 1899 had it not been for the uncharacteristic curiosity of Parnell about the South African connection, and for a chance shipboard meeting. Before that, however, South Africa was again in the Irish newspapers. James Carey, the Invincible who informed on his associates and whose evidence sent them to the gallows for the Phoenix Park murders, was sent to Natal to escape the vengeful wrath of the Irish advanced nationalists. On 29 July 1883, on board ship 12 miles off Port Elizabeth, he was shot dead by a labouring Irishman named Patrick O'Donnell. O'Donnell's extradition to England, his trial and subsequent execution proved a *cause célèbre* with nationalist Ireland, which was firmly sympathetic towards O'Donnell.

In the ensuing years Irish parliamentarians took the occasional interest in imperial matters. In 1882 there was unfounded speculation that the Zulu king, Cetshwayo, would visit Ireland. Interestingly Parnell vetoed two attempts to give an Indian nationalist an Irish seat in parliament on the grounds that it would cause trouble in party ranks and 'would not be clearly understood in Ireland'.[20] None the less the Irish MPs were quickly joining the parliamentary radicals as the watchdogs of the empire. During 1885 the Dublin mob cheered the success of the Mahdi at Khartoum. But all Irish interest in imperial matters waned at Christmas of that year when Gladstone announced his conversion to Home Rule.[21] The abortive 1886 Home Rule Bill specifically excluded further Irish representation at Westminster after self-government had been granted, a consequence of previous Irish disruption in the House of Commons.

In the aftermath of the defeat of the Home Rule Bill a second phase of the land war erupted. This was centred around the 'Plan of Campaign', a scheme which proved expensive to implement. In an attempt to raise funds various Irish parliamentarians went to America and Australia. But the most successful fund-raiser, albeit by accident, was the dishevelled J.G. Swift MacNeill.

In a by-election in February 1887 he had been elected to parliament for South Donegal. But his health was weak and he decided to take a voyage to the Cape to recover. On board the *Garth Castle* he met the South African mining magnate Cecil Rhodes, who was then unknown in Britain. The two men got on well, a surprising fact considering their different personalities. Rhodes was interested in Irish politics and persuaded a reluctant Swift MacNeill to address Irish home rule meetings in Kimberley, Port Elizabeth and Cape Town.

That Rhodes was sympathetic to Irish aspirations surprised MacNeill, but on the train between Cape Town and Kimberley Rhodes explained his scheme for imperial federation. He wanted Irish representation to remain at Westminster after Home Rule had been granted, a feature which had not been included in the abortive 1886 Home Rule Bill. This inclusion would then act as a model for the rest of the self-governing empire, which he hoped would then be allowed also to send representation to the House of Commons. This would effectively create an imperial British parliament. By way of encouragement he offered the Irish nationalist party the substantial sum of £10,000 if they would agree to retention of Irish members at Westminster. On his return to Ireland in late October 1887 Swift MacNeill visited Parnell at Avondale and told him of the surprising offer. Parnell, ever short of funds, readily agreed and got Swift MacNeill to write to Rhodes to this effect.[22]

It was not until June 1888 that matters progressed. By then Parnell's health was deteriorating. As he became more involved with Mrs O'Shea, so he became both more moderate and more remote from his colleagues. The late Professor F.S.L. Lyons noted this trend and pointed out that Parnell's interest in imperial matters seemed at times to transcend his desire to obtain an Irish parliament.[23] Thus the arrival of Rhodes in London created an intriguing distraction for Parnell. The two political giants — one the greatest imperialist of his day, the other the greatest nationalist — met on two or three occasions. After hard negotiations, during which Parnell appears to have dictated terms, an agreement was drawn up in three letters. Slightly amended versions of these letters appeared in *The Times* on 9 July 1888. Parnell got the better deal as he never agreed to oppose a Home Rule Bill which excluded continued Irish representation at Westminster. On the other hand he stated that he should 'cheerfully concur' if a bill included such a clause. For this Rhodes publicly agreed to supply £10,000 'to the funds of your party'. A further

£1,000 was offered by Rhodes' friend, an Irishman named John Morrogh. An initial cheque for £5,000 was sent to Parnell. *The Times* was indignant, asserting that Mr Rhodes 'apparently has never heard of Mr Parnell's celebrated statement that he could not set a limit to the aspirations of a nation'.[24]

The superficial picture one has of this affair is Rhodes hedging his bets and Parnell grabbing easy cash. The reality is far from this. Rhodes and Parnell respected each other, though Rhodes was more in awe of Parnell than Parnell of Rhodes.[25] In many respects the two men were of similar character. Both could be amazingly ignorant of issues or places, yet both possessed an extraordinary power over people, being able to command complete obedience from their respective underlings.

The accusation that Rhodes bought the votes of the Irish party cannot be substantiated.[26] Certainly the Irish did not cause trouble for him when he was negotiating the charter for his monopolistic British South African Company, but they did later oppose the Jameson raid in 1896, of which Rhodes was chief instigator. At that time Joseph Chamberlain caustically remarked, 'I imagine that the Irish will think they have done enough for their £10,000'.[27]

Rhodes' gift to Parnell mystified many in South Africa, including John X. Merriman.[28] Yet Rhodes seems to have been genuine in his overtures to Parnell. Perhaps the clearest sign of Rhodes' sincerity was the fact that in February 1891 Rhodes secretly gave the British national liberal federation £5,000 on the understanding that if a future Home Rule Bill did not include provision for continued Irish representation at Westminster, the money was to be returned.[29] This is not to say that the machiavellian Rhodes did not realise that his generous gift might not secure friends in an unexpected quarter.[30] As for Parnell, he increasingly came round to a genuine feeling that Rhodes was right and in December 1889 in private negotiations with Gladstone he strongly opposed the suggestion that after Home Rule Irish representation should be reduced from 103 seats to 32. That Gladstone intended to retain for Britain certain police and judicial powers in Ireland after Home Rule convinced Parnell that Ireland must retain her Westminster representation to safeguard her own interests.

By late 1889 Rhodes and Parnell had maintained as close a link as two men could who were notoriously lethargic at letter writing. It is interesting to note that Parnell wrote to Rhodes telling him of this dispute with Gladstone nine months before he raised it with his parliamentary colleagues.[31] When the second cheque for £5,000 was sent to Parnell is not clear, but it was certainly despatched.

An important development in cementing the link between Parnell and South Africa was the unopposed election to Westminster for Irish constituencies of two of Rhodes' lieutenants in South Africa. John Morrogh, whose

£1,000 donation accompanied Rhodes' first instalment, was returned for South-East Cork in 1889. He retained his seat until 1893, when he resigned. James Rockfort Maguire, 'a cultured, learned, dapper little Irishman', of whom it was said he could not even open a tin of salmon, had been with Rhodes at Oxford. From 1890 until 1892 this lawyer sat for North Donegal. In 1892 he defeated an anti-Parnellite candidate for the constituency of West Clare, but was himself unseated in 1895.[32] In the long run neither man succeeded in Irish politics. Maguire in particular blotted his copybook in Irish eyes by defending the now generally unpopular Rhodes at the House of Commons inquiry into the Jameson raid. In 1900, renouncing Irish nationalism, he stood unsuccessfully as a Liberal candidate in England. 'Is this not disgraceful from an Irishman?' was John Redmond's comment.[33]

But by 1900 the game had been long played out for Parnell and Rhodes' star was fast declining. The storm which grew around Parnell from November 1890 and erupted into full-scale conflict after the Committee Room 15 meeting of 1 December shattered not only Parnell's career but also Rhodes' hopes of imperial federation.

During the divorce and leadership crisis the two men kept in contact and met several times in early 1891. On one occasion Rhodes made his famous remark to Parnell, 'Can't you square the Pope?' It is said that on hearing of the O'Shea divorce petition naming Parnell as the co-respondent, Rhodes cabled Parnell the astute advice, 'Resign — marry — return'.[34] This was not dissimilar to John Devoy's opinion that Parnell should lie low for a while and go on a fund-raising tour of the Irish overseas.[35] Parnell did at one stage suggest he step down from the leadership, but this appears to have been a tactical gesture rather than a serious offer.

The year 1891 witnessed a full-scale political civil war in Ireland, a struggle that was to decimate Irish constitutional politics for a generation. In this battle, which for Parnell lasted until his death on 6 October, the name of Cecil Rhodes was not infrequently heard. At a speech delivered in Limerick on 11 January Parnell, attempting to prove his independence of the Liberals, contradicted Gladstone's assertion that the Liberal leader had made no proposal about Irish representation at Westminster at their meeting at Hawarden in December 1889. To prove this Parnell quoted from his letter to Rhodes on the subject which was dated 3 March 1890.[36] Tim Healy believed the letter had been 'castrated' by Parnell and expressed his hope that the Liberals would obtain the original and publish it.[37] But Rhodes did not deliver up his correspondence and Parnell won this round of the battle.

Two months after his Limerick speech Parnell, now warming more to the battle and encouraged by indications that the advanced men of Irish nationalism were swinging in behind him, delivered a rousing speech in the town of Navan. In this tirade he relished the prospect of 'royal Meath' becoming 'republican Meath'.[38] No doubt to Parnell's surprise and perhaps amusement, he received a rather pompous letter from Rhodes instructing him to hand over the £10,000 to charity. Despite what Parnell was to claim later, it is in fact doubtful if much remained of Rhodes' money. Besides Parnell was not so naïve as to give up what he had gained and in reply to Rhodes he glossed over the speech claiming, incorrectly, that he had been quoted out of context. That he bothered replying to Rhodes at all at such a juncture is of note.

What Rhodes thought of this response is not known, but the two men met later in March in the presence of the young proprietor of the *Freeman's Journal*, who was soon to rat on the Parnellites. Whether Rhodes was sorry for Parnell or whether, as is more likely, he understood that Parnell's lie to him about his speech was a political necessity is uncertain, but he obviously was impressed by Parnell for he offered him a further £10,000. Why Parnell refused this has never been satisfactorily explained. Perhaps the embattled Irish leader was more sensitive now about retaining his independence. He also may well have realised that Rhodes was now recognised as the principal imperialist of the age. To accept money from such a source might well give ammunition to his enemies. This second offer of money from Rhodes remained a secret until 1926.

If Parnell did think this, it was too late. The damage had already been done. In May Archbishop Croke in a speech at Kilteely queried the where-abouts of various party funds, including the Rhodes money. In a reply in a speech delivered at Wicklow Parnell lashed out at the archbishop's thinly disguised accusation of embezzlement. One by one he answered the questions regarding the different funds. Concerning the Rhodes money, he was vague, stating only that he had given some of it to the party treasurer and held some of the balance for 'the spreading of confusion amongst the enemies of Ireland (*prolonged cheers*), and the friends of English dictation (*renewed cheering*)'. He also proclaimed, 'as Mr Cecil Rhodes has not asked me how I spent the money, I don't think I need trouble myself about His Grace of Cashel's inquiry on the same subject (*applause*)'.[39]

Moving to the Morrogh £1,000, Parnell rejected the archbishop's allegation that Morrogh had told him that he had given Parnell the money on the morning he had been returned as MP for Cork. Avoiding mentioning what had happened to the money, Parnell's effective reply to this false accusation was, 'Either Mr Morrogh is untruthful, or His Grace is inaccurate (*applause*)'.[40] Next morning an anonymous article, most likely written by Tim Healy, entitled 'Stop thief', appeared in the recently founded anti-Parnellite newspaper, the *National Press*. It stated bluntly that for years Parnell had 'been stealing the money entrusted to his charge'.[41] As no legal action was taken by Parnell, the accusation of embezzlement was confirmed in the minds of his opponents. In fact, Parnell had little choice but to do what he did and promise to submit a balance-sheet of his finances to the party treasurer, William O'Brien, when he was released from prison.[42] It is doubtful whether Parnell knew what had happened to all the money. He could not manage his own personal finances. On the other hand, even if he could account for the money, he could not disclose his side's finances to the enemy. T.P. O'Connor believed that charges of embezzlement against Parnell could not have been substantiated.[43] The truth was Parnell had been outwitted and though he bravely soldiered on, visiting Ireland every weekend to address what at times were insignificant rural meetings, his cause was lost. His death on 6 October merely added pathos to the tale and enhanced the bitterness by creating the image of the colossus betrayed in his dying days.

It is not certain what happened to the South African money, though £5,000 appears to have been given to William O'Brien to use in aiding 'Plan of Campaign' evicted tenants.[44] This may be the £5,000 marked 'source unknown' in the 1888 finance books of the Irish parliamentary party. The total receipts of the party for 1888 amount to less than £10,000.[45] The first Rhodes £5,000 and the Morrogh £1,000 were paid by cheques. The second £5,000 was given directly to Parnell in cash. In a speech at Clonmel before the archbishop's attack on him, Parnell said this residue had gone into party funds, but in his reply to the archbishop in his Wicklow speech he claimed to have had some of the balance of Rhodes' money still in his possession. No explanation exists as to what happened to Morrogh's £1,000. It is likely that Parnell did give O'Brien a substantial sum and that the remaining money he retained, using it as circumstances necessitated. When he was given the money he was all powerful and it is doubtful if he ever contemplated the time when he would be called to account for his expenditure. There was a stubbornness about Parnell: he was the Chief and was not going to account for his actions to anyone. Thus he never disclosed the second Rhodes offer and his rejection of it, a fact that would have operated greatly in his favour. When he died, no secretly stashed-away funds surfaced to pay off his debts. The accusation of embezzlement has not been proved and is unlikely to be true. Be this as it may, the spectre of the Rhodes £10,000 haunted Irish politics for some years to come. In 1899 the Irish unionist leader Colonel Saunderson baited the Irish nationalists for their acceptance of the Rhodes money and their espousal of the Boer cause in the second Anglo-Boer war.[46] *The Times* was not slow to follow suit.[47]

But the Parnell-South African link did not end with the death of the Chief. Maguire, as an Irish MP, maintained contact between the Parnellites and Rhodes. On Parnell's death Maguire wrote to Rhodes:

I saw him [Parnell] four days before and thought him well and strong — Our position now is that the nationalist movement has been captured by the English liberals and the priests, who will always come to terms — Parnell could have exposed any deal they might make but I doubt anyone else doing so . . .The Priests in Ireland are the Dutch in the Cape, there you have the position.[48]

In 1893 the second Home Rule Bill did include provision for Irish representation at Westminster and Maguire took the opportunity to retrace the Rhodes-Parnell episode in the press.[49] Maguire was firmly in the Parnellite camp in these years, a fact which in part explains Dillon's attempt to hound him after the Jameson raid.[50] On the eve of the Boer war Maguire would finally part company even with the Parnellites.[51] In the interim, however, even after the Jameson raid had been widely denounced in Ireland,[52] Rhodes continued to interfere in Irish politics in support of the Parnellites. As late as 1896 the Dublin Metropolitan Police received the following report:

> That Colonel Rhodes has already given a large sum of money to Mr John E. Redmond for the purpose of maintaining his party, and that a further and much larger sum is expected from that gentleman. That the Parnellite party are favourable to Colonel Rhodes and the line of action taken by him for some months past, and by this means are said to be in a position to get almost any amount of money asked for.

Attached to this crime branch special file is a note which reads, 'From further inquiry we find it is Mr Cecil Rhodes and not Colonel Rhodes'.[53] To what extent and to what effect Rhodes involved himself in Parnellite politics after the death of the Chief is not known. The flames of two fires — that lit by Katharine O'Shea to destroy Parnell's correspondence after his death, and the blaze which devoured Rhodes' Cape home, Groote Schuur, and many of his papers — have ensured that this remains one of the best-kept secrets in Irish history.

J.L. Garvin, writing in the *Fortnightly Review* in December 1898, suggested that had Home Rule come to Ireland in Parnell's day, 'he would have become at once an imperial force as strong as Mr Rhodes'. Initially Parnell's interest in South Africa was obviously superficial, a vehicle to help secure his rise to eminence. But this could not be said of him ten years later. Rhodes appears to have interested him in the wider issue of empire and perhaps to have unwittingly created the image in Parnell's mind of himself at the head of an Ireland which would be, to use modern terminology, 'the commonwealth leader'.

Notes

1.   D.M. Schreuder, *Gladstone and Kruger* (London and Toronto, 1969), p. viii. See also British Library, Campbell-Bannerman papers, vol. xiv, Add. Ms. 41219 (215); and Erskine Childers, *The Framework of Home Rule* (London, 1911), p. 139.

2. See D.P. McCracken ed., *The Irish in Southern Africa, 1795-1910* (Perskor, Johannesburg, forthcoming in 1991).

3. For an account of the impact of events in South Africa on Irish politics, see D.P. McCracken, *The Irish Pro-Boers, 1877-1902* (Johannesburg, 1988).

4. James Joyce, *Ulysses* (London, 1937 edition), p. 610; and Seán O'Casey, *Pictures in the hallway* (London, 1942), p. 283. Parnell's body was placed in a lead casket immediately after death, thus making the outer oak coffin very heavy.

5. *Men of the Times, Pioneers of the Transvaal and Glimpses of South Africa* (Johannesburg, 1905), pp. 282-3.

6. The seven obstructionists were J.G. Biggar (West Cavan), E.D. Gray (Tipperary), G.H. Kirk (Louth), Capt. J.P. Nolan (Galway), C.S. Parnell (Meath), J. O'Connor Power (Mayo) and F.H. O'Donnell. Joseph Biggar had first begun this policy of filibustering as early as 1875.

7. *The Nation*, 11 August 1877.

8. *Hansard*, vol. 235, 25 July 877, col. 1809. See also vol. 236, 3 August 1877, col. 398.

9. *The Times*, 1 August 1877 and 4 August 1877. See also Parnell's letter in *The Times*, 30 July 1877.

10. F.S.L. Lyons, *Parnell* (Fontana, 1978), p.64.

11. F.H. O'Donnell, *The History of the Irish Parliamentary Party, 1870-1892* (New York, 1910), pp. 69, 216 and 461. O'Donnell visited Paul Kruger on four occasions when he was in London in July 1877. See also Conor Cruise O'Brien, *Parnell and his Party, 1880-90* (Oxford, 1957), p. 19n.

12. R. Barry O'Brien, *The Life of Charles Stewart Parnell* (London, 1910), p. 110.

13. L. Paul-Dubois, *Contemporary Ireland* (London, 1908), p. 145.

14. T.W. Moody, 'The New Departure in Irish politics, 1878-9', in *Essays in British and Irish history in Honour of James Eadie Todd* (London, 1949), p. 321.

15. *Hansard*, vol. 246, 26 May 1879, cols. 1265-6.

16. See Sir R. Anderson, *Sidelights on the Home Rule Movement* (London, 1906); Henri le Caron, *Twenty-five Years in the Secret Service* (London, 1893), pp. 169-70; and Special Commission Act 1888, minutes of evidence, proof, 5 February 1889, col. 2496.

17. J. Lehmann, *The First Boer War* (London, 1972), p.102.

18. ibid., pp. 226 and 292.

19. M.J.F. McCarthy, *Five Years in Ireland, 1895-1900* (London, 1903 ed.), p. 467.

20. Cruise O'Brien, *op.cit.*, p. 22n.

21. See, for example, *Hansard*, vol. 289, 26 June 1884, col. 1401 and vol. 296, 20 March 1885, col. 53; and the *Irish Times*, 19 October 1899. It should be noted that F.H. O'Donnell retired from parliament in 1885.

22. For a vivid account of this singular episode, read J.G. Swift MacNeill, *What I Have Seen and Heard* (London, 1925), chaps. iv and v.

23. Lyons, *op.cit.*, p. 66.

24. *The Times*, 9 July 1888.

25. This is likely but is challenged by one account. See R.I. Rotberg, *The*

Founder: Cecil Rhodes and the Pursuit of Power (Oxford, 1988), p. 231; and J.G. Lockhard and the Hon. C.M. Woodhouse, *Rhodes* (London, 1963), p. 167.

26. Arthur Griffith believed that Rhodes had bought the votes of the Irish party. See the *United Irishman*, 31 March 1900.
27. Chamberlain claimed he disliked Rhodes for three reasons: he had made an enormous fortune very rapidly, he was an Afrikander and he had given £10,000 to Parnell. Jeffrey Butler, *The Liberal Party and the Jameson Raid* (Oxford, 1968), p. 74.
28. Rotberg, *op.cit.*, p.232.
29. Rhodes House Library, Oxford, Rhodes papers, Mss. Afr. S.228 (vol. iii), C3A. See also J.G. Lockhart and C.M. Woodhouse, *op.cit.*, pp. 168-9.
30. See, for example, Rhodes House Library, Rhodes papers, Mss. Afr. S.228, C4, 9; C4, 37 and C127, 12.
31. Parnell's letter to Rhodes was soon to prove useful to Parnell as Gladstone tried to deny what had transpired at his Hawarden meeting with Parnell.
32. This is the parliamentary seat which was occupied from 1909 to 1918 by the former leader of the second Irish Transvaal Brigade, Colonel Arthur Lynch.
33. National Library of Ireland (NLI), Redmond papers, Ms. 15, 239(2), n.d.
34. J.C. Beckett, *The Making of Modern Ireland* (London, 1966), p. 403.
35. Lyons, *op.cit.*, p. 595.
36. *Freeman's Journal*, 12 January 1891; and *The Times*, 12 January 1891.
37. T.M. Healy, *Letters and Leaders of My Day* (London, 1928), 1.353.
38. *Freeman's Journal*, 2 March 1891.
39. T.M. Healy, *Why Ireland is Not Free* (Dublin, 1898), p. 46.
40. *Freeman's Journal*, 1 June 1891.
41. *The National Press*, 1 June 1891.
42. *Freeman's Journal*, 8 June 1891.
43. T.P. O'Connor, *Memoirs of an Old Parliamentarian* (London, 1929), II.275.
44. Lyons, *op.cit.*, p. 433.
45. NLI, William O'Brien papers, Mss. 13418-13477.
46. *Hansard*, vol. 78, 17 October 1899, col. 151. The Liberal party was also to be embarrassed when Rhodes' gift to Liberal funds became public in 1901. See *The Spectator*, 3 August 1901; and British Library, Campbell-Bannerman papers, vol. XI, Ms. 41, 216, ff. 124-5.
47. *The Times*, 18 October 1899.
48. Rhodes House, Oxford, Rhodes papers, Mss. Afr. S.228, C3A, vol. II, f. 193.
49. *The Times*, 5 June 1893. See also C.P. Taylor, 'Cecil Rhodes and the second home rule bill', in the *Historical Journal*, vol. XIV, no. 4 (1971).
50. See *Hansard*, vol. 51, 16 July 1897, col. 308.
51. See, for example, NLI, Redmond papers, Ms. 15238 (10).
52. See, for example, *Freeman's Journal*, 1, 3 and 19 January 1896.
53. State Paper Office, Dublin, Crime branch special papers, S/ex. 12013, 10 July 1896.

Katharine O'Shea and C.S. Parnell

Mary Rose Callaghan

When I was approached by a freelance editor to write a biography for Pandora Press to be part of a series on women's lives, I was given a list to pick from: Maud Gonne, Madame Despard, the Parnell sisters, I remember, were mentioned. I chose Katharine Parnell because I have always been fascinated by the period, and it seemed to me she had been given a raw deal by history. I didn't really know anything much about her, not even that there was already a biography published by Joyce Marlow in 1975. I only knew that she had had a bad press, and I discovered that this had filtered down to today, because the editor soon wrote that, yes, it was all right to write about Katharine Parnell, but that she had quite a job persuading the higher-ups in Pandora, who are dedicated feminists, that she was a fit subject to be investigating.

Katharine would never have entered history if she had not met Parnell. She was not a feminist, but a typical Victorian woman pushed by nineteenth-century morals and mores. Neither was she the heroine, merely the wife. Parnell actually called her 'Queenie' or 'Wifie' — which I tried to name the book. I lost that battle, however, but insisted that the name 'Kitty O'Shea' be in quotes on the front cover. It is only in quotes on the inside cover. Katharine hated the name 'Kitty' and nobody who knew her ever called her that. She was always Katie to her family. 'Kitty' was used most vociferously by Tim Healy at the time of the split in the Irish party and later taken up by the press.

In Victorian times it was a name with demi-monde, feline and coquettish associations. Yet it is as 'Kitty O'Shea' that Katharine Parnell has been remembered by the world. And the imputation still is that she was the married woman who ensnared the 'Uncrowned King of Ireland', destroyed his career, hastened his death and even prolonged a nation's struggle for freedom. The facts, however, are not so simple. They rarely are, and an historian often finds that something as seemingly simple as the mere establishment of a fact is in reality the most impossible task that he or she has. Many of the facts in the life of Katharine Parnell and her famous husband are a matter of indisputable public record. But some are not, and these hazy, often tenuous matters pose basic questions about the motives and characters of the chief actors in this dramatic story.

I had only previously written novels where I was free to invent — indeed that was the whole object of the exercise. But now I was writing a biography and had to stick religiously to sources. There were no living people to interview. Katharine died in 1921 and her children were also dead. Katharine's previous biographer, Joyce Marlow, advised me that the Woods, Katharine's family, would have nothing to do with me. She proved to be right, as I wrote to a Sir John Wood listed in Burke's Peerage, but received no reply. So I had to rely on written sources.

In Katharine's case, the chief one was her memoir, *Charles Stewart Parnell: His Love Story and Political Life*. This book was written in her later years, long removed from the events which were central in her life. Although it is particularly valuable for the inclusion of Parnell's many letters to her, the charge had been made that it was doctored, probably by her son Gerard, to present his father, Captain Willie O'Shea, in a more favourable light. That may well be, but major portions of the work are the only source for crucial matters and moments of Katie's life and seemed to me to be utterly authentic.

Her memoir does not, however, answer all of the questions and even glosses over some of the most significant. Its chief critic was Henry Harrison, who as a young MP and devoted follower of Parnell spent much time with Katie straightening out her affairs after his leader's death.

A second valuable source was a book about Katie's family, *A Century of Letters*, compiled by Minna Evangeline Bradhurst, Katie's niece, who seems to have been the family archivist. This book was privately printed and contains memoirs and letters written by Katharine's family, the Woods, which helped to bring them to life. It also had many letters from eminent friends like Trollope which provided insights into their life-style.

The British Library holds Katharine's letters to Gladstone and also letters from Willie to various people. Many of Katharine's political letters were not revealing, but in one particularly, where she pleads with Gladstone to intercede in a lunacy petition against her aged aunt, she came magically to life for me. Unfortunately I couldn't quote it in the book, as the letter was still in copyright.

The newspaper accounts of the day were also an important source, and the many books written about the period were of enormous help.

Denis Johnston said that he wrote a play about Swift in order to make psychological sense of him. And I soon realised that the process of writing a novel is not too different from writing a biography. Elizabeth Bowen says you don't *create* characters in fiction, you *find* them. It was the same for a biography. If you study the sources, the three principals emerge as characters. In trying to *find* Katharine's character, and inevitably Willie's and Parnell's, I felt like a detective. Why had they acted as they had? I concluded that the two most common motives in detective fiction were also theirs: love and money. Historians of the period have talked a lot about *love* as a motive in connection with Parnell, but never much about *money*. But I'll be coming back to that.

First we must consider Katharine's early life. Money was a recurring theme in a story which began in 1845 when she was born in Essex, England. Although her father, Sir John Page Wood, was a clergyman who had inherited his title, the Woods were only the minor aristocracy. The ambience was really upper-class gentry, the same class that had supplied Jane Austen with material for her novels a generation earlier. Indeed, the Woods were much like the Bennets of *Pride and Prejudice*. In both cases there was a family of girls to marry off. There was the same shortage of money, and the same hope of money in the background.

The family was able, interesting and cultured; politically they were Whigs with a tradition of liberalism. Katharine's mother, Lady Emma, was an artist who supplemented the family income by painting and, later on, by writing novels. She was the dominant partner in the marriage and thought to be a remarkable woman by all who knew her. She was a Florence Nightingale in her attitude to the poor and sick — cholera had come to England by then and was an absolutely dreaded disease, but there are accounts in *A Century of Letters* of Lady Emma's bravery in nursing sick infants along with her own.

Katharine was the last of her thirteen children, eight of whom were alive in 1845. At the time, the family lived in a damp vicarage at Cressing in Essex, but moved soon afterwards into Rivenhall Place, a nearby mansion which was considered one of the stately but derelict homes of England. The story goes that Sir John sent one of his sons out on horseback to the surrounding countryside to find a house suitable for his big family. The boy came back saying he had found a home his mother would love because 'it had a waterfall down the front stairs'.

Although the Woods seem to have lived well, they were chronically short of money. But there was a fairy godmother in the background who constantly came to the rescue. This was Maria Wood, Emma's elder sister, who had married Sir John's uncle, Benjamin. Because of this she was always called Aunt Ben. This aunt and her money were to have a considerable part to play in Katharine's fate, and consequently in Parnell's.

In many ways Katharine's childhood was idyllic. Like many a youngest child in a large family, she was brought up with a mixture of spoiling and neglect. Although one gets the distinct impression from her memoirs that she was neglected by her mother, she was her father's pet. As was usual for girls in Victorian times, she was educated at home. But by the time she arrived, the family could no longer afford a governess, so she was only patchily taught by her father. He instructed her in botany, while his curate told her about astronomy, an interest she was later to pass on to Parnell. Although Katie was interested in music and in her teens set poetry to music, there was no money for piano lessons. Yet she somehow persuaded an organist to teach her to sing and she delighted her parents by singing to their guests in the evening after dinner. A Victorian girl's job was to 'look pretty and keep her mouth shut'. Her object in life was to find a husband, if possible a rich one.

Visiting was an important part of life in Victorian times, and the Woods were eminently sociable. As well as important guests like Constable, Meredith and Trollope, Rivendale was constantly visited by handsome young officers, friends of Katharine's army brothers, Frank and Evelyn. Katie's older sister, Anna, who later became a minor Victorian novelist, had married one of these 'beautiful ones', but left him, the story goes, when she discovered that sex was expected of a wife.

Katharine first met Willie O'Shea on a visit with her sister Anna to her brother Frank's regiment. But she doesn't appear to have been impressed with him on this occasion. Indeed, she tells us in her memoirs, 'I found the elderly and hawklike Colonel of the Regiment far more interesting than the younger men'. However, they were soon to meet again, at her elder sister Lady Emma Barrett-Lennard's house, Belhus — Emma had done the proper thing and married money. Willie O'Shea, who was a keen rider with a dubious reputation as an Irish wit, had been invited for the weekend by her husband, Sir Thomas, who wanted him to ride a horse in a steeplechase. When it came time to go in to dinner, Sir Thomas asked, 'Who will she go in with, Milady?' 'O'Shee will go in with O'Shea,' was Emma's reply.

Willie was the most awful snob who spoke with a plummy English accent and constantly jeered things Irish. He always pronounced his name O'Shee, so this brought a ripple of laughter. It might also suggest that the Barrett-Lennards did not take their young guest too seriously but as a bit of a joke. In any event, it was the beginning of a courtship which was to last, with one lapse, till 1867 when Katie married him at the age of twenty-two.

As an Irishman and a Catholic, Willie would have been considered socially inferior to Katie, yet the Woods don't seem to have been typical of their intolerant class. Initially they welcomed him. Although he wasn't a particularly good catch, there could be money in the background and his Spanish relations were titled. The O'Sheas were a Limerick family of Castle Catholics who had fallen on hard times in the previous generation. Willie's father, Henry, a solicitor, had somewhat restored the family fortunes by specialising in the problems of bankrupt estates — a particular Irish problem at the time. He had spared nothing on the education of his only son who had been sent to St Mary's College, Oscott, a top English public school of the day. Although Katie wrote that 'Willie had no natural taste for learning,' he must have had some, because surviving mark books show him to have been well to the top of his class. After school he visited the Continent and became something of a linguist. He entered Trinity College, Dublin, but surprisingly did not do at all well. We can only speculate as to what he was up to. So in 1858, his father bought him a commission in the 18th Hussars, a regiment in the British Army, where as an accomplished rider he fitted in well. On his departure, his doting father told him to 'first become a smart officer; secondly do what the other men do and send the bill to me'.

Willie did just this.

Bills poured in for uniforms, mess expenses and gambling debts. And soon the fond father was complaining of the enormous expense of keeping his son in the army. When Willie presented a bill for £15,000, a terrible amount of money at the time, the poor father paid up, murmuring that if Willie continued spending, his mother and sister would suffer. So Willie agreed to resign from the army.

After this he went to Spain and Katie did not see him for some time. She next met him at a London party and she tells us in her memoirs that she did not recognise him as he had grown whiskers. These whiskers were a definite turn-off because Katie tells us 'a curious distaste for my love affair had grown up within me.'

Lady Emma had never been keen on Willie and she was the one who now sent him packing. Although it is unlikely that she knew he was probably already a heavy drinker and a reckless gambler, he was now without a job and so unsuitable husband material. Willie took this badly, but while he brooded in Spain, something happened which was to change everything — Sir John died suddenly.

This had a devastating effect on Katie. She fell into such an acute depression that Willie was immediately sent for by Lady Emma. It was a curious action. From reading the memoirs one gets the distinct impression that Katie was not overjoyed to see him. According to the conventions of the day, it could only mean that Lady Emma had changed her mind about Willie as a prospective husband. But why? Was it in deference to the memory of Sir John, who according to Katharine had liked Willie? Or did Lady Emma believe Willie had now abandoned his rakish army ways? Or was it simply that a change in the Wood family fortunes had brought about a changed view of Willie? Katie was now twenty-one and there was no other suitor in sight. An unmarried woman was considered an oddity and an embarrassment in Victorian times. Perhaps Willie was better than no one? Katie was pretty, but she had no unusual talents. Also she was bereaved and a depression might seriously damage her future marriage prospects.

It has to be said that in the beginning, Willie tried — for a short time. The couple went to Spain where he had banking connections. Katie seems to have liked Madrid, but the young couple were soon on their way back to England, as Willie quarrelled with his relations — quarrelsomeness was to be a feature of his adult personality. The next venture was a stud farm in Hertfordshire. But by now the cracks in the marriage had begun to appear. Willie was constantly absent, probably on drinking and gambling binges in London, leaving Katie to cope as best she could. Consequently, the stud farm was neglected and they went bankrupt. The farm was to be the first in a series of disastrous financial ventures.

The Woods now came to the rescue, sending money and renting the O'Sheas a house in Brighton. However, Katie's uncle, who was Chancellor of England at the time, refused to find Willie a job — finding a use for his dubious talents would henceforth be a constant theme in the story.

Despite this help, the next four years were to be unsettled, troublesome and lonely for Katie. At the end of them, her marriage had finally broken down. But she had at last found some security and freedom from financial worry as the companion to her rich Aunt Ben. Maria Wood paid her a salary and bought a house for her and the children across the park from her own. She even paid for Willie's rooms in London. For the first time in her life, Katharine was financially secure, if not actually independent, as the old woman was very demanding. Still, the arrangement suited everyone and was legally contracted. Maria Wood was then 82. What no-one realised was that she would live for the next fifteen years.

Having failed at everything he had so far attempted, Willie decided in 1880 to run for a seat in parliament. He was elected as a member for Co. Clare where he owned land. By now the O'Sheas had separated by mutual agreement, and he only came down to Eltham on Sunday to take the children to Mass.

It was time for the entrance of Charles Stewart Parnell.

Katie tells us in her memoirs that she hated dinner parties, and there is every evidence to believe that she was essentially private. But Willie now asked her to arrange a number of political dinner parties for him in London. To this she agreed. After all she had been brought up to the role of wife, but it must also be said that life would be better for her with Willie occupied. As leader of the Irish party, Parnell was invited, but did not respond as he was always most casual about opening his mail. Then when he finally did accept an invitation, he did not turn up. When Katharine was twitted by one of the other guests about the empty chair, she vowed that at her next party he would be there.

She went to the House of Commons with her sister Anna and sent in a note, asking him to come out and speak to them. Katharine tells us: 'He came out, a tall, gaunt figure, thin and deadly pale. He looked straight at me, smiling and his curiously burning eyes looked into mine with a wonderful intentness.' The attraction was instant. From then on their fates were linked.

When jesting Pilate said, 'What is truth?' he might have been voicing the lament of every historian and biographer. What might seem an easily verifiable fact is often the most elusive thing in the world to establish. And of the various classes of facts, probably the most elusive and tenuous to discover is what specifically happened between a man and a woman.

But we know from Katharine's memoirs and from Parnell's letters that the relationship between them developed quickly. Whenever she could, she would go and hear him speak in the House, and he would make a sign to her 'by certain manipulations of his handkerchief' to meet him later. Whenever he was away in Ireland, they corresponded constantly, and his notes now began 'My dearest love' and 'My dearest Wifie'. In the body of the letters were sentences like, 'If I return Thursday morning, my Queen may expect to see me about one o'clock.' And the conclusions were now signed, 'Always, your Charles' or 'Always your husband.'

I was asked recently what in my opinion attracted Parnell to Katie. Well, it is an unanswerable question. Why do we fall in love? I would say that Parnell was a very lonely man. He had been in politics since 1875, and that involved a rather hectic and homeless life: either travelling in Ireland or living in rooms in London. He came to Avondale, but only for the shooting season or to supervise his mining and quarrying. And although he was lord of the manor, it was, according to contemporary accounts, a frugal existence. Roy Foster, in his brilliant book *Charles Stewart Parnell, The Man and his Family* talks about life at Avondale. He quotes an incident where Parnell suggested to T.P. O'Connor on a visit that they go on a picnic. T.P. O'Connor, thinking he was in a Big House, expected some sort of sumptuous hamper of cold chicken and champagne. But Parnell went into the kitchen, cut off some hunks of 'oatmeal bread, buttered them, wrapped them up and off they set.'

Parnell did not have a real home. While others saw him as the great leader, Katharine knew he was a worn-out man. From the beginning she took care of his health and he soon gloried in Eltham's quiet domesticity. It was a place to retire to and potter around, pursuing absorbing hobbies. He took up book-keeping and astronomy; he spent hours making architectural drawings and assaying specimens of quartz from streams near Avondale. Indeed, he was so contented that Katie had ever greater difficulty in getting him to attend to affairs. She tells us in her memoirs, 'Many a day I have let him work up to the last possible moment, and then literally pulled off the old "cardigan" jacket he worked in and forced him into his frock coat for the House . . .' Sometimes he would have to catch the mail-train for Ireland, and she would have his clothes packed and ready but he would sit down and say, 'You are in a hurry to get rid of me; I will not go yet . . .'

In the case of Katharine and Parnell, certain points are abundantly clear, and the chief of these is his early, lasting and overwhelming attachment to her. What Katharine felt at one time or another is a bit more hazy and there are other central issues that have long puzzled historians and which have been interpreted quite differently.

One of the issues which puzzled them was Willie's knowledge of the affair. It also puzzled me. What did he know? And when? Was he the abused husband, as his son Gerard later claimed, or had he set up the whole thing for his own ends, as Henry Harrison claimed? Having studied the evidence, I at first concluded that of course Willie knew. He used his wife as bait to lure Parnell for his own ends and then turned a blind eye to their affair. That was in his character. But there are certain problems with this view. One is the problem of his concern for Katharine's child, Claude Sophie, who was born in 1882. Willie always doggedly believed she was his, even up to the divorce. If so, he couldn't have suspected that Katharine was sleeping with Parnell before 1882. But, although he claimed otherwise, by the time of the Galway by-election in 1885 he must have known. He was now just denying it publicly. Fear of blackmail is the only plausible explanation for Parnell's action in shoving him down the throats of the Irish party at that time.

But other aspects of Parnell's behaviour are not so easily understood. Many of his actions were incompatible with his proud and private character. We know from Katharine's memoirs that he quite quickly compromised her, bringing her into his private sitting room in Cannon Street Hotel in full view of members of the Irish party. It was not the thing for a Victorian married woman to be alone with a man in a hotel room. It is hardly the thing today. But from the beginning, Parnell acted with a lofty disdain for the opinion of others. Why then did he not soon ask Katie to divorce Willie and marry him? Why did he get involved in years of deceit and subterfuge? I could only conclude that he did so because of Aunt Ben's money. By today's standards the old woman was a millionaire. Katharine, along with the other Wood children, was to inherit a share of her fortune which was estimated at about £200,000. But if the truth about Parnell came out, Katharine knew she would definitely have been disinherited by her aunt. So it is easy to understand her motivation. Parnell's acquiescence is not so easily understood.

To Parnellites of a previous generation, it would have been seen as sacrilege to ascribe such human motives to their hero. But it seems obvious that he wanted the money. Not just for Katharine's sake, but because he needed it for himself as her future husband. He was not a businessman and Avondale was heavily in debt when he entered politics. It is to his credit that he was not a strict landlord. But he spent fortunes on quarrying and mining, which yielded little profit. Roy Foster brilliantly charts his shaky financial position. He quotes Sir Henry Lucy as saying that Parnell's premature death was contributed to by actual poverty. And according to his brother John, between 1881 and 1891, Parnell spent £90,000.

And remember, there was the matter of the Parnell Tribute which Parnell pocketed in 1883 without so much as a word of thanks. John Parnell wrote on this: 'I remember him in 1887, complaining of the financial difficulties in which he again found himself involved, and saying to me, "Well John, politics is the only thing I ever got any money from, and I am looking for another subscription now." I think he was serious when he said it, but, of course, a fresh tribute was not forthcoming.'

Aunt Ben's money was. It involved both Parnell and Katie in years of deception which in the end brought nothing but tragedy. But we are dealing here with people and not with the heroes of romance. The love of money may indeed be the root of all evil, but it is a dominating emotion for most of humanity.

Another puzzling question was Willie's decision to take the divorce action in 1889. After all, he had lain low for years. Why did he act now? He had most to gain by remaining Katharine's husband, yet he instituted proceedings on Christmas Eve of that year. Aunt Ben had died the previous May. But before that the Woods — that is Katie's brothers and sisters — had most callously tried to get the old woman declared insane and committed to an asylum. They had done this because she told them she was leaving Katie a bit more money than she was leaving them — after all, Katie knew her better and had looked after her for over ten years. But the Woods objected to this, so the old woman, who was no fool, responded by leaving Katie all of it. This drove the Woods to start an insanity petition in the courts. Katie responded quickly. She wrote to Gladstone, who sent his own physician to examine the old woman. He found her of sane mind, so when the petition came up it was thrown out.

After Aunt Ben's death, Willie's position remained uncomfortable, but it was not untenable. It was true that Aunt Ben's will had given everything to Katie, and had given it outside the terms of the marriage settlement, so that Willie could not touch it. Still, if Willie would not directly benefit, he had yet one large ace in the hole — if he made no public fuss, things could go on as they had and possibly they could go on even better. And there was another possibility: for a sufficient sum of money, he would allow Katie to sue him for divorce.

Willie subsequently gave two different versions of why he had at last taken action. One version was that Cardinal Manning had asked to see Willie's actual evidence of Katharine's infidelity and, when Willie sent him an incriminating letter, the Cardinal promptly passed it along to Parnell's barrister and solicitor, and that this perfidy caused Willie to act. A second story, written in a letter to Chamberlain, was that Willie and his son, Gerard, then aged 19, visited 10 Walsingham Terrace in Brighton where Katie and Parnell had moved after Aunt Ben's death. There they found some of Parnell's things which they chucked out the window. They then went to lawyers and settled that an action should be taken immediately.

However, it is Joyce Marlow's contention, and I have to agree with this, that the Wood family finally impelled Willie to launch the divorce action. Willie was still on friendly terms with them. With them he could share, although for different reasons, an animosity to Katharine. The Woods, of course, would have been delighted with a well publicised divorce action, which, whatever its outcome, would considerably have harmed Katharine's chances of the inheritance. Still, it must have been obvious, even to Willie, that if the money were divided among the whole family, his claim on a now smaller portion would be distinctly weakened.

All of the issues I have so far mentioned revolve around the Wood inheritance. It was a tale worthy of Dickens, with so many people waiting for an old woman to die. But one final question also puzzled me. This was to do with Parnell's last battle. Why did Katie not make him step down? She had been forceful before; why could she not act now? Parnell once told John Dillon, 'I have never heard that anyone could ever persuade a woman to do, or not to do, anything that she had made up her mind to do, no matter what the consequences to herself or others might be . . .' If I remember rightly, on that occasion he was referring to his sister Anna. But had Katie known he thought this, her actions in not opposing him at the end might have been different. Just as he had caved in to her about Aunt Ben's money, she now caved in to his ego in the last desperate fight for leadership. She knew what his health was, yet she caved in. Why?

But it is too easy to say what she should or should not have done. It is a biographer's task to report facts, not to pass judgement or to speculate on what might have been. Parnell was a supreme egotist and a stronger person than Katie was. After all, she had not been able to budge him in the matter of defending the divorce suit. But also the years of living as if life were a grand opera had taken their toll on her nerves. The years from Kilmainham to the last battle for leadership were a series of peaks and too few valleys. Too much had happened too quickly. In the end she had become a vine rather than a bough.

And after Parnell died, it was as if a light had gone out. No centre remained. Katharine disintegrated into nervous breakdown and wandered nomadically from rented house to rented house all over the south coast of England. Although I regretted that my book was dominated by Parnell, it was unavoidable. After he died, she disappeared from public life. So it was impossible to find out much about the last thirty years of her life. But some of her indomitability and courage remained, because she resurfaced at the time of the publication of her memoirs in 1914, which she wrote to make money, and which were quite a best seller at the time.

Having spent so much time thinking about Katharine, I came to like her. For the most part, she was a fighter. And if she wanted Aunt Ben's money, she also needed it. For years she had had to take care of Willie and her children. And one wonders what Parnell contributed to household expenses or to his children's upkeep in the years that he lived with her. Katharine does not tell us in her memoirs. She was always remarkable in her loyalty — to William long after he deserved it and then to Parnell. I thought she was best as a wife — the role to which she had been brought up. But when I sent my finished typescript to Pandora, the editors were unhappy with this conclusion and wanted me to be more critical of her. They wanted a different kind of book — something less 'wet'. I never discovered quite what this meant. After all, any biography is only one person's version of events. This was the gospel, according to me. I had *found* her character in the same way as I had *found* fictional characters and I could not change her now. But finally they decided it was all right and went ahead and published it.

Of course the publishers were right — Katharine was never the liberated woman a modern feminist might admire. She exchanged one monogamous relationship for another, which had more meaning but was no less iron-bound. But if feminism is to serve any purpose it should extol the forgotten virtues of loyalty and courage. It was not only the Joan of Arcs who were remarkable and who lost. It was also the Katharines.

The photograph of Katharine O'Shea (1880)
which Parnell had with him in Kilmainham,
and which he carried until his death.

The 'Appeal to the Hillsides': Parnell and the Fenians 1890-91

Frank Callanan

'I know', said Charles Stewart Parnell in private conversation in 1881, to a Fenian leader who doubted his power to deal effectively with English parties by Parliamentary action, 'I know I can bring English parties to their knees over this Home Rule question without risking anything like an insurrectionary movement. I cannot tell you how I will do it. Perhaps, I do not know exactly myself. But I am convinced that I can do it and that I will do it'.[1]

The unhistorical but superficially attractive interpretation of the split as a climactic chapter in a fixed and constant struggle for ascendancy between parliamentary nationalism and a unitary and historically invariant 'physical force' tradition — habitually linked to the implicit thesis of the Irish party succumbing belatedly to the death-wound of the split some twenty-five years after its infliction — continues to distort perceptions of Parnell's campaign in the split.

Perhaps the central criticism of Parnell in the split was that he embarked upon an 'appeal to the hillsides', which compromised his standing as a constitutional nationalist. Yet, while Parnell made an overt pitch for Fenian support, he did so in terms which neither derogated from his commitment to parliamentary action, nor marked a break with the classic politics of Parnellism. The definitive articulation of the 'appeal to the hillsides' came in a celebrated passage in Parnell's speech in the Rotunda on his return to Ireland immediately after his defeat in Committee Room 15:

> I have not promised you success, but I have said, and I repeat tonight, with all the force and energy that my poor words can give to the declaration — that if Ireland cannot win upon this line within the constitution she can win upon no other line within the constitution (*cheers*), and that if our constitutional movement today is broken down, sundered, separated, discredited, and forgotten, England will be face to face with that imperishable force which tonight gives me my vitality and power (*loud and prolonged cheers*), and without which we are broken reeds, bending and blown about by every puff of wind. And if Ireland leaves this path upon which she has trodden until she is almost in sight of victory, I will not for my part say that I will not accompany her further (*cheers*); but I shall claim for myself the right which each one of you has to consider [in] the future, to be warned by the mistakes of the past, and to shape his course as the side lights and the guide lights and head lights may best direct for the future success and prosperity of Ireland (*cheers*). You may ask what

I mean? Whether I intend to cross the Rubicon and burn my boats? I cross no Rubicon (*cheers*). I have no boats to burn (*cheers*); but my position is the position of 1880; and I say to you, and to all Irishmen — beware while you have time and while the power is still in your hands before you surrender for ever a force which you cannot control, the illimitable power of our race which has shown itself on these streets of Dublin tonight, without which I should be worthless and useless, with which I am strong (*cheers*), and with which at my side I pledge myself to push forward until we have either reached the goal, or until the majority of the Irish people tell me that the goal is not there, and that I must try some other method.[2]

It is surely more convincing to interpret this passage as a demonstration of Parnell's consummate mastery of Irish democratic politics, rather than as an equivocation in the pursuit of constitutional politics. In an arabesque of double negatives he affirmed the dependence of parliamentary action on continued popular support and on the achievement of effective results, a contention with which every contemporary constitutional nationalist would be constrained to agree. The reference to 'that imperishable force which tonight gives me my vitality and power', with its hint of insurgency, has a calculated Fenian resonance. Yet what gives the argument its rhetorical force is Parnell's recasting of the commonplace argument that if parliamentary nationalism failed physical force would take its place, so as to invest constitutional politics with enhanced vigour and urgency. With masterly elusiveness Parnell cheated Fenian ideologues of any substantive concession, by making the quintessentially Parnellian point that he alone was capable of leading the constitutional movement while constraining, and directing into constitutional channels, Fenian energies and sentiment. In the dancing syntax Parnell affirmed a constitutional purpose.

Rather than a rupture with his past, Parnell's speech was an avowal of constancy, an electrifying restatement of the premises of parliamentary action and an assertion that the Liberal alliance had not compromised the essential character of Parnellism. In response to the slackening of nationalist discipline and purpose wrought by the Liberal alliance, Parnell sought to achieve a sharpening of Parnellism's inner logic, a tautening of those tensions within Parnellism which provided its political dynamic. Parnell's 'appeal to the hillsides', such as it was, drew its force from the assertion that his overthrow could portend a Fenian resurgence. Parnell throughout his career systematically exaggerated the Fenian threat to his authority, to reinforce his indispensability as a leader, and to force the pace of constitutional reform. This had always been part of the armoury of Parnell's tactics: once deployed against the British government and party system, it was now directed within Ireland in furtherance of his quest to reconstitute his leadership.

Parnell's 'appeal to the hillsides' resided principally in his contention that constitutional action required to be justified in terms of its effectiveness. His

most seemingly extravagant rhetoric was reducible to the unexceptionable
commitment that he would desist from parliamentary politics when it became
in his judgement ineffectual: that he would in that event so advise the Irish
people, withdraw from politics and not impede the adoption by the country
of other political courses. His pledge was of intellectual honesty: 'I have not
misled you . . . I have never said that this constitutional movement must
succeed'. He promised that should parliamentary politics become demon-
strably barren he would avow this candidly rather than seek to deceive the
country by lending his authority to a perseverance in futile courses. It was a
daring and masterly argument. Without compromising his constitutional
purpose Parnell sought to turn his weakness to strength. With unflinching
suppleness he threw his full weight upon the paradox that he was at once the
only constitutional leader who commanded a degree of confidence among
Fenians, and the parliamentary leader who could most capably thwart and
defeat Fenianism. Through this dynamic counterbalancing Parnell sought to
create the matrix of his power.

Parnell at Kilkenny, in rejecting Davitt's taunt that he was engaged in an
appeal to the 'hillside men' and was leading young men into insurrectionary
courses, restated the argument of the Rotunda speech:

> I have not promised to lead them against the armed might of England. I
> have told them, so long as I can maintain an independent Irish Party in
> the English Parliament, there is hope of winning our legislature by
> constitutional means . . . So long as we can keep our Irish Party pure and
> undefiled from any contact or fusion with any English Parliamentary
> party, independent and upright, there is good reason for us to hope that
> we shall win legislative independence for Ireland by constitutional means
> (*cheers*). So long as such a party exists I will remain at its head (*loud
> cheers*). But when it appears to me that it is impossible to obtain Home
> Rule for Ireland by constitutional means — and this is the extent and limit
> of my pledge (*cheers*), that is the pledge which has been accepted by the
> young men of Ireland whom Michael Davitt in his derision calls the
> hillside men - I have said that when it is clear to me that I can no longer
> hope to obtain our constitution by constitutional and Parliamentary means
> I will in a moment so declare it to the people of Ireland, and returning at
> the head of my party I will take counsel with you as to the next step (*loud
> cheers*) . . . if the young men of Ireland have trusted me it is because they
> know that I am not a mere Parliamentarian; that I can be trusted to keep
> my word to them to go as far as a brave and honest heart can go on this
> Parliamentary alliance, and test it to the uttermost, and that when and if I
> find it useless and unavailing to persevere further, they can depend upon
> me to tell them so (*cheers*).[5]

While one might reasonably demur at the ingratiating use of the term
'mere parliamentarian', by which Parnell intended to recommend himself to

advanced nationalists, it hardly amounted to a detraction from his constitutional purpose. The phrase occurred elsewhere in Parnell's rhetoric in the split: 'although we may be mere Parliamentarians, we do not recognise, and we never admitted that we were permanent Parliamentarians', he declared to cheers at the banquet in Cork in March.[4] This represented little more than the assertion that constitutionalism was not an end in itself, but the most effective means to an end. It was further an assertion of his patriotic integrity, of incorruptibility in the face of parliamentary pomps and forms: 'I did not go to Westminster as a placehunter or to become an English party man'.[5] At Newry in March Parnell reverted to this subject:

> The Irish people accepted my declaration sixteen years ago that there was a fair hope and possibility of regaining our national rights by means of an independent Irish party (*hear, hear*). I did not pretend to you then that it was possible always or for ever to maintain independent members at Westminster. I told you often of the great dangers, the insidious influences which are always at work to sap the independence and integrity of Irish members there (*hear, hear*). I told you to beware of those influences. I told you that without an independent party I would take no part in Parliamentary action . . . I stand here today, unhappily, to commence a great deal of my work over again . . . I cheerfully look, and with confidence, for the decision to be given by the Irish people, and I will submit to no other decision (*applause*). And if that decision should be in favour of the slavery of our race, and the dependence of our people upon any English political party or statesman I shall bow to it, and I shall retire from constitutional agitation (*loud cries of 'never'*) and from public life. I shall admit my failure, while regretting it (*never*), but I will never be a party to misleading the men who have stood by me, the men who have given me the position which I hold today (*hear hear*), and I will never ask them to trust in a weapon which has proved to be blunted and corrupt (*applause*). But fellow countrymen, I am confident that that time will not come, and that the decision of Ireland when she is given the opportunity will be clear and decisive, and although we may not have as numerous a party as we had in 1885, it will be more solid, it will be stronger, its principles will be clearer, and more independent (*hear, hear*).[6]

What rendered even this pledge somewhat academic was that Parnell reserved to himself the judgement as to whether parliamentary methods in fact no longer held out any realistic hope of success, and so constituted himself the sole arbiter of the effectiveness of constitutional politics. He was notably evasive as to when the point at which constitutional politics could be considered to have failed might be reached. He conspicuously declined to equate a Parnellite defeat at the ensuing general election with the failure of constitutional politics. At worst his rhetoric contained an implicit threat to desist from constitutional politics in the event of a defeat so annihilating as to eliminate entirely the Parnellite representation at Westminster — an exceedingly remote prospect — and he did not commit himself even to this.

What appears initially as a pledge to withdraw from politics once he adjudged perseverance futile was rather an affirmation of his resolve to fight on so long as there was a Parnellite party in parliament. Similarly when Parnell declared at Balbriggan that if it ever became too evident to him that the struggle at Westminster was hopeless, 'I shall come back to the Irish people and I shall tell them that constitutional effort by parliamentary action has failed', he was careful to add that he had no more fear of that contingency arising than at any time in the preceding sixteen years 'although our discouragement at the moment may be great and heavy'.[7]

Parnell in the split thus contrived to couple a rhetorical play for Fenian support with a fierce and intense affirmation of his constitutional purpose:

> I shall stand upon this constitutional platform until they have torn away the last plank from under our feet. I desire to say here tonight that we can win on the constitutional platform. But if we cannot win upon it, well, I shall be prepared to give way to better and stronger men, and it can never be said of us that we have prevented better or abler men than ourselves from dealing with the future of our race.[8]

This is hardly the remark of a man despairing of constitutional politics or seeking to subvert public belief in parliamentary action.

Parnell throughout the split celebrated the establishment of the primacy of constitutional methods as an achievement of his own leadership. He declared that 'the Parliamentary weapon has now been brought within the grasp of the humblest peasant', and lauded 'this great constitutional weapon'.[9] Parnell's references to the ascendancy of parliamentarianism and the eclipse of physical force nationalism were on occasion imbued with a vague hint of menace, as at Tipperary in April:

> Tipperary has had to fight its own battles in the days gone by outside the constitution (*cheers*). Perhaps there is no other county in Ireland so little indebted to the constitution as the county of Tipperary ... However, these are reminiscences of the past which will never come again. As an apostle of constitutional methods I should be ashamed of myself if it were necessary for those bygone times to return.

Yet he proceeded to develop his argument with impressive temperateness:

> We can contend for the first time in history upon an equal footing within the constitution for our rights . . . Permit not then, fellow countrymen, these forces, these weapons of precision, sharpened as they have been by years of exertion, to be directed against yourselves, and the men proved to be good in your cause.[10]

Parnell's characteristic technique was to induce Fenian sympathisers to impute to him a deeper affinity with their views than he actually possessed. He achieved this by conveying a sense of heightened understanding of Fenian sensitivities, and an intimation that his practice of parliamentary politics was not hidebound by that bourgeois Catholic nationalist constitutionalism which excited particular Fenian mistrust. Accusations of Fenianism levelled against him served Parnell's purpose particularly well. In response to Davitt at Kilkenny, he declared 'when anybody has the audacity to taunt me with being a hillside man I say to him that I am what I am because I am known to be an honest and unchanging Irishman'.[11]

To Harcourt's taunt that he was espousing 'Fenian Home Rule' he retorted: 'I tell Sir William Harcourt, who derides Irish nationality and terms it Fenianism, that unless he and the English Liberal party recognise this spirit they may bid goodbye to the attempt to reconcile Irish public opinion or to settle the Irish question'.[12] The concluding portion of Parnell's last speech on an Irish platform was addressed to this subject:

> . . . we do not subscribe to Sir William Harcourt's doctrine that the legitimate independence of Ireland means a recourse to the resources of Fenianism, of outrage, and of dynamite. We tell Sir William Harcourt that in using those words he is a liar. Ireland has a right to her legitimate freedom, and when Sir William Harcourt defines our platform according to that fashion we see his measure of sympathy for Ireland, and the desire of the new leader of the Liberal Party to give Ireland her legitimate freedom.[13]

Parnell's rhetoric in the split was not without precedent in his career. His assertion in the manifesto that the integrity and independence of a section of Irish members had been 'apparently sapped and destroyed'[14] had been prefigured in pronouncements at the outset of his career, when he used the time-hallowed theme of the deleterious effect wrought by sustained presence at Westminster on the patriotic fibre of Irish members to invest parliamentary politics with a sense of urgency and purpose that it had previously lacked, so as to render the constitutional struggle 'short, sharp and decisive like a bayonet charge'.[15] From the outset he had warned against 'contaminating influences' in the House of Commons and declared he was not one of those who believed in the permanence of an Irish party in the House of Commons because of his conviction that 'sooner or later the influence which every English government has at its command . . . will sap the best party you can return to the House of Commons'.[16] At Tralee, in January 1891, Parnell cited a remark he had made in the town some twelve years earlier to the effect that the air of London was 'very contaminating'.[17]

Parnell had dramatically restated this caveat in a speech at his zenith in May 1889, when he stated he would not remain in the House of Commons once it had become very clear that parliamentary nationalist efforts to achieve self-government were unavailing:

> The most advanced section of Irishmen, as well as the least advanced, have always thoroughly understood that the parliamentary policy was to be a trial and that we did not ourselves believe in the possibility of maintaining for all time, or for any lengthened period, an incorrupt and independent Irish representation at Westminster.[18]

This speech has been rightly interpreted as a corrective adjustment necessitated by his dismissal of Fenianism as a political force in his evidence to the Special Commission.[19] Parnell sought thereby to renew his strange rapport with Fenianism, conveyed in allusive hints of imaginative affinity and historical sympathy, which rendered his firm and unyielding containment of Fenianism endurable to its adherents. He sought to convey then, as he would again in the split, that he alone of parliamentarians had an innate understanding of the predicament of the Fenian sensibility. What might be called Parnell's affective compact with Fenianism was that he would pursue a constitutional solution in a manner which would not gratuitously wound Fenian susceptibilities, and that he would ensure that the values and politics of the Home Rule state were not those of a supremacist conservative Catholic nationalism.

On Parnell's death the perceptive correspondent of the Gladstonian Liberal *Manchester Guardian* who covered the Kilkenny and Carlow elections attested to his abiding reserve:

> As one heard him speaking to an Irish audience in Carlow, or even in Kilkenny, one seemed to sense the secret of his power over Irishmen in the high degree in which he possessed two or three distinctly un-Irish qualities. In his best speeches he never followed his audience. He always led them. Complaisance to their hearers is nearly always a vice of Irish speakers. Mr. Parnell was constantly pulling his audience back, constantly moderating a sweeping sentence that had been uproariously cheered with some exception or statement that brought a dead silence upon everybody. As one heard him, for instance, in the fine speech — scarcely reported in England — that he made at Bagenalstown on the day before the polling at Carlow, one felt that the standard of value for Irish public assertion was rising . . . But even the written speech gives little idea of the high reserve of Mr. Parnell's delivery . . . When he spoke thus he was the embodied corrective of Irish national faults, and the complement that the national character needs before it can attain completeness and efficiency.[20]

This commentary serves as a corrective to Healy's caricature of Parnell as a cynically ruthless saboteur of constitutional politics, and to the complementary extreme nationalist myth of Parnell.

It is true that Parnell's assertions of the contingent nature of constitutional action acquired in the split an emphasis and occasionally a crudity which disconcerted many contemporary nationalists. Yet Parnell could validly, and did fiercely, assert the unity of his career and the constancy of his political principles. His campaign in the split constituted a furious challenge to the anti-Parnellite contention that the success of the movement under his tutelage had rendered redundant the principles he had laid down at the commencement of the struggle.

After the Kilkenny election, Parnell brought to prominence the issue of amnesty for 'political' prisoners convicted for treason felony arising out of the dynamite campaign of 1883-84 in England. Though the advocacy of amnesty, based on humanitarian considerations and on juridical doubt as to the correctness of the convictions, was common to Parnellites and anti-Parnellites, Parnell, while invariably coupling his references to the subject with a deprecation of physical force, contrived to transform the amnesty question into a bridge between Parnellism and Fenianism.

Parnell sought to identify himself closely with the amnesty issue in speeches at Limerick and Waterford in January 1891, in the latter of which he extravagantly asserted that 'the question with which my mind, heart and soul has been identified from the first moment of my entry into politics has been the question of amnesty which founded the home rule movement, which brought myself and others to Irish life'.[21] In late February Parnell agreed to attend an amnesty rally, and expressed his desire to enrol as a member of the Amnesty Association of the National Club.[22] At the rally, in the Phoenix Park in April, Parnell determinedly sought to appropriate the amnesty issue for his own political purposes. He exploited the opportunity it presented for an attack on the Liberal Party, alluding to 'the remarkable coincidence . . . that the Liberals have always been distinguished for making political prisoners and the Tories for letting them out again'. Parnell, notorious for his habitual eschewal of poetic allusion, was in unwontedly lyrical mood, and it is difficult not to discern some trace of cynicism in the maladroit sentimentalism of his declaration, prompted by a downpour, that 'the quality of mercy is not strained, it falleth like the gentle rain from heaven'. He asserted that 'I have always thought that the most beautiful prayer in the English language is that which asks the Almighty to have mercy upon all prisoners and captives'. Rather more characteristically, he added, 'I know the language of petition and of supplication is not what is asked of us by those men if they could speak to us'. He declared that 'mere politicians, mere Members of Parliament, should feel a sense of shame in standing to plead the case of the political prisoners'.[23] This denigration of parliamentarians *vis-á-vis* Fenian prisoners was Parnell's most abjectly ingratiating use of the term 'mere parliamentarians', and could only tend to validate the brutally exclusionary rhetoric which Healy directed against him in the split.

In the House of Commons in July, Parnell moved a reduction in the prisons vote to advocate the granting of political status to the prisoners, and a measure of amnesty, canvassing the possibility that they had been convicted 'owing to a most disgraceful plot on the part of the Irish police and Home Office of that day' — the latter being a reference to Harcourt's Home Secretaryship. He warned: 'You will always have political prisoners so long as the Irish question remains unsettled'.[24] Supporting a clemency resolution of John Redmond a week later, Parnell argued from the demonstrated obsoleteness of the dynamitard strategy: 'These conspiracies, even in America, have now been abandoned for many years, and nobody now wishes to blow up the British Empire with dynamite — an idea which has passed out of the view of the most extreme Irishmen'.[25] So it was that Parnell's last three speeches in the House of Commons were concerned with the issue of amnesty and the plight of political prisoners.[26]

The anti-Parnellites denounced Parnell's ostentatious espousal of the amnesty issue as wholly cynical, and warned that Parnell's advocacy of their cause was likely to militate against the interests of the prisoners themselves. The *National Press* accused Parnell of neglecting the three Phoenix Park prisoners, the 'hapless remnant of a terrible conspiracy', in favour of the dynamitards whom Parnell believed to have 'friends in Ireland', and warned that his opportunistic adoption of their cause would hinder their release, which could only be urged 'on grounds of clemency and expediency'.[27] It charged that a fatal mistake had been made in permitting amnesty to be identified with 'the failing and degraded cause of Parnellism': 'The result of the alliance of Amnesty with Parnellism . . . tends to double-bolt the doors of those prisoners'.[28] William O'Brien intervened to charge Parnell with failing to respond to representations on behalf of the prisoners prior to the split, a charge Parnell denied.[29]

Parnell's evidence to the Special Commission had placed his relations with Fenianism under extreme strain. His writing of Fenianism out of contemporary Irish history had approached the patriotic recantation which diehard Fenians believed to be the ineluctable nemesis of the parliamentary politician.[30] His treatment of the amnesty question in the formation of the Home Rule movement permitted him to atone for his wounding of Fenian susceptibilities. The issue of amnesty had acted as a catalyst in the emergence of the Home Rule party under Isaac Butt: Parnell sought in the split to enlarge the significance of its circumstantial role, and thereby to acknowledge the involvement of Fenians in the shaping of the Home Rule movement.

Parnell declared at Waterford in January that the Home Rule movement owed its existence to 'the upheaval of feeling on behalf of those imprisoned sufferers in 1870 . . . they are the men whose sufferings led to the foundation of our movement and without whom we should be nought'. At Listowel in September, Parnell went so far as to assert 'it would be no exaggeration of me to say that to the question of amnesty belongs most of the success which has attended the constitutional movement of later years'. This a flagging Parnell, in limp and hackneyed vein, attributed to the patriotic inspiration afforded by Fenian prisoners at a time when parliamentary politics were sunk in disfavour.

> It was the sacrifices and the sufferings of the men of '65 which kept alive during many long years the spirit of Nationality in the heart of the Irish people. If the betrayal of Keogh and Sadlier in 1852 had caused the hottest Irishmen to despair of the future of the country, these men in those days did not despair, and the national spirit of Irishmen burned with renewed vigour as a consequence of their enterprise and their sufferings (*cheers*). For them there were no honours and rewards; for them there was no applause of crowded public meetings; for them there was no seat in Parliament, which many of your latter-day Nationalists think the crown of the Irish patriot's ambition.[31]

Parnell at Limehouse in May similarly contrived to pay historic tribute to Fenianism in adumbrating a 'history of Irish reform'. The achievement of reform in Irish history was due to 'the courage and union of the Irish people alone':

> . . . no English statesman, from Gladstone to Balfour, has ever done anything for Ireland until he had first tried by imprisonment, persecutions, by penal servitude — aye, and by executions — to destroy the unity of our race and the independence of our people (*applause*). That is the history of Irish reform, and the English friends who come here tonight to instruct us in Irish politics [a reference to hecklers] do not know the history of Catholic Emancipation early in the century, when it would not be conceded by England to Ireland until the English Ministry told the Sovereign and the Parliament that unless it was conceded Ireland would be lost to England (*applause*). They forget the history of the passage of the Irish Church Act, and of the Land Acts of 1867 and 1870, when these measures were yielded to the intensity of Fenianism which were denied to the considerations of justice (*applause*). It was not until — to use Mr. Gladstone's own words — 'the explosion at Clerkenwell had tolled the chapel bell' that even his conscience was awakened to the terrible injustice and crime of supporting an alien Church of Ireland out of the pockets of the masses of the Catholic people (*applause*).[32]

Parnell's dubious 'history of Irish reform' promiscuously linked Parnellism with O'Connell and with Butt, and pointedly if obliquely with Fenianism, in terms with which it was difficult for any contemporary nationalist to take exception, availing of the admitted effect of the Clerkenwell explosion in arousing Gladstone's conscience to an awareness of injustice in Ireland.

Parnell's veiled tribute to Fenianism, archly couched in the form of an historical acknowledgement, arguably went further than his political purposes rendered strictly necessary or desirable. Yet it presented also the creative obverse of Parnell's so-called 'appeal to the hillsides', whereby he sought, as he had throughout his career, to embrace Fenianism within an ambitiously conceived constitutional movement. It was a renewal of one of the classic motions of Parnellism, the implicating gesture, the drawing inward of Fenianism to within a unitary nationalist movement. In according to Fenianism a deliberately exaggerated measure of credit for the success of nationalism under his leadership, Parnell was seeking to encompass Fenianism within a quintessentially Parnellian synthesis.

To assess adequately the rapprochement between Parnell and Fenianism it is necessary to consider the nature of the Fenian allegiance which Parnell attracted, and in particular the politics of John O'Leary, James Stephens, and other Fenians in the split, an essay in the renewal of the complex equivocality with which Parnell was regarded within the Fenian movement. That in turn requires a reconsideration of the nature of contemporary Fenianism. Twentieth-century nationalist and republican ideologues have obscured the complex and diverse character of late nineteenth-century Fenianism, and the sharp discontinuities which demarcate Fenianism in the era of Parnell from its professed successor movements, discontinuities so sharp as to render problematic and tendentious the concept of a 'Fenian tradition'. That calculated ideological misrepresentation has influenced *à rebours* modern liberal historiography, eventuating in the tendency to project anachronistically on to the Parnell era the malaise of twentieth-century Irish republicanism.

What united Fenians of the old school was a commitment to Irish independence, in the attainment of which they were willing to countenance a resort to physical force. Their conception of legitimate physical force was however so severely circumscribed ethically and so militarily obsolete as to render it somewhat platonic. Old Fenians such as John O'Leary adhered to a severely chivalric code of martial honour. Even James Stephens, the most intransigent keeper of the physical force flame outside the United States, discountenanced atrocities and was wedded to an engagingly archaic concept of open military engagement. He remained unswervingly faithful to the single strategy of the 'battle on Irish soil'. 'I have never believed', he declared quixotically, 'in anything but a stand-up fight'.[33] The first stirrings of a dynamite strategy, prefiguring modern terrorism, elicited the sharp disapprobation and disdain of the old guard. Irish-American extremists such as O'Donovan Rossa had no fiercer critic than John O'Leary.

The high Fenianism of O'Leary and others moreover was not confined to the espousal of national independence, but extended to a deep hostility to the political influence of the Catholic clergy (as well as latterly of the substantial tenant farmers), to the point where one dispassionate contemporary looked to Fenianism as 'the bulwark of the civil rights of the Irish laity',[34] a prophecy of which the split can be considered a partial fulfilment. This pertains to the neglected radical aspect of Fenianism, which was to be subsequently betrayed.

The condition of Fenianism in 1890-91 was of decline and disarray, a state of affairs brought about by the objective predicament of a movement which lacked any discernible strategy with which to confront the changing prospect of Irish politics. That predicament had been excruciatingly sharpened by Parnell himself, whose masterly pursuit of a parliamentary strategy consummated the eclipse of Fenianism. In the words of one of the most perceptive chroniclers of Fenianism, 'Parnell had crowded the IRB out of public life, and out of the public mind in Ireland'.[35]

Parnell in the split commanded extensive Fenian support. A substantial minority of the Dublin Parnell Leadership Committee were members of the Irish Republican Brotherhood, while others were sympathisers, and this pattern was reproduced across the country. While not formally sanctioned by the Supreme Council of the IRB, the support of Parnell by individual Fenians was openly connived at, and influential members of the Supreme Council such as O'Leary, Wyse-Power and P.N. Fitzgerald were themselves active Parnellites.[36]

Fenian support for Parnell represented a much-needed accretion of campaigning strength, partly compensating for the drastically atrophied state of the post-split National League, and the active opposition of the clergy. The principal purpose of the establishment of a network of Parnell Leadership Committees standing outside the formal structure of the National League was presumably to accommodate Fenian scruples, so as to permit Fenians to adhere to the Parnellite organisation without being obliged actually to join the National League.

Parnell in the split enjoyed the support of men formerly opposed to him. P.N. Fitzgerald for example had been described by Davitt in evidence to the Special Commission as 'a very extreme man . . . a bitter opponent of the Land League and Mr. Parnell's policy'.[37] Yet while Fitzgerald was an opponent of Parnell, he was one of the 'advanced' men with whom Parnell had throughout his career remained on speaking terms. Parnell told the Special Commission that Fitzgerald was one of his Cork constituents, and 'an advanced man who is very much opposed to my policy and to the Land League from first to last . . . He considers that we are demoralising the Irish people and drawing them away from the true path'. He was on personally friendly terms with Fitzgerald and they conversed whenever they met: 'He always tries to reason me out of the errors of my ways and I try to reason with him and neither of us has any success'.[38] Parnell's evidence illumines the nature of the Parnellite-Fenian axis in the split: rather than an abrupt *volte-face*, a sharp resiling from constitutional purposes, Parnell in the split sought to turn to political advantage those relations which he had always taken care to maintain with influential Fenians and 'advanced' men individually.

Parnell, the *Spectator* wrote close to the end, had 'nothing respectable left him, except Mr. O'Leary and the old-fashioned Fenians — a body of men not numerous but composed in part of really high-minded men'.[39]

Underlying John O'Leary's adherence to Parnell's cause in the split was a deep and complex affinity between the two men masked in the prior history of their relations. O'Leary had resisted overtures from Parnell at the outset of his political career to endorse his parliamentary policy, then in its early obstructionist phase, and had held aloof from the New Departure, proclaiming that the Fenians were not 'a transacting party'.[40]

The split rejuvenated the sixty-year-old O'Leary, and liberated him from the dogmatic aloofness he had previously felt obliged to maintain from Parnell: 'I condemned many things he said and did in the past, and I condemn them still, but I have ever held that in him, and in him alone, rested all our hopes from constitutional action'.[41] O'Leary returned from London, where he had been living, to campaign for Parnell. He became an active Parnellite, joining the Parnell Leadership Committee and becoming a member of the working executive of its fund. He collaborated with Parnell: significantly he was reported as engaged in a lengthy consultation with Parnell at Westminster after Dillon and O'Brien had on their release declared against Parnell. He was to be, with James Stephens, a prominent mourner at Parnell's funeral.[42]

O'Leary was prompted to rally to Parnell's defence in the first instance by the Gladstone letter, declaring that Parnell 'is not now other than he was because Mr. Gladstone and the whole howling voice of prurient British hypocrisy has been heard'.[43] The support of O'Leary and other Fenians owed much to Parnell's abiding capacity, in the fierce strength of his resolve, to engage Fenian respect. Their support reflected a romantic predilection for Parnell's independent strength of character as against the conformism of the anti-Parnellite 'combination'. Thus of the Parnell manifesto O'Leary wrote that 'there was a man — whether a good or a bad one was beside the point — behind it: But what is behind the manifesto of the now notorious forty-five? Simply an old woman, or possibly several, for a more nerveless, boneless, sapless production I never remember to have read'.[44] This response was shared by W.H. Mitchel, brother of John Mitchel, who prior to his death in January 1891 twice endorsed Parnell in the split.[45] Mitchel declared that Ireland would be slow 'to replace his strong affirmative personality by a committee of negatives', observing that while Parnell was not blameless, his virtues outweighed his vices: 'Moreover his faults are common, while his virtues are rare'. Parnell was to be preferred to his opponents: 'Against him are all the big wigs, all the political wiseacres, all the specious reasoners, all the high-collared respectabilities'.[46] In like vein, Arthur Griffith twenty years later condemned the replacement of Parnell by a committee, substituting for his judgement 'the conglomerate wisdom of the Irish party'.[47] The most dramatic, almost Carlylean, statement of Parnell's faculty to enlist support on the strength of his human qualities, which informed the allegiance of many Fenians, came ironically from a Parnellite priest, Nicholas Murphy, in 1895: 'Parnell may have had many sins but one sin he had not, that of cant. With all his dross he was a man, fiery, real, from the great fire-bosom of nature itself'.[48]

There is an important and neglected second dimension to the rapprochement of Parnell and O'Leary in the split. O'Leary was and remained the most trenchant adversary of agrarian nationalism, of which his critique strikingly complemented Parnell's policy on land purchase in the split. O'Leary forcefully articulated the distaste of the Fenians of the old guard for agrarian agitation — the commingling of nationalism and the drive for proprietorship which they believed to detract from the integrity of Irish nationalism. O'Leary in 1883 denounced Parnellite agrarian publicists as 'a set of loose principled agitators as have ever disgraced Irish politics'.[49] With the Plan of Campaign his distaste intensified. O'Leary forswore sympathy for 'these pets of the agitators — the strong farmers', and morally disapproved of the withholding of rents.[50] O'Leary carried his attack on the Plan of Campaign and its progenitors into the politics of the split. He denounced the debacle of the Smith Barry tenants in Tipperary as the result of 'a piece of cowardly cruelty on the part of Mr. William O'Brien with no intellectual reason behind it save that of lying to England' — which was to say, misrepresenting the condition of Ireland for the supposed benefit of the Liberal-nationalist alliance.[51]

O'Leary in March 1891 actually challenged Parnell publicly to justify his continued support of the 'New Tipperary' project, the most self-evidently disastrous demarche of the Plan of Campaign, which he denounced as 'this tragic farce'.[52] He thus prefigured and helped to inspire the increasing vehemence of Parnell's condemnation of the Plan of Campaign. Parnell's position on the Plan of Campaign and the implicit critique of the excesses of agrarianism which underlay his rhetoric in the split, conformed increasingly to that of O'Leary and other Fenian critics of agrarian nationalism. Behind Parnell and O'Leary's opposition to the Plan of Campaign lay a common concern with the disposition of social power in Ireland, and a shared apprehension of the predominance of a Catholic nationalist proprietorial order.

O'Leary's support for Parnell was not uncritical. As if somewhat defensively asserting the doctrinal soundness of Fenian support for Parnell, he declared in mid-September 1891:

... if Mr. Parnell were dead tomorrow, I and men like me, who are above and before all things Irish nationalists, should never dream of following the party of clerical dictation and compromise with England. We go with Mr. Parnell so far as he goes, and insofar as he goes, for Irish freedom.

This argument strikingly complemented Parnell's almost contemporaneous declaration at Listowel on 13 September ('If I were dead and gone tomorrow, the men who are fighting against English influence in Irish public life would fight on still'). O'Leary thereby insisted that his endorsement of Parnell was not purely a matter of personal allegiance, but involved an issue of principle, which the nature of the forces arrayed against Parnell threw into high relief.[53]

Parnell's ally of old, John Devoy, in the United States, rallied to his defence, cabling at the outset: 'Retirement means chaos, leaving Ireland at mercy of English whims and Irish cranks. Retention involves temporary hurt but ensures final victory'. Devoy however proved unable to fulfil his promise of increased financial support from Irish Americans, reflecting Parnell's general failure to attract the financial assistance he had hoped for from American nationalists. Devoy's endorsement of Parnell proved unavailing, as did his peace initiative of August-September 1891.[54]

In September 1891 the old Fenian leader James Stephens returned to Ireland from Paris, like a phantom from the picaresque *demi-monde* of Fenian exiles, but one whose legendary intransigence had sanctified his name among extreme and sentimental nationalists alike. Stephens had declared for Parnell at the outset of the split, and his return to Ireland was sponsored by Parnellite sympathisers. *United Ireland* established a fund to purchase a cottage for Stephens in Ireland, to which, if the paper is to be believed, Parnell very shortly before his death telegraphed an endorsement and forwarded a subscription. The Parnellites ostentatiously feted 'the old rebel chief' on his return. *United Ireland* archly declared that Stephens would be consoled to learn that 'though Fenian methods are not the methods of our times, at least Fenian courage and Fenian spirit, and Fenian nationality are not dead today'.[55]

Stephens returned to Ireland on 28 September on the ship on which Parnell was making his last crossing to Ireland. While according to *United Ireland* they had 'long been anxious to meet each other', each was unaware of the other's presence. Three days later Parnell was at his request privately introduced by a Parnellite MP, Patrick O'Brien, to Stephens at a cottage in Sandycove, outside Dublin. The fact of this meeting was only disclosed by O'Brien on the third anniversary of Parnell's death. O'Brien recalled a rather flat exchange:

'I am indeed proud to know you, Parnell, and I am sorry we did not meet sooner in life, as we might have done something for the freedom of

Ireland,' was the salutation of the venerable rebel as he grasped the hand of Parnell, who replied, 'Yes Mr. Stephens, and I am sorry too, for I believe we could have done much together'.[56]

There is no reason to doubt O'Brien's assertion, published in Stephens' lifetime, that the encounter took place. It accounts for Stephens' otherwise inexplicable references to Parnell as his friend: he cabled to the National Club the day after the death of 'my revered personal friend and the noblest Roman of them all', and later, weeping over the death of 'the noblest Irishman of our time', laid a wreath on Parnell's grave inscribed to the memory of 'my sincere friend'.[57]

The assignation recalled the 'New Departure' (to which, however, Stephens had not himself been a party). It is above all a demonstration of Parnell's unremitting tenacity, less than two weeks before his death, in his declared purpose of starting over again from the beginning his work of creating an independent Irish party. The meeting was not, in the phrase the Dublin *Daily Express* applied to Parnell's visit to Tralee in January, a revisiting of 'the glimpses of the moon'.[58] It did not represent the affirmation of a mystical nexus with Fenianism. Rather Parnell, without derogating from his constitutional purpose, was reworking his old formula and mechanically amid the ruins of his leadership re-laying the foundations of his power.

Turning away from the 'old guard', Frederick J. Allan, a prominent young Fenian and radical activist in Dublin, rationalised Fenian allegiance to Parnell in more progressive terms. He asserted that even the sympathy for Parnell created by the Gladstone letter could not have assured him of the active Fenian support he received, which was elicited rather by the intervention of the Irish Catholic hierarchy of the 'English' side. Extreme nationalists had, Allan argued, for generations struggled to break the alliance of the Catholic church and English power: 'When therefore, the real fight in Parnellism burst upon us, it found many of us only too ready to carry out into the open a battle which for so long had been kept beneath the surface, and in which the clergy had hitherto all the advantage of position, and every opportunity of choosing their ground'. He considered that Parnell's Rotunda speech had 'contained nothing that really would carry the support of Irish Revolutionists', but that the domestic struggle against ecclesiastical influence took precedence and determined Fenian allegiance:

> ... those men, whose vision was quickened by bitter experience, knew as they stood beside Parnell that night that the real issue in the Parnellite fight was to be fought out in Ireland, and would not be with England, but with that power in Ireland which had thrown in its lot with the British Government in every great crisis of our national life.[59]

Allan's views, while reflecting radical nationalist opinion in Dublin rather

than mainstream Fenian sentiment, convey the significance of Fenian opposition to the political role of the Catholic church in determining Fenians'
support of Parnell in the split.

More representatively, an unnamed 'physical force man' and acquaintance of Parnell's sought, after Parnell's death, to account for what he lucidly
described as the phenomenon of Fenians rallying to Parnell 'even while it
seemed to bring them deeper and deeper into courses that they would never
have taken but for him'. The cause of this seemingly perverse allegiance lay,
he suggested, in Parnell's 'thinly veiled hatred of England', and in the
treachery of his opponents. Perhaps, the writer surmised, 'it was because he
never degraded the deep national feelings of Ireland'.[60] The candid concession of this Fenian obituarist that Fenian support for Parnell compromised
Fenians rather than Parnell is to be contrasted with a markedly cruder
assessment of Parnell written six years later, which reflects the emergence
of an extreme nationalist myth of Parnell: '... the farther we recede from his
epoch the clearer becomes his personality, and the higher he towers above
his contemporaries . . . Instead of growing timid, like some other constitutional leaders, he developed bolder national views as he advanced'.[61] Such
were the perspectival tricks of nationalist historical retrospect: the further
nationalist ideologues receded from the era of Parnell the more readily could
his political purpose be misconstrued in terms of their own agenda.

Fenian allegiance to Parnell is probably best interpreted in terms of
instinct rather than any belief that Parnell was making any substantive
concession to Fenianism. Those Fenians who adhered to the Parnellite cause
in the split were motivated by a respect for Parnell personally, and for the
fierce resolve which marked his style of constitutional politics, which did
not exhibit the demeaning political beggary and social deference towards
English politicians which Fenians regarded as the endemic vices of parliamentary nationalism. Fenian support for the Parnell of the split cannot be
adequately accounted for in terms of what would have been, in Fenian terms,
an ideologically highly dubious gamble on Parnell forsaking constitutional
action. The most cursory consideration of the earlier course of Parnell's
career could have left Fenians under few illusions about Parnell's tenacity
of purpose as a constitutional politician. He had ruthlessly subordinated
Fenianism as a political force before, and there was little reason to believe
he would not do so again. Dillon, years later, wrote admiringly of 'the steely
fibre of Parnell, who did not fear or hesitate to fight Fenians at the election
of 1880, altho' it was they who created his movement'.[62]

It is true that Fenianism stood to gain from the sundering of the Irish party,
and in the event of Parnell's final defeat, from the bitterness and disillusion-
ment of his followers. If such considerations cannot have failed to influence
Fenians in the split, there is little in the ardour of Fenian support for Parnell
in the split to suggest that such cold revolutionary calculation was uppermost

in their minds. Fenian support for Parnell in the split was more gratuitous than might appear. The objective circumstances of the split, a contest which pitted Parnell against Gladstone, the Church and the forces of conservative Catholic nationalism represented by Healy and the Sullivans, sufficed to ensure Parnell of a high degree of Fenian support. What occurred was a reprise of the tactics which Parnell had adopted at the outset of his career, strikingly conveyed in Davitt's description of Parnell's relations with Fenians at the time of the New Departure: 'Parnell *shut his eyes* and held out his hand for money and help'.[63] What was termed Parnell's 'appeal to the hillsides' was largely by way of a guarded reciprocating gesture. Fenian backing for Parnell was inspired by respect for Parnell as a politician whose integrity as a nationalist they believed uncompromised by parliamentary action, as evidenced by his break with Gladstone. That backing was moulded by common enmities and antagonisms, and sealed in the split's deepening controversy.

While a later generation of more doctrinaire nationalist ideologues would seek to divert the Parnell myth to their own purposes, and lay claim to his political legacy, their treatment of his historical persona revealed a guardedness and a wilful preciseness which suggests an inhibiting awareness of how close Parnell had come to success by parliamentary methods, and an intimation of the awkward implications which a consideration of his career raised for their political project. 'The pale and angry ghost of Parnell' was narrowly edged out of the curious nationalist pantheon devised by Patrick Pearse, which comprised Wolfe Tone, Thomas Davis, James Fintan Lalor, and John Mitchel. Parnell stood on its threshold. Slipping elusively from argument into imagery, Pearse described Parnell as 'less a political thinker than an embodied conviction; a flame that seared, a sword that stabbed'. Parnell's instinct was, he asserted, 'a Separatist instinct'.[64] P.S. O'Hegarty, conceding that Parnell was a constitutional leader, and kept strictly within the constitutional framework, added that he was a constitutional leader with what he described as 'the root of Nationalism firmly within him, who used constitutional language in the tone and temper and with the intellect of a Separatist'.[65] More straightforwardly, using Parnell as a stick with which to beat his successors in the leadership of the Irish party, Arthur Griffith laid down what became an axiomatic proposition of Sinn Féin: 'the era of constitutional possibilities for Irish Nationality ended on the day Charles Stewart Parnell died'.[66]

Parnell's rhetoric was misconstrued, originally in the polemical onslaught of Healy and Davitt, devised to marginalise Parnell in the split, and in a curious collusive dialectic thereafter magnified in the myth of Parnell fostered after his death by extreme nationalist ideologues, which has served in turn to provoke the excessive acerbity of the assessment of the Parnell of the split in modern liberal historiography. There was an 'appeal to the hillsides' in the sense of a play by Parnell for Fenian support. However the term, insofar as it is used to suggest a resiling by Parnell from constitutional purposes, is profoundly misleading. Parnell in the split struggled desperately to turn to his advantage what had been perceived as his unique strength as a nationalist leader, what William O'Brien had termed 'Mr. Parnell's peculiar quality, that he exercised a spell over extreme and moderate men alike'.[67] He was not engaged in the undoing of what was his greatest achievement, vaunted in his observation to Alfred Robbins that while he was depicted as a dangerous revolutionary, he had ensured that the Irish people espoused constitutional courses: 'If it had not been for our movement most of them would have become Fenians long before this'.[68] However ruthless or vehement Parnell's rhetoric in the split, it remained squarely within the grid of parliamentary politics, subordinated to his purpose of reconstituting his authority as the leader of a constitutional nationalist movement. Throughout the split, he did not cease to speak as the prospective premier of a Home Rule Ireland.

The 'appeal to the hillsides' is central to any re-assessment of Parnell's campaign in the split (conventionally dismissed as a lapse into frenzied and opportunistic incoherence) and to a retrieval of the lost integrity of his career. His last campaign, although it was not to bring him victory, affords a classic study in his political technique, and exemplifies his unique capacity as a nationalist leader. It is due as much to his unflinching professionalism as a politician whose purpose was tempered by the enlightened scepticism of power, as to the romantic *éclat* of his personal tragedy, that the remembrance of Parnell should have outlasted the longest of Irish centuries.

Notes

1. *Westminster Gazette*, 30 Sept. 1893, Letters from Ireland, Avondale, Part II.
2. *Freeman's Journal, 17 Dec. 1890.*
3. *Freeman's Journal,22 Dec. 1891, Kilkenny.*
4. *Freeman's Journal, 18 Mar. 1891.*
5. *Freeman's Journal, 22 June 1891, Balbriggan.*
6. *Freeman's Journal, 9 Mar. 1891.*
7. *Freeman's Journal, 22 June 1891.*
8. *Freeman's Journal, 23 Feb. 1891, Longford.*
9. *Freeman's Journal, 23 May 1891, Belfast; 22 June 1891, Balbriggan.*
10. *Freeman's Journal*, 28 Apr. 1891, Tipperary banquet.
11. *Daily Express*, 22 Dec. 1890, Kilkenny.
12. *Freeman's Journal, 21 Apr. 1891, Ballina.*
13. *St. James' Gazette*, 7 Oct. 1895, quoted *United Ireland*, 12 Oct. 1894. The article is unfortunately anonymous, but purports to be an account of the latter part of Parnell's Creggs speech omitted when the evening ran late and the reporters left for Dublin.
14. *Freeman's Journal*, 29 Nov. 1890.

15. Quoted in Henry Harrison, 'Memories of an Irish Hero', *Listener*, 22 Mar. 1951, vol. 45, pp. 445-6.
16. *Nation*, 30 June 1877, 6 Nov. 1880, quoted in F.S.L. Lyons, 'Political Ideas of Parnell', *Historical Journal*, XVI, 4 (1973) p. 754.
17. *Freeman's Journal*, 19 Jan. 1891, quoting speech of 9 Nov. 1878. Parnell at Kildare warned against 'the very powerful engines of contamination which the English parties have ready at hand' (*Freeman's Journal*, 24 Dec. 1890).
18. *Freeman's Journal*, 24 May 1889.
19. F.S.L. Lyons, *Charles Stewart Parnell* (London, 1977, Repr. 1978), pp. 444-5; see also C.C. O'Brien, *Parnell and His Party* (Oxford, 1957), p. 234, n.1.
20. *Manchester Guardian*, 8 Oct. 1891.
21. *Freeman's Journal*, 12 Jan. 1891, Limerick; *Freeman's Journal*, 26 Jan. 1891, Waterford.
22. *Freeman's Journal*, 27 Feb. 1891.
23. *Freeman's Journal*, 6 Apr. 1891, Phoenix Park.
24. *Hansard*, vol. 356, cols. 443-9 (27 July 1891).
25. *Hansard*, vol. 356, cols. 1171-4 (3 Aug. 1891).
26. *Hansard*, vol. 356, cols. 363-70 (24 July 1891); cols. 443-9 (27 July 1891); cols. 1170-4 (3 Aug. 1891). See also *Irish Weekly Independent*, 10 Oct. 1896, Frank McDonagh, 'Parnell in Parliament . . . Maiden Speech and Last Words'. Even after Parnell's death, amnesty endured as a Parnellite theme: Redmond charged in 1894 that Parnell would have succeeded in prevailing upon the Conservative Home Secretary to grant amnesty were it not for the opposition of Harcourt, the Parnellite *bête noire* (*Irish Weekly Independent, 6 Oct. 1894, J.E. Redmond, 'Mr. Parnell and Amnesty'*).
27. *National Press*, 12 Aug. 1891.
28. *National Press*, 28 Aug. 1891.
29. *National Press*, 2 Sept. 1891, O'Brien to *National Press*, d. 1 Sept. ; *Freeman's Journal*, 3 Sept. 1891, Parnell to *Freeman's Journal*, d. 2 Sept.
30. See *Irish Weekly Independent*, Oct. 1894, F.J. Allan, 'Parnell's Legacy'.
31. *Freeman's Journal*, 14 Sept. 1891.
32. *Freeman's Journal*, 14 May 1891.
33. *Freeman's Journal*, 21 Feb. 1881, interview.
34. T.W. Rolleston, 'The Archbishop in Politics', *Dublin University Review*, Feb. 1886, p. 103; noted, C.C. O'Brien, *Parnell and His Party*, p. 130 n.1.
35. P.S. O'Hegarty, *A History of Ireland under the Union* (London, 1952), p. 633.
36. Marcus Bourke, *John O'Leary* (Tralee, 1967), pp. 204-5.
37. *Special Commission Proceedings*, vol. 9, pp. 440-9, 8708, 3 July 1889.
38. *Special Commission Proceedings*, vol. 7, p. 276, q. 61, 670-5, 7 May 1889.
39. *Spectator*, 26 Sept. 1891.
40. T.P. O'Connor, *Charles Stewart Parnell, A Memory* (London, 1891), p. 52; Katharine Tynan, *Twenty-Five Years* (London, 1913), p. 77.
41. *Freeman's Journal*, 10 Mar. 1891, 'O'Leary to the honorary secretaries of the Parnell Leadership Committee', d. 7 Mar. 1891.
42. Marcus Bourke, *John O'Leary* (Tralee, 1967), pp. 202-3; Katharine Tynan, *The Middle Years* (London, 1916), p. 25; *Freeman's Journal*, 10 Mar. 1891; *Freeman's Journal*, 6 Aug. 1891.

43. *Freeman's Journal*, 1 Dec. 1890, O'Leary to *Freeman's Journal*, d. 30 Nov.
    O'Leary is almost certainly the 'old Fenian leader' referred to by R.
    Barry O'Brien who attributed his action in supporting Parnell to the Gladstone
    letter: R.B. O'Brien, *The Life of Charles Stewart Parnell* (2 vols., London,
    1899), ii, pp. 252-7.
44. *Freeman's Journal*, 13 Dec. 1891, O'Leary to *Freeman's Journal*, d. 12 Dec.
45. *Freeman's Journal*, 23 Jan. 1891.
46. *Freeman's Journal*, 16 Dec. 1891, Mitchel to *Freeman's Journal*, d. 12 Dec.
47. *Sinn Féin*, 7 Oct. 1911.
48. *Irish Weekly Independent*, 28 Sept. 1895, Nicholas Murphy to *Irish Weekly
    Independent*,
49. John O'Leary to John Devoy, d. 9 Nov. 1882, in William O'Brien and
    Desmond Ryan (eds.) *Devoy's Post Bag* (Dublin, 1948, 1953), 2 vols, ii, p.
    222.
50. *Nation*, 27 Sept. 1890; see Marcus Bourke, *John O'Leary* (Tralee, 1967), pp.
    195-9.
51. *Freeman's Journal*, 8 Jan. 1891, O'Leary to *Freeman's Journal*, 7 Jan. 1891.
52. *Freeman's Journal*, 19 Mar. 1891.
53. *Freeman's Journal*, 15 Sept. 1891, O'Leary to *Freeman's Journal*, 14 Sept.
    1891; quoted in*Times*, 16 Sept. 1891. Marcus Bourke is surely wrong to
    interpret this avowal as reflecting a waning of enthusiasm for Parnellism on
    O'Leary's part and a reversion to old certitudes (Bourke, op. cit., p. 206).
54. O'Brien and Ryan, op. cit., pp. 316-29; T.D. Williams, 'John Devoy and
    Jeremiah O'Donovan Rossa' in T. W. Moody (ed.), *The Fenian Movement*
    (Dublin, 1978), p. 96.
55. *United Irishman*, 3, 10 Oct. 1891; *Freeman's Journal*, 27 Apr. 1891.
56. *Irish Weekly Independent*, 7 Oct. 1892, Patrick O'Brien, 'Two Irish
    Chieftains: The Old Guard and the New'.
57. *Daily Express*, 8 Oct. 1891; *United Irishman*, 31 Oct. 1891; *Freeman's
    Journal*, 26 Oct. 1891. The meeting provides the missing link in Owen
    Dudley Edwards' account of the interrelationship of the careers of Parnell and
    Stephens in his postscript, 'Stephens and Parnell', to Desmond Ryan's *The
    Fenian Chief* (Dublin, 1967). Parnell in 1880 had briefly met Jeremiah
    O'Donovan Rossa, the most extreme of physical force nationalists. He
    disclosed to the Special Commission that he had met Rossa in the breakfast
    room of the Philadelphia Hotel where he was staying and had 'a few minutes
    conversation' with him. Parnell was surprisingly not pressed further on this.
    He instructed his own counsel that the introduction had been effected by his
    rampantly Anglophobic American mother: 'I came down to breakfast and saw
    him talking to my mother who introduced him to me'. (*S.C.P.*, vol. 7, p. 58, q.
    58, 992 [1 May, 1889]); *Special Commission Brief*, NLI, Parnell Proofs, p. 57.
58. *Daily Express*, 17 Jan. 1891.
59. *Irish Weekly Review*, 6 Oct. 1894, F.J. Allan, 'Parnell's Legacy'.
60. *United Irishman.*, 10 Oct. 1891, 'Mr. Parnell as I knew him' by 'A Physical
    Force Man'.
61. *United Irishman*, 9 Oct. 1891, 'The Chief's Tactics'.
62. Dillon to O'Connor, Dillon Papers, TCD Ms. 6744, f. 970. The context was an

unfavourable contrast of Ramsay Macdonald with Parnell.

63. Davitt to R. Barry O'Brien, 6 Dec. 1893, Davitt Papers, TCD Ms. 9377.
64. Patrick Pearse, 'Ghosts' (Dec. 1915), in *Collected Works of Pádraic H. Pearse, Political Writings and Speeches* (Dublin and London, 1922, p. 241).
65. P. S. O'Hegarty, *A History of Ireland Under the Union* (London, 1952), p. 597.
66. *United Irishman.*, 8 April 1899.
67. *Special Commission Brief*, NLI, O'Brien Proofs, p. 27.
68. *Birmingham Daily Post*, 8 Oct. 1891.

ABOVE: "Conspicuous moderation" — "Our speech is now as smooth and soft as one of William's collars. The only 'big, big D's' we know are dynamite and dollars."

BELOW: "Coercion" — "We are all patriots of the stamp that brag and run away; Whene'er we see a Bobby's lamp we call another day!"

Cartoons from *The Irish Green Book*

Charles Stewart Parnell and his Doctors

J.B. Lyons

Doctors stand in history's obscure corners saying little about their prominent patients. This is in keeping with the traditional confidentiality of medical practice and if an individual doctor ventures to 'tell all', as Lord Moran did about Winston Churchill, his disclosures may elicit protest. Just a few years ago, Dr Stephen Lock, editor of the *British Medical Journal*, was rapped across the knuckles by the General Medical Council, the official body responsible for the supervision of medical ethics, when an obituary notice in his journal revealed that General Orde Wingate, the legendary leader of the Chindits, attempted to cut his throat when deranged by cerebral malaria. Dr Lock did not accept the unexpected reprimand for the alleged breach of medical secrecy, and the ensuing controversy appears to indicate that relaxation of close secrecy is justifiable sooner or later, where public figures are concerned.[1] A 'thirty year rule' was mooted but it may be argued that there are advantages in publishing records during the lifetimes of contemporaries whose comments may be valuable.[2]

Sufficient time, almost a century, has elapsed since the death of Charles Stewart Parnell to place that unexpected event well beyond the limits of the strictest sanctions. Nobody is likely to object to my review of his health. It is, indeed, surprising that Parnell's theatrically appropriate demise has received so little scrutiny.[3] New facts are no longer likely to be adduced but consideration of the known clinical features of his illness in the light of modern knowledge may be informative.

Could his death have been avoided? And if he had survived would he, like Daniel O'Connell and Isaac Butt, have lived on to experience political extinction in senility? I shall not attempt to answer the second question but I hope to supply a credible diagnosis and I shall say a little about the doctors who attended him. The closest to Parnell was Dr J.E. Kenny, a fellow-prisoner in Kilmainham where Dr William Carte, the prison Medical Officer, was also in attendance. Sir Henry Thompson FRCS, a leading London urologist, was first consulted by Parnell in 1886 at the insistence of Mrs O'Shea who 'had heard that he was very clever'. During the fatal illness a Dr Towers of Brighton was called.

Doctors

Charles Stewart Parnell was born in Avondale, Rathdrum, Co. Wicklow, on

27 June 1846. While at school in Yeovil, Somerset, he contracted typhoid fever, then an endemic disease. His medical attendants at that time remain unnamed but the illness was followed by a phase of emotional or nervous instability and the boy was taken by his parents to be seen by Dr Forbes Winslow, a Cavendish Square alienist, author of *Health and Body and Mind*. Some time later Parnell came down with scarlet fever.

Joseph Edward Kenny was born in Dublin in 1845 and was thus almost Parnell's exact contemporary. By 1881, when they were both lodged in Kilmainham jail, to their mutual political interests had been added the bond of a doctor-patient relationship. Kenny was a well-established practitioner, having studied at the Catholic University Medical School, Cecilia Street, graduating LAH in 1868 and taking the diplomas of the College of Physicians and Surgeons of Edinburgh two years later. He was then living at 71 Lower Gardiner Street and was Medical Officer to the North Dublin Union Hospital. During the smallpox epidemic of 1872, he was placed in charge of the fever huts and was commended for his handling of the situation.

Elected to the Executive Committee of the Land League on 21 December 1880, Dr Kenny's patients included a number of politicians whom he was permitted to visit when they were jailed. He travelled to Portland to see Michael Davitt on 3 March 1881 and again in June and went to Naas to visit Andy Kettle, whose transfer to Kilmainham he recommended. He attended his sick patients in Kilmainham regularly. When unable to do so, he sent his brother, Dr Robert D. Kenny, in his place. Less involved in the political sphere, Dr R.D. Kenny was featured in *Ulysses* by James Joyce, whose mother was his patient — 'Dr Bob Kenny is attending her'.

Parnell was jailed on 13 October 1881 and on October 24th the warrant for Dr J.E. Kenny's arrest as 'suspect' under the Protection of Persons and Property Act was enforced and he was taken to Kilmainham. He was dismissed by a sealed order of the Local Government Board from his post at the North Dublin Union Hospital but as a measure of ironic compensation was now in a position to observe patients who were fellow-prisoners more closely. The official medical officer at Kilmainham jail since 1880 was Dr William Carte and while his professional relationship with Kenny seems to have remained amicable, their points of view were widely separated. They clashed on several occasions in their expressions of opinion and like Dr Robert Gover, the chief medical inspector of the English Prison Board, who felt that Kenny's fears for Davitt's health were not genuine but directed towards seeking his release, Carte may have listened to Kenny with a measure of incredulity.

Carte was not by any means in the tradition established by his 18th-century predecessor, Dr Trevor, whom Freida Kelly in her *History of Kilmainham Gaol* calls 'the atrocious Dr Edward Trevor'. Born in August 1830 at Woodlawn, Newcastle, Co. Limerick, William Carte was reared in

Tasmania but obtained his professional education at the Royal College of Surgeons in Ireland. He graduated in 1852 and proceeded to the Fellowship in 1874, having meanwhile served in the Crimea. He held the post of surgeon to the Royal Hospital, Kilmainham, from 1859 until his death in 1899. A vice-president of the RCSI, his commercial interests included the Dublin Tramway Company (of which he was chairman), the Civil Service Building Society and other companies.[4]

The State Paper Office holds copies of the reports Dr Kenny issued after his visits to Kilmainham and those written during his own imprisonment when sometimes he sat up all night if John Dillon or Michael Boyton were acutely ill. His petitions to the General Prisons Board for their release usually elicited contradictory assessments from Carte but Kenny's persistence resulted in the eventual discharge from prison of Dillon, Boyton and Andy Kettle.[5]

On 15 November 1881, Dr Kenny expressed alarm about Parnell's loss of appetite, insomnia and sciatica. 'As I may find it necessary to Faradise Mr Parnell [he wrote] and perhaps give him Hypodermic Injections of Morphia after he goes to bed at night I have to request permission to visit him at night at 8 o'clock or 8.30 o'clock p.m.' Two days later he reported that sulphur baths and electrical stimulation had been beneficial; there was less pain and Parnell slept better. 'I made a careful examination of him last night and though I find his heart's action a little improved I find no reason to alter the opinion I expressed concerning him some time since. His liver also has latterly become very torpid and inactive and is beginning to be very troublesome.'

Parnell, on the other hand, explained to Mrs O'Shea the need 'to invent little maladies for myself from day to day in order to give Dr Kenny an excuse for keeping me in the infirmary, but I have never felt better in my life.'

Dr Kenny's vindictive dismissal from his hospital post caused anger in nationalist circles and led to questions in the House of Commons. The Chief Secretary refused to have the sealed order withdrawn 'as that would be an admission, not justified by the circumstances of the case, that it was not within the duty of the Government to issue it.' Kenny was entitled, however, to apply for the readvertised post and if appointed, his years of service would count for superannuation purposes. He was released from prison in February 1882 and towards the end of March was reinstated by the Guardians of the North Dublin Union. Gladstone later conceded that the Chief Secretary had been in error. He could imprison Kenny as a 'suspect' but could not as a 'suspect' dismiss him.

Parnell was released on parole on April 10th to attend the funeral of a nephew who had died in Paris from typhoid fever. He re-entered Kilmainham on April 24th to be released finally on May 2nd. John Howard Parnell[6] believed that his brother's health 'certainly suffered by his imprisonment' but this is unproven and the next event of clinical relevance was his visit to Sir Henry Thompson at 35 Wimpole Street. Thompson was emeritus professor of clinical surgery and consulting surgeon to University College Hospital. He was London's leading urologist, having operated on Leopold I, King of the Belgians and Napoleon III, Emperor of the French.[7]

Accompanied by Katharine O'Shea, Parnell went to see Sir Henry Thompson on 6 November 1866, presenting himself as Mr Charles Stewart and not revealing his actual identity until a later visit. He was so apprehensive that he deputed his companion to go in first to explain to the doctor just how he was feeling. He stayed in the waiting room while she went into the consulting room where Sir Henry Thompson had just arrived in a tearing hurry and a foul mood.

'Look, look, *look!*' he exclaimed. 'Look at the clock! What is the matter? I have a consultation in a few minutes.'

Coolly she remonstrated, saying that 'her' patient would never stand such a brusque reception. Sir Henry recovered his poise and became a model of kindness. His speciality might lend credence to the suggestion that Parnell had 'Bright's disease', an ill-defined progressive kidney disease. A more likely explanation, if he did have intermittent fever, is chronic pyelitis (a low-grade renal infection) but Mrs O'Shea attributed his ill-health to a nervous breakdown brought on by overwork.[8] This may well be so and Sir Henry's prescriptions may have been mainly dietary. His publications included *Food and Feeding* (1880), and *Diet in Relation to Age and Activity* (1886), books which went into many editions.

Parnell's speech to the Eighty Club in 1888 refers to this period and is in keeping with a reactive depression:

I was ill, dangerously ill. It was an illness from which I have not entirely recovered up to this day. I was so ill that I could not put pen to paper, nor even read a newspaper . . . I was so feeble that for several months, absolutely up to the meeting of Parliament, I was positively unable to take part in any public matter, and was scarcely able to do so for months after.

The element of self-pity is obvious and his behaviour at that time contrasts remarkably with his failure in the fall of 1891 to heed medical advice and his ability to write letters from his sick-bed in Brighton a few days before his death.

Whatever the nature of Sir Henry Thompson's ministrations, he certainly gained Parnell's confidence and the latter was to consult him (by post rather than in person) in those critical days in October 1891. He collected Nankin blue and white china which Whistler helped to catalogue, and was famous as a host for his 'octaves' — dinners of eight courses, for eight people at eight o'clock. 'The guests were as carefully chosen as the food, and for a quarter of a century the most famous persons in the worlds of art, letters,

science, politics, diplomacy and fashion sat at his table in Wimpole Street.'
One might wonder if Charles Stewart Parnell earned the accolade of an
invitation.

Parnell's Dublin doctor, meanwhile, had been elected to parliament. Dr
J.E. Kenny represented the south division of Co. Cork from 1885 until 1892.
He did not rank among the party's orators but was active during question
time and spoke briefly on many subjects. He took advantage of his position
to ask the Chief Secretary why deranged patients in the North Dublin Union
had been refused admission to the Richmond District Lunatic Asylum, and
he intervened in the debate on the Dublin, Wicklow and Wexford Railway
Bill to urge that the line should run on the eastern side of the Custom House
instead of on its western side where it would destroy the view.

'We are likely', he said, 'to have a Home Rule Parliament for Ireland
before long, and it would be unfortunate to call upon the new Parliament
sitting in Dublin, the very first time they meet, to remedy the evils which this
Parliament is now about to perpetrate.' His advice went unheeded.[9]

Parnell wrote to Kenny on 19 January 1888 to ensure his attendance in
the House of Commons for the discussions on the Local Government Bill.
'I am very unwilling to ask you to come over, but I think I ought now to do
so, and I hope that you will be able to stay for ten days or a fortnight'.[10] The
disruptive effects of a parliamentary career on Dr Kenny's practice must
have been considerable and when he supported Parnell after the divorce, he
forfeited his post as consultant to Maynooth but, in July 1891, he was
appointed coroner for the city of Dublin.

The vicissitudes of Parnell's troubled life are material to my theme only
as occasions of stress. Dr Kenny remained loyal to the Chief throughout. He
had referred to the love-affair when writing to John Dillon on 1 January 1890,
showing little concern for the moral aspect but worried in case Parnell should
suffer by it. 'I believe he is much more sensitive than he gets credit for, but
this in my opinion is our plain duty, that come what will we are bound to
stand to him as one man and show that no amount of obloquy will displace
him from his position as our leader.' Dr Kenny was present during the
protracted debate in Committee Room 15 when Parnell's calm demeanour
was transformed by anger until he seemed on the verge of physical assault
on his opponents. And when a young poet, Katharine Tynan, marvelling at
Parnell's apparent detachment as he was ushered into the Rotunda by a
torch-lit procession, remarked to J.E. Kenny who was standing beside her,
'He's the only quiet man', the doctor disagreed. 'Outwardly', he said, and
looking again she noticed Parnell's flashing eyes and dilated nostrils.

Struck by Parnell's total absorption as he sat down to prepare the manifesto on his return to Brighton on November 26th, Katharine O'Shea decided
not to dissuade him from carrying on — 'even if it killed him I must let him
fight . . . it was himself — the great self that I loved, and that I would not

spoil even through my love, though it might bring the end in death'. Ostensibly a noble sentiment, but what woman true to her real nature would not beg her lover to save his life and let the cause go hang? The objectivity of biographers and historians when dealing with this period is vitiated by 'hindsight'. Knowing that Parnell died within twelve months of the divorce and 'the split', they are inclined to herald pathology gratuitously and to link cause and effect without reference to any particular disease process. Even the exemplary F.S.L. Lyons[11] describing Parnell sleeping before the fire in the Victorian Hotel, Kilkenny, chose ominous words: 'He looked like a dying man.' But by the next day the resilient leader's energy returned and not until September 1891 do we find Dr Kenny wishing to curb his activity.

Mrs O'Shea's description of her lover's 'tall, gaunt figure, thin and deadly pale' derived from the early days of their acquaintanceship when his health and vitality were not in question. As early as 1877, after an ordeal in the House of Commons, he seemed to be 'worn out and looking terribly old.' Parnell's appearance was deceptive and to balance the statements of those who saw him as wasted and ailing, may be set the words of a man who saw him attacking the premises of the *United Ireland*, crowbar in hand, breaking his way in and facing the crowd from an upstairs window: 'I looked at a tiger', the spectator said, 'in the frenzy of its rage. Then he spoke and the tone of his voice was even more terrible than his look.'

The harbingers of doom who thought Parnell looked awful may later have crowed 'I told you so' but actually his death on 6 October 1891 was so sudden and unexpected that Sir Henry Thompson was shocked and distressed when the evening papers carried the news. Despite what Parnell had endured, he was tolerably well in the winter of 1890/91. Arriving in Dublin on the morning of December 10th, he was taken to Dr Kenny's house in Rutland Square. The breakfast room was full of men all talking at the same time. Parnell sat by the fire looking thoughtful and saying nothing until Mrs Kenny entered the room and approached him.

'Mr Parnell, don't you want something to eat?'

'That's just what I do want', he replied.

'Don't you see that the man's worn out,' Mrs Kenny said to those nearby, 'while you all keep talking and debating.' As the noise abated Parnell sat to the table. 'I'm hungry as a hawk', he said.[12]

For all his apparent frailty, he could travel for hours in bitter weather. Standish O'Grady encountered him on an outside car on a dreadfully cold day in 1891. 'Parnell was muffled in the most copious manner, quite a hill of rugs, cloaks and shawls'.[13]

June 25th, 1891 was his wedding day and during the campaign for the

Carlow by-election he was exceptionally good-humoured despite Andy Kettle's predicted defeat. On his return to Brighton in the second week of September, his wife thought he looked ill and worn. She made him rest and urged him to consult Sir Henry Thompson. He refused, saying he could not spare the time. 'I'm not ill', he said, 'only a little tired.'

'I sent him off bright and happy', Mrs Parnell wrote, recalling his departure for the meeting in Creggs, but his letters to her referred to pain in his left arm which is notable as the presenting symptom of a mortal illness. From Morrison's Hotel he wrote to Dr Kenny:

My Dear Doctor,

I shall be very much obliged if you can call over here to see me this afternoon, as I am not feeling very well, and oblige. Don't mention that I am unwell to anybody, lest it should get into the newspapers.

Dr Kenny told him not to go to Creggs but Parnell insisted on going and one may wonder if in assuming the dual role of political subordinate and medical attendant the doctor had not sacrificed his authority over his patient, who set out by train from Broadstone Station at 7.30 p.m. In response to calls for a speech he came to the carriage window and asked to be excused for health reasons. He had been ordered by his doctor, he explained, not to go to Co. Roscommon.

A crowd had gathered to greet him in Athlone and while the train was in the station it was discovered that a Parnellite supporter had fallen on the line and been killed. From Roscommon Station Parnell was driven to Mitchell's Hotel, where he made a short speech. Next day he drove to Creggs, about seven miles away, and after the addresses of welcome from various branches of the GAA and National League at Kearns' Hotel, the meeting was held in the main street where a temporary platform was erected.

Parnell explained that he was not in the best of health and said: 'Nothing but the desire not to disappoint all the true men that I see around me overcame the orders that I was to go to bed last night when I arrived in Dublin. However, I do not think that any material damage will come to me from this meeting. If I was to allow the suggestion of such a thought we should have our enemies throwing up their hats and announcing I was buried before I was dead, and although a man on the other side of forty cannot do the things he used to do in the days of his youth, still I intend to bury a good many of their men.'[14]

His macabre levity, which was rewarded with cheers and laughter and his promise that they would find him physically improved when he next visited them, shows that he had not the least suspicion of the potential gravity of his symptoms. He returned to Dublin by the night mail and stayed for three days with Dr Kenny, who prescribed champagne. Then, disobeying doctor's orders, he travelled to London on September 30th and after a Turkish bath, went on to Brighton.

Glad to be home, he sat before a blazing fire and ate a fairly good dinner before being helped up to bed by his wife, who rubbed him with firwood oil and packed the left arm with wool. Evidently he was well enough to talk to the dogs, Grouse and Pincher, and to plan for the future with his wife. He refused her plea to have Sir Henry Thompson down — 'No, the fee would be enormous at this distance' — but agreed to write to him.

Next morning he felt better and, after a good breakfast, he sat in bed, smoked a cigar and made notes for a speech. He discussed renting a house nearer to London and later wrote to his solicitors about a mortgage, and to Dr Kenny who was secretary of a committee set up to provide a home for James Stephens, the Fenian.

Feeling less well on Sunday morning, he agreed that a local doctor should be called and was more optimistic after he had been seen by Dr Jowers.

'My husband was in great pain on Monday . . . ' Mrs Parnell recalled. He attempted to get out of bed but was too weak to do so. On Tuesday he was flushed and feverish. Dr Jowers came twice and promised to call early next morning. The last moments of her husband's life have been described by his widow.

> Late in the evening he suddenly opened his eyes and said: 'Kiss me, sweet Wifie, and I will try to sleep a little.' I lay down by his side and kissed the burning lips he pressed to mine for the last time. The fire of them, fierce beyond any I had ever felt, even in his most loving moods, startled me, and as I slipped my hand from under his head he gave a little sigh and became unconscious. The doctor came at once, but no remedies prevailed against this sudden failure of the heart's action, and my husband died without regaining consciousness.[15]

The cause of death on the certificate signed by Dr Jowers — 'rheumatic fever 5 days, hyperpyrexia, failure of the heart's action' — must be received with a measure of scepticism, though on arrival in a sick-room where the patient's arm was carefully packed in wool, a rheumatic process may have been readily accepted by the doctor. 'Whoever heard', Parnell's mother asked with consuming sarcasm, 'of rheumatism passing from a man's left arm and killing him in a single night?' Her disbelief would be unnecessary today: the pain of coronary heart disease can be confined to one or other arm, yet presage coronary thrombosis and cardiac arrest which slays in an instant.

Let us now review the medical evidence, however incomplete. Diagnosis is not an intuitive process but an intellectual exercise in which three groups of facts are sifted:

    1. The patient's symptoms and physical condition (clinical picture);

    2. The family medical history;

    3. Spectrum of relevant pathology and diseases (differential diagnosis).

Clinical Picture

What little is known of Parnell's physical condition in his forties indicates that because of poor circulation Sir Henry Thompson advised him to keep his feet warm. Having gone through a period of wildness in his youth he drank wine in moderation but smoked heavily.

Evidently the symptoms he mentioned when writing to Sir Henry Thompson from Brighton did not seem alarming to the surgeon who felt entitled to reassure him. The fullest account of his illness is that given by Mrs Parnell, who referred to left arm pain but gives us no reason to believe that there was swelling or discoloration. She does not specify the site of the pain he suffered on Monday, on which day he experienced 'a sudden horror that he was being held down by some strong unseen power.' He was sleepless, flushed and feverish but no details are available as to the level of the fever.

The *Freeman's Journal* reporter stated that Parnell complained of 'a severe pain in the chest' at Creggs and referred to 'extreme agony' shortly before his death.[16]

Family History

Parnell's great-grandfather, grandfather and father died unexpectedly in middle age. Sir John Parnell, the second baronet, who was given to the pleasures of the table, died suddenly 'at the height of his exaltation', aged fifty-seven. His son, William Parnell, MP for Wicklow, while on business in Dublin in January 1821, caught the 'chill' which led to his death a few days later at forty-four years of age. John Henry Parnell, the great politician's father, when suffering from what is euphemistically termed 'rheumatism of the stomach', in June 1859 insisted on playing for Leinster Cricket Club against Phoenix, despite the contrary advice of Sir Henry Marsh, a leading physician. He was taken ill in the Shelbourne Hotel after the match and died there next day, being then forty-eight years old.[17]

Differential Diagnosis

With Parnell's family history and smoking habits, an illness commencing with left-arm pain progressing to some degree of general weakness and ending suddenly suggests atypical coronary insufficiency (angina pectoris) causing coronary thrombosis with myocardial infarction and cardiac arrest, a sequence of events not diagnosable in 1891. Some degree of fever is to be expected, possibly attaining 103°F.

The differential diagnosis includes cancer (unlikely), pneumonia and rheumatic fever. Many were cut down in the prime of life by pneumonia in Victorian times but the clinical picture of this disease was readily recognised.

And besides, in the throes of pneumonia a patient is prostrated and not disposed to disobey his doctor's instructions. Adolescents and young adults were the selected victims of rheumatic fever, a disease temporarily crippling through involvement of many joints and unlikely to kill in its acute phase. Dr William Osler saw only one death in 456 cases (1897).[18]

Before re-affirming coronary thrombosis (myocardial infarction) as the probable cause of Parnell's death, the question of 'hyperpyrexia', i.e. a temperature greater than 106°F, must be considered. Was this factual or a 'red herring' introduced when Dr Jowers was called back to Walshingham Terrace close to midnight on that wet, windy night, arriving to find his patient dead, and influenced by the distraught woman's reference to the burning lips? 'The fire of them, fierce beyond any I had ever felt . . .'

Was 'hyperpyrexia' merely a convenient surmise to explain the dire turn of events? Fever at that level is characterised by delirium and stupor. These were not features of Parnell's illness according to his wife and, as F.S.L Lyons had pointed out, 'It is not likely that she would forget the least detail of the poignant climax to the supreme event of her life . . .'[19] Neither does she mention the ritual application of cold packs and sponging of the extremities customary in hyperpyrexia. A doctor's examination, peering at the tongue, tapping the chest and the like, bewilders anxious relatives but when the thermometer is produced they know what he is about. Is it credible that earlier in the week Jowers recorded a temperature above 106°F and did not mention it to Mrs Parnell who in turn would surely have highlighted it in her book? Was hyperpyrexia, then, a conjectural figment of the doctor's fertile imagination? Later, Dr Jowers told the press, in the presence of those of Parnell's colleagues who had come to Brighton, that 'he had a thin and weak heart', a statement hardly warranted by the evidence available to him.[20]

If the validity of the hyperpyrexia is thus impugned, coronary thrombosis remains far the most likely diagnosis and it is quite possible that, had Dr Kenny's advice been accepted and had Parnell rested instead of overtaxing himself in dreadful weather at Creggs, his life would have been prolonged.

Sir Henry Thompson

Sir Henry Thompson wrote a letter of condolence to Mrs Parnell on October 7th, expressing himself deeply interested in knowing 'what was said, or supposed to have been the cause of the fatal result.' He wrote again on October 10th, inviting her to call on him when she felt up to it. He assured her of Dr Jowers' experience and capability. Her husband could not have been in better hands. Nothing further could have been done.[21]

'If I were to regret anything', Sir Henry continued with supreme self-confidence, 'it would be that he had not found a spare half-hour to come to see me *some time ago*. Let me see then how his strength was and whether he could not be fortified a little for the wearing life he was leading.'

Having been knighted in 1867, Thompson was elevated to a baronetcy in 1899. He was particularly interested in astronomy and had a private observatory at his country house. He presented a giant telescope manufactured in Dublin by Sir Howard Grubb to the Greenwich Observatory in 1897.

The last of Sir Henry Thompson's 'octaves', the 301st, was given shortly before his death on 18 April 1904. His remains were cremated, a procedure which he had promoted, as President of the Cremation Society, until its legality was finally accepted.[22]

Dr Jowers

F.S.L. Lyons's biography mentions 'Dr Benjamin Jowers, junior' but the Jowers practitioners in Brighton were Frederick W. Jowers of 27 and 28 Old Steyne, and his sons, Reginald and Lancelot.[23] It was Dr Reginald Jowers of 29 Norfolk Square who was called in by Mrs Parnell but the death certificate was signed by F.W. Jowers who, with his son and a third (unnamed) doctor, had performed a superficial post-mortem examination in view of the rumour that Parnell had committed suicide. The Press Association reported Dr Jowers Senior as saying 'that a more straightforward case, or one presenting fewer difficulties either in the way of treatment or diagnosis he had never met with', a statement that was certainly a masterpiece of disingenuousness. A very experienced man with a larger practice, Dr Jowers Senior, was consulting surgeon to the Sussex County Hospital and FRCS (elected as a Member of twenty years' standing). He died on 17 May 1893 in his 63rd year.[24]

Dr Reginald Jowers, FRCS, a practitioner of five years' standing in 1891, was then thirty years old and honorary assistant surgeon to the Sussex County Hospital. In his statement to the press he said: 'Mr Parnell died from . . . what is popularly known as excessively high temperature and failure of the heart's action . . . The case is one of the plainest I have ever attended, and there is not the slightest ground for some of the doubts that are said to have been expressed about it'.

Educated at Winchester and St Bartholomew's Hospital, Reginald Jowers maintained the family tradition in Sussex and held the office of president of the Brighton and Sussex Medico-Chirurgical Society. During the Great War he served in the 2nd Eastern General Hospital with the rank of lieutenant-colonel. He died in 1937 after prolonged disablement from sub-acute-degeneration of the spinal cord, then an untreatable condition.[25]

Dr Kenny

Parnell's funeral was the largest in Dublin since Daniel O'Connell's. With the Redmonds, Edward Leamy, Henry Harrison and other close associates, Dr J.E. Kenny stood by the grave.[26] The last message written by Parnell was sent to Kenny: 'Rejoice that a movement is to be made to provide Mr Stephens with a resting-place during the last years of his life — Parnell'.

Kenny defeated the anti-Parnellite candidate, T.D. Sullivan, and was elected MP for Dublin's College Green division, holding the seat from 1892 until his resignation in 1898. A founder and director of the *Irish Independent*, he was a regular playgoer and a supporter of the Irish Literary Theatre. His unexpected death on 9 April 1900 resulted from septicaemia following a dental extraction.[27] At his funeral to Glasnevin, the wreaths included one from Frank Benson, the Shakespearean actor, with an appropriate inscription from *The Merchant of Venice*:

> The dearest friend to me, the kindest man,
> The best conditioned and unwearied spirit
> In doing courtesies and one in whom
> The ancient Roman honour more appears.

His brother, Dr Robert D. Kenny, died on 30 July 1909 and was interred on August 3rd at Golden Bridge Cemetery, Inchicore. James Joyce, who was visiting Dublin, attended the funeral as, more relevant to my theme, did old Andy Kettle and his son, T.M. Kettle, MP. A wreath was sent by Bob Kenny's colleagues on the Parnell Memorial Committee: 'With sincere sympathy at the loss of an old and valued friend and faithful follower of Parnell.'[28]

When the Parnell Monument was unveiled on 1 October 1911, Tom Kettle published a tribute from which the following lines are taken:

> Tears will betray all pride, but when ye mourn him,
> Be it in soldier wise;
> As for a captain who hath gently borne him,
> And in the midnight dies.[29]

Notes

1. Lock, S., 'A question of confidence,' *British Medical Journal*. 288, 123-125, 1984.
2. Loudon, I., 'How it strikes a historian,' Ibid, 288, 125-126, 1984.
3. Lyons, J.B., '"What did I die of?" The last illness of Charles Stewart Parnell,' *Irish Mededical Journal*, 78, 223-226, 1985.
4. Cameron, Sir Charles, *History of the Royal College of Surgeons in Ireland*, 2nd ed., Dublin: Fannin, 1916.
5. State Paper Office, CSO, Registered papers, 40461/81.
6. Parnell, John H., *Charles Stewart Parnell: A Memoir*, London: Cassell, 1916.
7. *Plarr's Lives of Fellows of the Royal College of Surgeons of England*,

London: RCS, 1930.
8. O'Shea, Katharine. *Charles Stewart Parnell: His Love Story and Political Life*, London: Cassell, 1914.
9. Hansard, 318, 884-885, 2 August 1887.
10. NLI Ms. 15, 735.
11. Lyons, F.S.L., *Charles Stewart Parnell*, London: Collins, 1977.
12. O'Brien, R.B., *The Life of Charles Stewart Parnell*, London: Smith, Elder, 1898.
13. O'Grady, Standish, *The Story of Ireland*, London: Methuen, 1894.
14. *Freeman's Journal*, 28 September 1891.
15. O'Shea, *loc. cit.*
16. *Freeman's Journal*, 8 October 1891.
17. Foster, R.F., *Charles Stewart Parnell: The Man and his Family*, Hassocks: Harvester Press, 1876.
18. Osler, William, The *Principles and Practice of Medicine*, London: Pentland, 1897.
19. Lyons, F.S.L., *The Fall of Parnell, 1890-1891*, London: 1960.
20. *Freeman's Journal*, 9 October 1891.
21. O'Shea, *loc. cit.*
22. *British Medical Journal*, ii, 357, 1937.
23. *Medical Directory*, 1891.
24. *British Medical Journal*, i, 1201, 1893.
25. *Lives of Fellows of the Royal College of Surgeons of England, 1920-1951*, London: RCS.
26. Leamy, Margaret, *Parnell's Faithful Few*, New York: Macmillan, 1936.
27. *Medical Press*, 3 May 1909.
28. *Freeman's Journal*, 4 August 1909.
29. Kettle, T.M., *Poems and Parodies*, Dublin: Talbot Press, 1916.

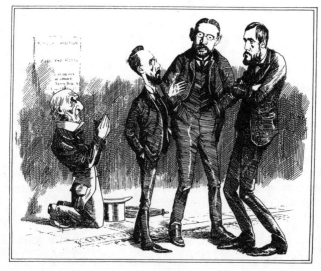

"The Allies" — "For we're the original friends of the Nation. All the rest air a paltry and base fabrication." — Biglow. Cartoon from *The Irish Green Book*.

Parnell: The Lost Leader

Seamus Deane

Parnell has been written into Irish history and into Irish literature; where the history ends and the literature begins is so difficult to determine that it might be easier and wiser to abandon the ostensibly strict distinction between them and acknowledge that they are both fictional modes that have developed different functions. The professionalisation of this difference is a nineteenth-century phenomenon; it was then that history and literature became specifically academic disciplines. It is sufficient for our present purposes to say that the standard rhetorical procedure for separating one discipline from the other consists in assigning to the historian a respect for 'reality' and 'facts' and in granting to the literary artist a plenary indulgence for all the sins committed against these in search of his or her 'truth' or artistic requirements. I am not going to pursue the issues I have raised here with any vigour; I merely raise them to remind you that with Parnell — as with any such figure — we are dealing with representations in words of an individual and career and that representation is an exercise that employs a particular rhetoric.

I shall restrict my remarks to the representation of Parnell by Yeats and Joyce. In our retrospect, they are the dominant figures in the creation of the so-called myth of Parnell and that is, in itself, sufficient reason to give them priority. In addition, it is widely recognised that their respective visions of Parnell are only legible in relation to certain preoccupations in their own work. So Parnell can be ranked with Swift, Wilde, Hugh Lane, Synge and a number of others as one of the 'heroic' figures in a Yeatsian portrait gallery that is itself a construct in and of his poetry; that heroic image may have more in common with an aristocratic or authoritarian ideal of leadership than with any specific features of Parnell himself. He has simply been recruited as a member of the Yeatsian family — or, more precisely perhaps, and with due respect for Yeats's occult interests, as one of the Yeatsian familiars. Similarly, Joyce's reputed obsession with betrayal finds in Parnell a gratifyingly spectacular example of treachery on a national scale; Parnell is the political analogue for the artist, the hero besieged by the mob, the Irish hero brought down by his own people at the behest of their English oppressors. Literary Parnellism is certainly inclined to view the crisis of the great leader's life as a parable about authority and most particularly as a manifestation of the Irish Catholic incapacity to possess it because of some radical fear of it. But, for the present, let the point stand: the Parnell of Yeats and Joyce is an imaginative construct through which we can the better read them without entertaining any ambition thereby of being the better able to read him. I offer this cliché for what it is. It is important because it is a cliché and because it is successful in erasing many issues — like the difference between history and literature — with which it pretends to deal.

Parnell is a product of Parnellism. Parnellism is a set of rhetorical procedures for the reading of the Irish past that Yeats and Joyce, with many others, perfected in the period between 1890 and 1940. The first and most important of these procedures was to formulate the Parnell crisis as a confrontation between two forces, one embodied in Parnell himself, the other in the Irish people. This is so obvious that it deserves repetition. Parnell is one agent; the Irish people are another. Each of these agents is then constituted as having a radical bias of personality. Parnell is austere, remote, self-contained, disdainful; the Irish people are, under his influence, an organised community that has, nevertheless, an irresistible longing towards the delinquency and volatility of the mob. This 'mob' impulse is precipitated by the divorce proceedings. The fear of the mob had been one of the bequests of the counter-revolutionary reaction to France since 1789; in Ireland, it took on a local colouring in the opposition to O'Connellite politics and the mobilisation of the Catholic masses. Indeed, both Yeats and Parnell rehearse the standard attacks on O'Connell's demagoguery, on his populism and garrulity, unfavourably contrasting these with Parnell's solitariness and his lack of eloquence. All the stereotypes of Irishness are contradicted by Parnell, confirmed in the Irish people. The conflict between these two agents is one between a highly individuated selfhood and, to adapt a Yeatsian phrase, 'common greenness'. Parnell almost made the Irish into individuals; that was the real version of Home Rule that he offered. Once they refused it, the battle for individuality was resumed by the artist, availing of the long romantic tradition of radical selfhood to support his position. Parnell is, in that respect, the leader who almost redeemed the Irish from their oppression; but what he revealed was that the oppression was not inflicted by the English alone; the Irish had introjected the oppression; they had become experts in oppressing themselves. That was why they hated individuality, why they hated the artist and why they turned upon Parnell. They could not take on the responsibility of becoming themselves; they turned instead into the infernal mob condition to which earlier in their history they had been reduced.

'Ivy Day in the Committee Room' is, of course, the story in which Joyce's Parnell figures most prominently, although it is through his absence that his presence is most felt. All the stories in *Dubliners* move from repression to epiphany, from a condition of moral inarticulacy to a moment of revelation, even if the revelation is nothing more than an exposure of the initial condition. The *ethos* of Dublin and the *pathos* of the individual Dubliners are interfused. In 'Ivy Day', the gloom and the dilapidation of the committee room, the banked fire, the cheap futilities of the conversations and, above all, the shadowiness of the scene all conspire to remind us that this is Ireland in the despondent years after Parnell's fall. Parnell is a shade, Ireland is in his shadow; Ireland is an underworld populated by shades; the Parnell crisis is shadowed forth again by the dispute about the kind of reception to be accorded to the adulterous English King Edward VII. Dublin is apparently going to welcome the King of England who is adulterous, having destroyed the uncrowned king of Ireland for the same fault. This is a wake for Parnell, haunted by the mysterious figure of the spoilt priest, celebrated by drink — payment for political services — and by bad poetry, sentimentally received. Funeral, wake, underworld, shade, shadow, depression, repetition — these are the indications of the famous Dublin paralysis that has been brought on, in this case by the shock of Parnell's downfall. The stupefaction of this world is complete. The Irish, having destroyed their leader, have lapsed back into that sodden state of lachrymose concussion from which he had threatened to liberate them.

There are more political subtleties in the story than this reading offers, but they do not undermine it. More immediately pertinent is the final burst of 'eloquence' by Hynes when he recites the poem 'The Death of Parnell'. It is this piece of doggerel that finally unites everyone and that, of course, is part of the irony. But the revelation, such as it is, merely makes explicit what had been implicit in the story and is an effective ending because it is, in its gross way, so articulate about Parnell and what had been done to him and to his memory. Joyce is fond of the 'eloquent' closure, the gesture that finally brings words to a voice or a theme that had been silent. In *A Portrait of the Artist as a Young Man*, Stephen Dedalus who has been the object of the narration finally becomes the narrator himself. His voice is released to us through his diary entries and his annunciation of his programme shows him to be now the producer of a language of which he had previously been the recipient. So also, Molly Bloom in the final Penelope section of *Ulysses*, achieves that runaway 'female' eloquence that brings the novel to a close, providing it with the woman's voice that had been up until then excluded. In *Finnegans Wake*, Anna Livia Plurabelle becomes the universal voice, the river embracing the ocean, the individual voice merging into the general noise out of which that book emerges and into which it returns. In effect, Joyce's fiction is constantly elaborating the drama of the return of the repressed, of the speaking out of what had been latent and disturbing. In 'Ivy Day', it is the saga and myth of Parnell that finally gets spoken; its shadowy presence up until then had been lurking within the committee room, the crime that had to be admitted so that a reason for the condition of Dublin could be found. But Parnell's death does not explain the pathological state of the inmates of the room. It is their pathological state that explains why Parnell was destroyed. The source of that is in the national character of the Irish people. It is their destiny to be slaves and, in their revolt against this destiny, to be confined to a bogus and eloquent lamentation about it. Their dreadful blarney is the index of their servitude. Parnell, being silent, reserved, hesitant, is, on that account, an individual. A certain aristocratic hauteur defined the person who had selfhood, not the blether and kitsch sentiment of the democratic rabble. Joyce's valorisation of 'silence' (along with 'exile' and 'cunning') as the mark of the artist, the extraordinary personage, brings him close, at times, to Yeats's vision of personal and spiritual integrity.

It would be a mistake to see Joyce's or Yeats's Parnell as a constitutional nationalist. That would be too tame a role for either of their purposes. Joyce consistently associates Parnell with the Fenians — not just through the 'phoenix flame' of Hynes' recitation, but much more specifically in the famous Christmas dinner scene in *Portrait* and in his essay 'Fenianism'. Mr Casey, Simon Dedalus's guest and friend at the dinner table, is a Fenian who served time for his beliefs. Parnell himself appealed to the Fenians when in extremis, in his last campaign over the heads of his Irish parliamentary party supporters. The complicated relationship between Parnell and the Fenians is reduced by Joyce's representation to a close liaison in which both parties seem to share a common insurrectionist aim. Yeats also had the old Fenian John O'Leary as one of his icons of noble rebellion, contrasting them — in a manner redolent of the present time — with the coarser, more vulgar and violent revolutionaries of the present. Perhaps the main attraction of Fenianism was that it had never been defeated. Despite 1867, Fenianism survived, in various guises, as a freemasonry of those who were against the British presence. Fenianism was the sea in which the IRB fish swam. Brutal jail sentences, clerical condemnation, the rise of the Home Rule movement and the Land League, reprints of patriotic song books, most especially *The Spirit of the Nation* - which got a de luxe edition, replete with Celtic gold and green entwinings and harps, in 1882, the year Joyce was born — aided its survival. In Joyce's own words,

the Fenianism of 67 was not one of the usual flashes of Celtic temperament that lighten the shadow for a moment and leave behind a darkness blacker than before.

Fenianism was as different from Emmet's rebellion, or Young Ireland's 1848 fiasco, as was Parnell from O'Connell. In terms of military incompetence and clownishness, there is not much to choose between 1848 and 1867; nevertheless, the choice was made because, it would seem, 67 was regarded as an origin for Fenianism while 48 was a finale for Young Ireland. More importantly, Fenianism had the reputation, assiduously fostered by James Stephens and his allies, of being an *organised* movement. It was not a mere impulse, not a twitch of the Celtic nervous system. It was, in Joyce's view, a movement that would change the character of the Irish people. This is close to the heart of the Fenian appeal for Joyce and his association of Parnell with the movement. It would change the national character of the Irish people; it might finally relieve them of their junior status as molten Celts and make them into truly individuated Parnellites. Joyce appreciated that, between them, the Fenians and Parnell were achieving the beginnings of a psychological revolution in Ireland. Parnell's destruction — for which the Fenians could not be blamed, as they had, in his view, remained steadfast — was an act of self mutilation, a turning back into the underworld of servitude even as the Home Rule sun arose above the divorce court and Committee Room 15.

In short, Joyce's version of Parnell was part of his analysis of the aborted progress of the Irish people from colonial slavery to near-freedom. The double empire of London and Rome weighed so heavily on Ireland because they had grown to love their enslavement and to fear freedom and its responsibilities. What Parnell had tried to do politically, with the help of the Fenians, Joyce envisaged himself as doing in art, with the very minor help of shadowy forerunners like James Clarence Mangan and in despite of the fake Celticism of W.B.Yeats, Synge and company. Ibsen was the literary Fenian; Joyce would be literature's Parnell — except that he would not be dragged down. He would get Home Rule for art; with him, modernism would truly begin and so too would Irish literature. He would be the uncrowned king of Irish letters and the first writer to give to the Irish people a representation of spiritual freedom.

This summary description of the early and enduring phase of Joyce's Parnellism says nothing of the formal aspects of his work, especially of those remorseless, gentle inflections of repeated words and phrases that make his text shimmer uncertainly in a series of incremental vaguenesses, like something out of Debussy. Oddly, this is quite compatible with the unsparing 'scrupulous meanness' of the writing in *Dubliners*. Everything is exact, yet resonates with indeterminate possibilities. A story like 'Ivy Day' is both an acrid critique of Dublin eleven years after the death of the Chief and also a mournfully poetic evocation of the lost leader.

Ulysses and the *Wake* are another matter. This is not the place for an inventory of their varied formal experiments and effects, but the Babel of these works grows out of the more formal, univocal language of their predecessors. For my immediate purpose, it seems remarkable that the heterogeneity of Joyce's later texts coincides with a diminution of the Parnellism that had been so evident in the early books and in the Italian essays and lectures. The 'Cyclops' episode of *Ulysses*, for instance, which is a focus for variant versions of Irish history and different varieties of hostility towards the British empire and its scandalous record, has nothing of note on the Parnell crisis. The other references to Parnell are slight indeed: Bloom recalls a trip with his daughter Milly around the Kish lighthouse in a boat called *Erin's King*; in the Nighttown sequence, the mob turns on Bloom, calling for his lynching and shouting, 'He's as bad as Parnell was, Mr. Fox!' — Fox being one of the pseudonyms Parnell used during his liaison with Katharine O'Shea; Bloom also remembers Parnell's hat being knocked off in a fracas in a newspaper office in December 1890 and that he, Bloom, returned it to his owner. There are, perhaps, half-a-dozen other references of this kind. Even the obsession with betrayal, so evident in the opening episode, is associated with Oscar Wilde more than with Parnell. In the *Wake*, he appears, but in no major role and with no remarkable frequency — not nearly so often as, for example, de Valera. Did Joyce's Parnellism die as the last, painful decade of the nineteenth century faded and other forces and other people came to dominate the Irish scene? The answer is yes; but there is another factor to be considered.

The later works are stylistically different from the earlier, in part because the whole basis of Joyce's critique of the Irish situation has altered. The Irish people have found their voices. The plural is important. All the pastiche and parody, all the colloquial conversations and ruminations, the songs, the puns, witticisms and so forth are signs of a diversity that contrasts strongly with the fixity of character and the univocal performances previously displayed. Joyce is no longer stereotyping the aristocratic leader and his plebeian followers, just as he is no longer positing the ideal of the remote artist against the philistine mob. He is still preoccupied with the effects of internalised guilt, with the victim's tendency to self-blame for the triumph of his victimiser. Bloom and HCE are both victims of some original fault — Bloom's father's conversion, the condition of being a Jew or a cuckold or, in Earwicker's case, the anxiety about that original and unspecified thing that happened in the Phoenix Park, the Dublinised version of the Garden of Eden. But he sees this issue in a more various light. The racial propensities of the Irish were no longer for him a legitimate basis for a reading of the Irish situation, as they had been in relation to the Parnell crisis. This is true, even though the conventional anthropological distinctions between the Irish and the English had become part of the political discourse of the period. One has only to glance at the mass of writing on Celts, Gaels and Anglo-Saxons to see this, and Joyce exploited it to comic effect in the 'Cyclops' episode of *Ulysses* already mentioned. Remember Matthew Arnold in *Culture and Anarchy*:

And then the difference between an Irish Fenian and an English rough is so immense . . . [The Fenian] is so evidently desperate and dangerous, a man of a conquered race, a Papist, with centuries of ill-usage to inflame him against us . . . But with the Hyde Park rioter how different! He is our own flesh and blood; he is a Protestant . . .

This is the preacher of the new hellenism Joyce mocks in the opening chapter of *Ulysses*. It is this species of racial characterisation that Joyce abandons; in abandoning it, he also abandons his Parnellism.

Yeats never abandoned either anthropologically derived versions of national character nor his preoccupation with the phenomenon of racial degeneration, both of which elements played a large part in his construction of his version of Parnell. Racial character and degenerative tendencies were part of the intellectual equipment of the pseudo-scientific avant-garde, led by men like Sir Francis Galton who set up a travelling laboratory in Ireland in the 1890s to record ethnic measurements of skull, jaw, distance between the eyes, etc. Yeats gave this kind of thinking a suitably apocalyptic historical frame. In his commentary of 1935 on the poem 'Parnell's Funeral', he spoke of the four bells that struck, at equally divided intervals, to mark the ending of major historical phases of Irish experience. The first came with the Flight of the Earls; the second with the Battle of the Boyne; the third with the arrival of French revolutionary influence 'among our peasants'; and the fourth with the death of Parnell. He then describes how he went to Kingstown to meet Maud Gonne off the mail-boat one October morning in 1891 and found an immense crowd there to meet the body of Parnell and escort it to his grave. At Glasnevin — and he cites Maud Gonne and Standish O'Grady as witnesses — a star fell as Parnell's body was lowered into the grave. The bitterness of the Parnell dispute was such, according to Yeats, that it changed Dublin from 'a well-mannered, smooth-spoken city' into the 'foul mouth' he mentioned in 1913 in his first Parnell poem 'To a Shade'. But it also brought with it 'free discussion', the 'passion for reality' and the 'satiric genius that informs *Ulysses*, *The Playboy of the Western World* . . . . Yeats goes on to mention the Christmas dinner scene in Joyce's *Portrait*, and then adds:

> We had passed through an initiation like that of the Tibetan ascetic, who staggers half dead from a trance, where he has seen himself eaten alive and has not yet learned that the eater was himself. As we discussed and argued, the national character changed, O'Connell, the great comedian, left the scene and the tragedian Parnell took his place. When we talked of his pride; of his apparent impassivity when his hands were full of blood because he had torn them with his nails, the preceding epoch with its democratic bonhomie, seemed to grin through a horse collar. He was the symbol that made apparent, or made possible that epoch's contrary . . .

In the poem itself, as the crowd gathers under O'Connell's (the Great Comedian's) tomb to watch the burial of Parnell, and the star falls again, two epochs of Irish history are conjoined and separated simultaneously. What is taking place is a terrible sacrifice. Earlier heroes like Emmet, Fitzgerald and Tone were murdered by 'strangers'; but Parnell is our own victim.

None shared our guilt; nor did we play a part
Upon a painted stage when we devoured his heart.

Yet the motley Ireland that came out of this sacrificial devouring of the hero need not have continued if, as the second section of the poem avers, de Valera or Cosgrave, even General O'Duffy had eaten Parnell's heart. At one level, the destruction of the hero is an act of self-mutilation on the part of the community; at another, mythic or ritual level, the absorption of Parnell's great example might have restored the Irish community to itself. But, finally, he has, like Swift, passed away from us in bitterness and his legacy is lost. For this loss, the only recompense is the enrichment of him as a symbol.

This is highly charged drama indeed. Even in 1913, in 'To a Shade', Parnell is advised not to return to the squalid Dublin that is, in its way, akin to the Dublin of Joyce's 'Ivy Day'. In 'Come Gather Round Me Parnellites', from *New Poems* (1938), Parnell is keeping company, in the surrounding poems, with Roger Casement, the O'Rahilly and 'The Wild Old Wicked Man', one of Yeats's own personae. So it is evident that Yeats is anxious, in a much more explicit way than Joyce, to set Parnell in an historical context that will identify his role in modern Ireland. He is different from the others — de Valera, Cosgrave, the O'Rahilly, Casement — in one obvious and important respect. He preceded them. They achieved what they did without the benefit of his influence; instead they received only from him the tragic gesture that he embodied. Although all of them were remarkable men, they did not create, out of their own individuality, a community that would — in a gloss on Yeats's own phrasing — gratify the imagination. The O'Rahilly earned the definite article before his name by writing it out in his blood as he lay dying. The ghost of Casement is beating on the door to gain admission to the company of heroes; and even the Yeatsian wild old wicked man chooses an ironic second-best, solace from suffering in sex, not in religious belief. These maimed heroes are the bitter heritage of Parnellism. Like the Tibetan sage he wrote of, Ireland has come out of a trance, mutilated, and still unaware of the fact that it has maimed itself. Here Joyce and Yeats are singing in unison. Parnellism, of the literary kind, is an analysis of a self-destructive impulse. But where Joyce began by reading that impulse as arising from the national character of the Irish people and ultimately abandoned that diagnosis, Yeats retained, developed and expanded it into a chiliastic account of a degenerative movement both in Irish and in European civilisation.

The most powerful images associated with the downfall of Parnell are those of the crowd, the mob, the animal ferocity of the Joycean 'wolves', the degenerative effects of the Yeatsian 'contagion of the throng'. The second half of the nineteenth century saw the development of 'crowd theory' (Morel, Le Bon, Tarde, Spencer, Sighele). In a sense, Yeats stayed loyal to the Parnell myth because it focused that fear of the mob that was a composite of many things (revolution, urban development, growth of metropolitan populations, the consequent rise in crime, disease and in uniformity, popular literature, etc.) and that he, in his Protestant Anglo-Irish fashion, readily associated with the Catholic democracy that the 'Comedian' O'Connell had forged. Parnell was the Protestant hero who almost stayed the degenerative process, the tragic figure who would have made Ireland into a political and social community but who had been overcome by mob hatred. Thus a new phase of civilisation began, the dark phases of the moon, and everything individual, beautiful, lofty was threatened with extinction. Catholic Ireland — all those later political heroes — had been cut off from the influence of Protestant Ireland. The fury of the mob, in destroying that by which it had believed itself to be oppressed, had succeeded only in performing a grotesque act of self-mutilation from which it would not readily — perhaps not at all — recover. Yeats's Parnellism is, thus, a much more potent brew than Joyce's. Crowds crucify saviours. It was the crucified Parnell that lay like an emblem for Yeats across the threshold of modern Ireland and of the modern world. In his work, Parnellism is the central feature of a tragic politics; in Joyce's work, the tragic element fades into a celebratory account of the release of the Irish people from the stereotype that had been instrumental in bestowing upon the fall of the great leader such a sombre freight of doom-laden associations.

"He never hoped before; but now he hopes and breathes, because he has got the alliance of Mr. Parnell." — W. E. Gladstone, 24th November 1885. Cartoon from *The Irish Green Book*

Select Bibliography

Bew, Paul, *C.S. Parnell*, Gill's Irish Lives, Dublin, 1980.

Bew, Paul, *Land and the National Question in Ireland, 1858-82*, Dublin, 1978.

Clark, Samuel and Donnelly, James S. Jr (eds.), *Irish peasants: violence and political unrest*, Manchester, 1983.

Clark, Samuel, *Social origins of the Irish land war*, Princeton, 1979.

Cooke A.B. and Vincent, *The Governing Passion: Cabinet Government and Party Politics in Britain, 1885-86*, Harvester, 1974.

Curtis, L.P. Jr., *Coercion and Conciliation in Ireland, 1880-1892: a Study in Conservative Unionism*, Princeton and Oxford, 1963.

Foster, Roy, *Parnell: the man and his family*, Harvester, 1976.

Geary, Laurence M. ,*The Plan of Campaign, 1886-1891*, Cork, 1986.

Hammond, J.L., *Gladstone and the Irish nation*, London, 1938.

Lyons, F.S.L., *Charles Stewart Parnell*, London, 1977.

Lyons, F.S.L., *The Fall of Parnell, 1890-91*, London, 1960.

Moody, T.W., *Davitt and Irish Revolution ,1846-82*, Oxford,1981.

O'Brien, Conor Cruise, *Parnell and his Party, 1880-91*, Oxford, 1957, 1964.

O'Brien, R. Barry, *The Life of Charles Stewart Parnell, 1846-1891*, 2 vols, London, 1898.

O'Shea, Katharine [Mrs C.S. Parnell], *Charles Stewart Parnell: His Love Story and Political Life*, 2 vols, London, 1914.

Solow, Barbara, *The land question and the Irish economy, 1870-1903*, Cambridge, Mass.,1971.

Vaughan, W. E., *Landlords and tenants in Ireland, 1848-1904*, N.P. 1984.

Arrival in Dublin.

ARRIVAL IN DUBLIN.
"DRAWING MR PARNELL PAST THE OLD PARLIAMENT HOUSE.